AUG   19

HOW TO
THINK LIKE
A CEO

HOW TO THINK LIKE A CEO

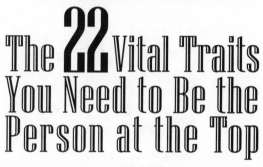

The 22 Vital Traits You Need to Be the Person at the Top

D. A. BENTON

WARNER BOOKS

A Time Warner Company

Warner Books, Inc., 1271 Avenue of the Americas, New York, NY 10020

A Time Warner Company

First Warner Books printing: July 1996
10 9 8 7 6 5 4 3 2 1

Library of Congress Cataloging-in-Publication Data

Benton, D. A. (Debra A.)
    How to think like a CEO: the 22 vital traits you need to be the
person at the top / D.A. Benton.
        p.   cm.
    ISBN 0–446–51800–X
    1. Executive ability.   2. Leadership.   3. Executives—Interviews.
I. Title.
HD38.2.B4625   1996
658.4'092—dc20   95-43182
                                                            CIP

Book design by Giorgetta Bell McRee

Acknowledgments

Special thanks go to my parents, Fred and Teresa Benton, who introduced me to the business world at a young age and inspired me to "get in there and tackle it." I'd also like to thank them for teaching me to live, not just earn a living.

To my husband, Rodney Sweeney. I wish all women could be so lucky to have a partner like him.

To my friend and business associate, Pat Straley. She never lets me off the hook and never lets me take a shortcut.

To my editor, Joann Davis, and to the other pros at Warner Books.

To my agent, Mike Cohn.

And to some tremendous friends: Nancy Albertini, Delores Doyle, Ernie Howell, J. M. Jones, Dr. Kelly Kesler, Lawrence Land, Shelley Monfor, Winona Siu, and Inge Trump.

Debra Benton
Benton Management Resources
2221 West Lake Street
Ft. Collins, Colorado 80521

Contents

PART TWO

PART ONE

Understanding the CEO is a critical step for moving up the mountain. You'll avoid getting fired, get promoted more quickly, and prepare yourself for taking the lead. *Plus*, it makes the climb more exhilarating and fun for you!

CHAPTER 1

Basic Equipment

What gear does the modern climber need to make it to the top of the corporate mountain?

You can become a CEO—a chief executive officer—in your career lifetime. It is not the unreachable pinnacle once reserved for those born with a silver spoon in their mouth, who went to the right school, who know the right people, the privileged group. Tomorrow's top chiefs will get there on their merit. Their—and *your*—entitlement will be based on the utilization of the required traits needed to operate, influence, and lead at high levels. There are no "secrets" left unearthed for the chosen to follow. *You* are the chosen, if you want to be one of them.

This book is for people who haven't reached their summit—*yet*. It lays out the equipment—err, *qualities*—they will need to pack on their climb to the top of the corporate mountain.

Because maneuvering through various levels of a corporation is analogous to moving up a mountain, I've used mountain climbing in this book as a metaphor for learning to think like and become the person at the top. To make it to the top of a company, you must pass through tricky and scary situations, just as you would on a mountain.

To scale rocky heights, your first move must be to establish a firm footing: You must learn the ropes to overcome obstacles, move on, and take the lead. A solid foundation of vital traits gives you a substantial base from which to operate. Knowing exactly what's demanded of you gets you through problems and shoots you out ahead of others.

To get the firm footing you need, you must learn from those who have already reached that seemingly inaccessible pinnacle.

It's smart to see what experienced climbers know. You might be surprised to discover that you have all of the necessary gear already. Now you just need to approach the mountain and decide where to climb— and how high up to go.

To learn what experienced climbers know I went to where they are, at the top: the chief executive officers (CEOs) who have made the ascent themselves. I've picked some of the best mountaineers there are and included their experiences so you can witness the various qualities required and learn to make them your own.

You may not actually aspire to be the chief executive officer of your company, but you may still want to be the chief accountant, salesperson, administrator, or MIS person, or principal, division manager, editor, or head of whatever group you are in. *With the right gear you can be.*

This book is intended to give you a better understanding of the qualities that "chiefs" of organizations have and *how to make them your own*. Throughout the book I'll refer to actual chief executive officers and give you their perspectives because they have successfully made the climb themselves over several years and are best qualified to tell you what it takes from the very firmest of foundations.

Remember: Perhaps your current goal is not to get to the top of the hill but simply to avoid being pushed off. That's okay. (You may be more of a "hiker" than "climber" in the vernacular of this book.) To keep your job, or to move up, you still need to understand what a chief (i.e., your boss) expects from you.

As you learn the ropes you may decide it's not that difficult to stretch for the next ledge. You may want to take on the exhilarating, challenging, and usually fun route of scaling to the top. But even if you just want to do a good job at the level you are at and be rewarded for it, that alone would make this book worth reading.

Yet there is more.

If you understand how the chiefs run the show:

- You'll avoid getting fired.
- You'll get promoted more quickly.
- You'll enjoy the quality of work life you want and deserve.
- And—if you do decide you want to be the Big Boss, the CEO, someday—you will have the right equipment.

If you are working for a CEO it's important to know what makes him tick. You need to discover what his priorities are for the short term and long term. You'll want to know what he's instinctively good at as well as his blind spots.

In addition to avoiding being fired and maybe getting promoted, a main benefit to you of understanding how the CEO thinks is financial. You want your company to be a valuable business entity and to make money so you can make money. You can't afford not to know the boss, to understand how he plans to make the company more successful. You have to talk to him and ask questions. You have to read him a lot. *You* have to *push him occasionally. It's unreasonable to think he should do that for you. . . . And the higher up you go, the more critical this is.*

—JERRY HENRY
Senior Vice President
and CFO, DuPont

Important note: Most of the time I'll use "he" when referring to CEOs because they are predominantly male. But I will also use "she" occasionally, because women are progressively joining those ranks.

You'll avoid being fired.

In simplest terms, the employee who satisfies the boss keeps his job. A lot of people fail because they aren't aware of what the boss wants. If you ignore the work needs and wants of the boss, if you think he has stupid requests, if you think "that's not my job," you just might get fired.

Understanding your boss may be as simple as asking him and others around him what he values. For example, you might learn he likes "dates" attached to "tasks." Therefore you provide specific schedules of work activity with deadlines. Tell him what's been finished, and *when*. And what's next, when. And on and on. It's that basic.

> *Understanding the boss is critical to career success. When I've hit rocky patches on the job, it's often been because I didn't understand what was expected of me, and sat back and waited to be told. Now I know better. I ask, What's important to you? What's absolutely essential to getting my job done? Understanding the boss gives me confidence and clarity.*
> —TAMMY TIERNEY
> Editor, *Kansas City Business Journal*

A recent client of mine, a vice president of international marketing, told me, "My CEO's hobby is the printed word. He'll read a book on grammar on an airplane rather than a novel. Using poor grammar won't get you fired, but knowing the value he places on good grammar makes you careful about what you say and how you write to him."

You'll get promoted.

Bosses are always evaluating who will advance next. Top people topple from their positions overnight. Your company's leaders and your company's competitors are constantly looking to "pick off the best" and replace those who have just toppled.

Getting promoted does not require genius. It requires continued attention to details, tenacity, understanding effective chiefs, and doing a little more than the next person.

A friend of mine who works as a financial manager for a large energy company told me, "I learned this about my boss. Sometimes he helps people out financially or in some other way, he gives them a real break. But the next time he really sticks it to them. I may not like it, but at least now I understand it and I'll decide how long I'll put up with it."

> *You have to realize that whether your CEO moved up the ranks or was recruited into the company you work for, she got there because she fit into the culture. Understanding what she is about will help you understand what is valued in that organization.*
> —CAROLYN DUFF
>   President, WomenWorks, Inc., and
>   author of *When Women Work Together*

You'll enjoy the quality of work life you want and deserve.

You probably want to live and survive and thrive in business, rather than just plod and toil. You probably want to greet each day with praises rather than curses. Humans who do the right stuff in life deserve such happiness.

A professional business life can be a great source of enjoyment. It produces general prosperity and helps one avoid the rather miserable state of unemployment.

> *Understanding the boss is just projecting yourself into how they might think. It's like you face a situation and ask yourself, How would Clint Eastwood or Beetle Bailey or the CEO handle the situation? It can be fun to think this through. The negative of that situation is that people don't come up with their own solutions, don't use their creativity, sometimes limit themselves, and play it too safe. The positive of the situation is that if they have a CEO who is the most experienced, has the most wisdom, uses the best judgment, is well equipped to lead, run, or direct the organization in the normal and abnormal course of events—well that person should be emulated. The question employees have to decide is, Is my CEO really that good?*
> —GREGG MILLER
> President, RACOM Corporation

An executive secretary I spoke with (who wished not to be named to protect the confidentiality of her boss) makes it her practice to learn what her boss values in addition to doing her job. "I know who to put through on the telephone and who not to put through. If he stays until 8:30 P.M., I stay until 8:30 P.M. I know the image he has created and how to support it. I know when to prod, when to help, when to back off. Because of his high-profile position, I took a special course on being a bodyguard so I could play a small role in protecting him, or at least spotting danger." She showed me a Polaroid photo of his desk. "This is how it looked when he left a week ago. I take a snapshot of it every time he leaves to make sure it is identical upon his return. It helps him feel organized and in control despite long absences."

How has this secretary been rewarded for her understanding of the CEO's work needs and acting on this understanding?

Not only has she kept her position over many years with regular pay increases, she got promoted— *to president*. Her boss created a separate company for his private investments and made her president of it "because she was doing all the work anyway," he explains. Her CEO recently bought her a full-length mink coat at Christmas, and he relocated his offices to a different part of the country to better satisfy her health needs. The secretary turned mountaineer and her husband regularly have use of the CEO's beach house for weekends. She enjoys a high-quality work life.

If you do decide you want to be the Big Boss some-day, you will have the right equipment.

The fact is, you need to think like a CEO long before you become one. People who make it to the top act and think like they are "number one" before they actually become number one. They've learned it's critical to adopt the view from the perch while aspiring to it. They demonstrate time and time again that one can operate within that frame of reference. Any job thoroughly understood becomes fairly simple and workable. After you become a top climber, most mysteries will become apparent to you. The purpose of this book is to make them apparent *before* you get there.

> *If you want to wear the chief's shoes some-day it is a good idea to understand what he did to get them. Don't make the same mis-takes; learn what he would have done differently, and do it. And sooner than later, you'll be tying your laces.*
> —JEFF BARENS
> President, The Barens Group

If in your career plans you think you will wait until you are working closer in the chain of command to corporate chiefs before you try to comprehend that world, you will have waited too long. If you conclude that it really doesn't matter if you understand the boss, that all you need to do is your job, you are wrong. If you rationalize that at your level it isn't that critical, you are incorrect. And if you reason that thinking like a chief isn't necessary until you hold the title, then you are really off target.

> *The problem is that employees get trapped into doing their piece or part of the work and don't see the business as a whole. The CEO has the entire entity to be concerned with. Employees have to grasp that and be able to work with it.*
> —PHIL WILKINSON
>   Principal, Network Programs, Inc.

Employees mistakenly rationalize, I'm too busy doing my job. And anyway, if anyone is doing the understanding it should be my boss. If you wait for that ideal situation to happen, you may wait for a long time. A computer manufacturer accounting manager told me, "I avoid him [the CEO] like the plague. I just do my job and carry on. I wish he'd pay a little more attention to me. But he's very happy letting me alone. I notice I do the same to my subordinates. I guess we become our boss."

> *Occasionally I've heard someone say I don't care enough for people. That hurts me deeply. If they knew me they'd know I do care. That misunderstanding comes from some generalization that bosses aren't caring people ... but I can understand misconceptions. When I was a young person starting with the company I'd see the boss take an*

*hour-and-a-half lunch while I sat at my desk
with a sack lunch getting a half hour. I incorrectly thought the CEO had no worries
and not much to do. Now that I run this operation, I know there is not a lot of heavy
lifting at the top but it's still hard work.*
> —JACK LUNDBERG
> President,
> Denver Sala/Svedala Industries, Inc.

You may ask, Isn't the CEO's role and power dimin-
ishing? Aren't companies turning upside down, putting
chiefs on the lowest rung instead of the highest rung of
the ladder, so they truly serve their people? Don't team
decisions take precedence over dictatorial decision-
making from the top? Aren't employees supposed to be
empowered by management now? And doesn't all of
this mean the CEO isn't that important anymore? *No.
Definitely not. Not now nor in the future.*

Every group of any size needs a lead person, someone who takes responsibility for making decisions,
guiding teams, selling ideas, managing crises, and
generally conquering the mountain before them.
Paths to the top are pretty narrow. There isn't a lot
of room. A lead person makes the ascent and others
support him. You can be that head person if you
want. It is up to you to take the responsibility.

*What should an ambitious career person do
to become a CEO? Understand the people
above her/him. Get results.*
> —LOLA SCOBEY
> President, Audio-Therapy Innovations

It's a self-fulfilling prediction. You learn from chiefs about chiefs. You take on the vital traits. You stand out from the crowd of people afraid to stand out or unwilling to put the effort out. You get slotted as the leader. You forge ahead. You get to the top. You are invaluable to the rest who are also attempting the climb. Your role and power only increase.

You are the one who will win. You know that any time you fully comprehend something or someone you can better deal with it or them. *My objective is to bring you up close to CEOs you wouldn't normally have access to,* to unlock their mystique and any power over you. As good as you already are, you'll do better when you fully realize what they want and need. You will deal more effectively with the boss—and in time have the tools required to become the chief.

Comprehending the chief slot does not mean being artificially chummy to powerful people. It does not mean developing a friendship you can flaunt among your peers. It is not about psyching someone out or positioning yourself to manipulate or exploit. It is not bar-hopping with the boss to become a crony. The purpose is to understand the leader so you can work better with him or her, understand what he or she values, minimize problems for yourself, structure the way you work, and decide if you want the job someday.

> *Simply treat the boss like your best customer—find out about him.*
> —JOEL A. SCHLEICHER
> COO, Nextel Communications, Inc.

How to Think Like a CEO is divided into two parts. Part One will lay out the 22 Vital Traits that successful chiefs have and how to make them your own. The mystery of why some people make it to the top and some don't, when they are all equally competent in the job, is revealed to you. No one wants an unknown power presiding over them. If you follow the right path and utilize the right ropes, you'll be the one who reaches the pinnacle of power.

This book is intended to make you aware of the 22 Vital Traits so you can more confidently and quickly acquire those necessary qualities. By having a near-perfect model, you can better evaluate those you work with as well as set your own self-development objectives. As you complete chapters 3, 4, and 5 (detailing the 22 Vital Traits), you will notice clear changes in how you view yourself and how you view others.

You will learn the major and minor differences between the entrepreneurial chief and the professional manager—the mountaineers of corporate America. Understanding their makeup minimizes mistakes you might make on your climb up.

To begin with you'll learn about near-perfect chiefs, then the not-so-near-perfect ones. The fact is, sometimes people who lack some of the 22 Vital Traits still succeed in scaling lofty heights. That creates an obstacle to your climb. The secret for you is not to learn the wrong lessons from the not-so-near-perfect chiefs.

Part Two of *How to Think Like a CEO* is for

moving up. First you develop the necessary qualities of chiefs, then you have to put them into use. This means you want to know what routes other climbers took to get to the top. Succeeding chapters lay out what to expect when you make your move from the "number-two" to the "number-one" slot.

You will also get a clear view of the chiefs' jobs and what they get paid for doing them. Reading what "top mountaineers" actually do, what they want in the people around them, and how they deal with their own bosses provides you accelerated learning and insights into the world at the top.

At its best, climbing a corporate mountain is as fun, engaging, and invigorating as any activity you can be involved in. If you are unprepared, it can be a miserable disaster. With the correct information you will discover the joys of doing friendly battle with any "rockface" or obstacle presented and will be impatient to go out and test yourself again and again.

BASIC EQUIPMENT SUMMARY

If you understand how chiefs run the show—and learn to think like them *before* you are one— you'll become one yourself sooner.

You also:
- will avoid getting fired or passed over,
- will get promoted more quickly, and
- will enjoy the quality of work life you want and deserve.

CHAPTER 2

The Right Ropes

Understanding the most basic climbing tools, as the experienced climbers—err, chiefs—know

In my book *Lions Don't Need to Roar: Using the Leadership Power of Professional Presence to Stand Out, Fit In, and Move Ahead* (Warner Books, 1992), I had researched what successful people do to be memorable, impressive, credible, genuine, trusted, and liked. I interviewed people who had achieved in their field to learn how they set themselves apart from the rest in an effective manner. More than one hundred people were personally interviewed for my book, including the CEOs from companies such as Avis, Fruit of the Loom, Colgate, ARCO, Heinz, Adolph Coors, MTV, Time-Warner, General Instruments, Pan Am, and ESPN, retired Admiral Elmo Zumwalt Jr., former U.S. presidential candidate Senator Gary Hart, the publisher of *Forbes*, the editor of the *Wall Street Journal*, the owner of the Seattle Mariners, and the authors of the mega-bestselling books *How*

What Is a CEO?

No, *CEO* does not stand for "Crafty, Energetic, Overachiever." It stands for Chief Executive Officer. It's a modern term invented to describe the job of the individual who manages the executives in a company. Theoretically, the CEO puts the right executive in the right job at the right time. He or she could be called a field marshal. But FM doesn't look as good as CEO behind a name on company stationery.

The title of president is often redundant with CEO. Although widely accepted for describing the head of the executives, its legal meaning holds the real importance. Banks require a "president" for a legal signature. The IRS goes after the president and treasurer if the company doesn't pay taxes. Internationally the president or CEO is likely called "managing director."

There can be lots of chiefs in a company: Chief Executive Officer, Chief Operation Officer, Chief Financial Officer, Chief Administrative Officer, Chief Information Officer, Chief Legal Officer, Chief Investment Officer, Chief Whatever.

The Chief Operation Officer (COO) is occasionally the president. The COO manages the business operations, reporting to the CEO. The COO carries out the plans of the CEO and is frequently the second in command.

The Chief Financial Officer (CFO) usually reports to the CEO (as does the CIO). CFOs frequently become the CEO. In tough times the CFO seems to stand for Chief Firing Officer because they do the reporting and recommendations on how much personnel overhead a company can afford.

The CIO usually means Chief Information Officer as in computer and software information. It can also mean Chief Investment Officer.

The Chief Administrative Officer (CAO) title is used less frequently and is foggy in the description of his duties. It means different things to different organizations but is generally the same as a CFO with additional administrative, strategic planning, legal, business development, human resources, and corporate communication responsibility.

Regardless of the exact official title, this book is about the top people in an organization—the chiefs who have the financial fire power to make and back up decisions that ultimately affect you and me.

to *Swim with the Sharks*, *Games Mother Never Taught You*, and *Anatomy of an Illness*, to name a select few. From the numerous conversations I found *how those people think, act, and interrelate to set themselves apart from others.*

Lions Don't Need to Roar detailed how effective people think about themselves, think about others, and think about life. I elaborated on how the effective individual walks into a room, shakes hands, sits down, and begins a business conversation. Posture, eye contact, gestures, voice, facial expressions, body movement, and physical presence were dissected. Then I provided a prescription for going beyond communicating to truly bonding with people by expecting acceptance, touching, asking questions, using humor, being personal, asking favors, and other behaviors of confident and competent people. From my research I profiled the personal management strategy of successful people.

The research for *How to Think Like a CEO* again involved interviewing those recognizable names listed above as well as more than one hundred additional successful CEOs—people who have already made it to the top, so to speak. I knew that controlling one's effect on others was a critical step in becoming an effective individual, but I knew that climbing corporate mountains involved more. One has to truly understand people who carry the most authority, power, and dominance in an organization—the people who oversee and sway a career. Those are the corporate chiefs—the people who have triumphantly made the treacherous climb themselves.

So I set out to learn about and understand the CEO

and other chiefs in business. I asked seminar attendees and employees of client companies around the
country the same question: What would be beneficial
to know about the top individuals in your company?
From their responses I developed a list of questions,
the answers to which will provide you with important
information about an organization's "chief":

- What traits do effective chiefs have?
- Why do some chiefs turn out to be so ineffective?
- How does one become CEO?
- What exactly does the CEO do?
- Who bosses the boss; what constituents does he
  have to satisfy?
- What do chiefs look for in people they hire, pro-
  mote, and fire?

*Of course most CEOs want to be understood
by their people; I need to be understood by
mine. It's critical to get the work done. Sometimes CEOs will complain to a subordinate,
"I can't believe you can't see what I'm thinking." When the employee protests, "I can't
read your mind," CEOs respond, "Dammit,
you should at least be trying!"*

*People used to think the CEO was un-
reachable. Ten years ago that may have
been true. Today it's easier than it ever has
been to reach the boss and learn about his
thinking. In my company, with e-mail,
phone mail, fax, and my physical presence*

*in the building, people can access me
twenty-four hours a day.*

*I naturally want my employees to produce
good work, but I also expect them to understand me. I expect them to do internally for
the company what I do externally for the
company. They need to understand me as I
understand other CEOs and our customers.
That is what makes the process work.*

*We are the leading golf course designers in
the world. Every guard-gated community
and country club we've developed started
with some CEO's idea. Most of them
wanted a course tailored to their own interests and their friends. I needed to find out
what they wanted to keep them happy yet
separate that from what the market
wanted. . . . I can usually tell by playing a
game of golf with them what kind of businessperson they are. Then I have to convince
them of the difference between what they
want and what the market will support. I
have to understand that person to do that.*

*That is my external role. My employees'
internal role is to develop the same understanding of me to keep our company's operations running smoothly and profitable.*

—PERRY DYE
President, Dye Designs International

It was very interesting conducting my initial survey
of what people wanted and needed to know about the

CEO of their company. The first reaction from nonchiefs I talked with was, "I hadn't really thought about it, particularly to the extent that I could do anything about it. The CEO is the CEO and I'm just a [pick one: engineer, data processor, accountant, salesman, assistant to . . . , secretary, administrator, teacher, department head, and on and on, up and down the line]." The person at the pinnacle of power in the company was thought to be unreachable, untouchable, unquestioned, *unknown*. And that top person seldom had any intention of changing that. But when people started thinking about the possibility of getting to know and understand the person in power, so they could work better with that positioned being, they got excited. *They got empowered!* Maybe not in the way the current management gurus talk about empowerment but in the true sense of it. When people thoroughly understand the unknown, its *power* over them vanishes. When the mystery, mystique, and misunderstanding of the unreachable wanes—well, that's exciting!

The reaction from CEOs was equally interesting when I told them I was doing research on how to understand CEOs and other chiefs. It wasn't warmly received by everyone. No one wants to be analyzed—particularly the big boss. He is the least studied person in the organization. He's scrutinized and criticized the most, but not really *looked at*. Some CEOs dismissed the significance of studying CEOs. (Remember, they don't like to be inspected. As Steve Cornforth, a partner at Price Waterhouse in Toronto, puts it, "They don't like to be too introspective about why they got there. It might jinx them.") But many more CEOs became as intrigued about the study as their subordinates because *they don't know how CEOs think*. As Larry Kirshbaum, president of my book publishing company, Warner Books, remarked to me upon the announcement of my study, "Good grief. Good luck." As it turned out most of the CEOs I interviewed were very helpful because they wanted to contribute and they were curious what others would say.

> *There is no one group of thought that deals with all CEOs. You are dealing with human beings with different personalities, temperament, experience, intellect, age, education, upbringing. There is not one pat group.*
> —LEONARD ABRAMSON
> CEO and President,
> U.S. Healthcare

CEOs want to think they are individuals. (Don't we all?) They don't like to admit to a stereotype. They don't want to be categorized and labeled. They don't want to follow some prescription. But in reality they do. *They have to, to do the job they need to do.* And you may say, Well, I work for a guy who follows no pattern. He is totally unpredictable and sometimes irrational. He is certainly not smart, dynamic, or charismatic. And he doesn't care a cent about his people. Yet he is still the CEO! HOW?

As in any walk of life the best and brightest don't always succeed. Sometimes the ones who don't *apparently* deserve it do make it to the highest level.

But not that often. Usually the cream does rise to the top, as they say on the farm. Instead of looking at the *dis*similarities between CEO A compared to CEO B, I looked at the similarities. Those traits are much more prevalent.

There *are* plenty of similarities.

SO WHAT IS A NEAR-PERFECT CHIEF?

One morning in the Denver airport's United Red Carpet Lounge, a group of insurance company award winners were convening for a flight to an incentive-trip destination. Company executives and salespeople were meeting, shaking hands, and enthusiastically talking about their trip. A regional vice president was taking a star salesman and his wife around the room to meet the corporate honchos. The six-feet-two-inch CEO of the insurance company was walking to a corner work area where he'd set up a makeshift desk with a phone and his papers. Out of the corner of his eye, he saw the regional vice president and salesman. In an attempt to avoid them, the CEO hunched his head and shoulders down to reduce his frame to about six feet, hastened his step, and went out of his way around a pillar. But the vice president saw him and took the nervous salesman and his wife in hand to introduce them to Mr. Big. The CEO was trapped. He had to stop and meet them. He couldn't avoid it even though he wanted to. With a feeble smile and a trite exchange of words, he shook hands, studied his coffee cup, and stuffed his free hand in his pocket while the vice president explained the salesman's success. The CEO did nothing to appear interested or impressed, only impatient. He mumbled congratulations and turned and hurriedly walked away, avoiding others who might try the same thing.

The CEO had an opportunity to make the salesman and his wife feel like heroes. Instead he made them feel like heels.

This CEO is *not* what I'm talking about in a near-perfect CEO. (Although, I admit, there are too many like him out there.)

A near-perfect CEO in that situation would have deliberately positioned himself close to the doorway so he'd be first to greet everyone entering. He would stand energetically, with a smile, and initiate handshakes, small talk, and pats on the back. He'd have personally taken the star salesman and his spouse to the other executives and sincerely praised the accomplishments of the salesman in front of others. Maybe he'd ask a question or two that would let the vice president look "big" in front of his salespeople. Perhaps the CEO would make a humorous comment to ease the tension of the people talking with him. He could note some detail about the sales record. He'd appear to be sincere and congenial. Then Mr. Big, at an appropriate time, would graciously excuse himself to return to his post to be available to calm the next nervous salesperson entering the room. That's a near-perfect CEO.

To become a near-perfect CEO you have to be a near-perfect number two, three, four, and on-down-

the-line person. It takes work, effort, and commitment to get to the top ledge, and when you get there,
you have to keep on working at it to stay there.

> *As a general rule, leaders have become lead-*
> *ers because they've done more, been better,*
> *worked harder, and somehow differentiated*
> *themselves in some ways. They've accom-*
> *plished this more or less on their own all*
> *along the way.*
> —GREGG MILLER
> President, RACOM Corporation

It is critically important for you to work for a first-
rate CEO. They run a good operation, are less apt to
fail, and are less likely to go out of business. You are
less liable to lose your job. Plus they set better exam-
ples while teaching better lessons. The kind of person
you admire and work for is the kind of person you'll
become.

(One retired CEO friend of mine read this part of
my book during the early editing and said to me, "I
never worked for anyone I admired or tried to emulate. I always felt unfortunate in this matter.")

It will be no surprise to you that a *real* CEO is only
a *real human being* who happens to have a certain
job—like an astronaut or doctor has a certain job. It
takes specific traits to execute the job effectively—to
be near-perfect. Not all CEOs have all of the traits in
use all of the time. Some of the chiefs interviewed
simply did not demonstrate the traits during our time
together. They may possess the necessary qualities

and I just didn't see them, or maybe they don't. When CEOs are asked directly to discuss CEO characteristics, they seldom acknowledge them because

- they haven't specifically identified their traits,
- admitting traits would be too revealing,
- they don't want others to know the useful characteristics.

But the vital traits—the attributes that make up the right stuff to get to the tallest peaks—are there if you know how to look.

You should be able to recognize a good percentage of these qualities in your own CEO. Most important, these are traits you should consider developing for yourself.

The CEOs I interviewed for this book try to do a good job. In my view, they try to be *near-perfect*. Not one of them would use those words together, of course. Most try to use a majority of these traits during good times and bad times in a steady, proven manner of effectiveness.

CEOs—the Mr. or Ms. Bigs out there—are just folks! Folks like you and me and the people we know. In my twenty-year career of working with CEOs, I've found some are ten times wealthier, nicer, smarter, more honest, or better looking than others. Some are ten times dumber, meaner, more dishonest, or downright nastier than others. Some CEOs are intellectual nerds, not the charismatic figure you'd expect. Many are definitely not politically correct.

Many are salt-of-the-earth, good-character, productive types, while others are simple profit moguls.

Some came from silver-spoon backgrounds, some from the other side of the junkyard; some had lived in villas in the Mediterranean, some had lived in their cars for a period of time. (I've worked in sixteen countries around the world and many more different cultures than that. There is no difference between CEOs anywhere in the world—they just speak different languages.)

Despite how high up you are or how far away from your level they are, one thing is certain: A CEO's personality, character, drive, and spirit will affect you now and in the future.

My professional job is to provide advice, outside opinion, and expertise in professional development to CEOs and their mid- and senior-level managers. I've had to learn to understand, influence, persuade, negotiate with, sell to, present to, and deliver bad news (and good news) to heads of large and small companies, hospitals, universities, financial institutions, associations, utilities, other consulting businesses, and government agencies. I must understand what makes them tick.

Although few people recognize it early enough in their careers, for them to accomplish their business and career goals they need to understand the major presence of important chiefs in their business life. Most people think that that insight will not be available to them until much later in their careers. But in *How to Think Like a CEO* it is available, and you can begin identifying with those top people—starting now.

Through my research I've tracked patterns that

run through the people who scale lofty heights in life. The result is 22 Vital Traits that make up the right stuff you need to work your way to the top.

It's not enough to list a trait like "leadership." What does that mean? There is so much mystery (and misinformation) in a label like that. My search was to discover what *exactly* such a label means. The following traits dissect what "leadership" and other labels actually entail.

In *The Effective Executive*, Peter F. Drucker wrote, "To be reasonably effective (as an executive) it is not enough for the individual to be intelligent, to work hard, or to be knowledgeable. Effectiveness is something separate, something different. But to be effective also does not require special gifts, special aptitude, or special training. Effectiveness as an executive demands doing certain—and fairly simple—things." I wanted to find those "fairly simple" yet often missed things.

Rich Karlgaard, editor of *Forbes* technology supplement *ASAP*, writes, "I have interviewed Bill Gates (founder and CEO of Microsoft) three times, most recently while accompanying him on a five-day, five-city tour. Not once have I heard Gates talk on a subject resembling management theory. . . . The entire Gatesian theory for managing Microsoft is . . . simple stuff. But effective management in the real world is simple."

When you read and study the 22 Vital Traits you'll find that I report on my findings and simultaneously make recommendations for you to make them part of your own gear.

Upon reading the traits of near-perfect chiefs you

may react, So what is new? Sometimes research just verifies what you already suspected, sometimes it uncovers something you didn't know or would never have guessed. Sometimes it points out that which is so obvious it is completely overlooked—the simple things.

You might say, My boss isn't anything like that! You may be right, but you may be wrong. Unless you've posed questions directly to him, heard his response, watched him in action, observed his nonverbal reaction to things close-up, asked more questions, and thoroughly succeeded in cutting through his professional public persona, you may not really know him.

Hopefully your next reaction will be, You know, when I think about it, the really effective "Mr. and Ms. Bigs" really are the way Benton says they are; interesting. And better yet, I think I can do that too!

THE RIGHT ROPES SUMMARY

There are 22 Vital Traits that successful chiefs have.

You must make them your own.

Read carefully (and reread) about them.

Intelligently observe the vital traits in others.

Work on improving your own qualities to surpass yourself as well as others.

Chapter 3

Approaching the Climb

How near-perfect chiefs size up themselves, others, and life

NEAR-PERFECT CHIEFS ARE:

---

1. SECURE IN SELF

2. IN CONTROL OF ATTITUDE

3. TENACIOUS

4. CONTINUOUSLY IMPROVING

5. HONEST AND ETHICAL

6. THINKING BEFORE TALKING

7. ORIGINAL

8. PUBLICLY MODEST

1st VITAL TRAIT: SECURE IN SELF

Sometimes the biggest obstacle isn't the climbing—it's yourself.

An extremely necessary attitude that a chief requires is being secure in himself. This attitude must be carried both inside one's head and outside in one's demeanor for the public to see.

John Bianchi grew his hobby business of making leather holsters for himself (he was a police officer at the time) into the largest manufacturer of leather holsters and belts for law enforcement officers and the military in the country. His company, Bianchi International, was a privately held company sold to Huntington Holdings, where John remained as a consultant until his contract expired and he became the spokesman for Safari Inc. (a competing manufacturer of leather goods). John Bianchi has tremendous charisma in a macho industry. When he shows up at a trade show booth, men line the halls to get the chance to see and meet him. The scene takes on the appearance of a country-western singer meeting his fans. He is a star in his industry. He was also a friend of John Wayne, personally making holsters the Duke used in his movies. In addition to his personal and business successes he attained the rank of brigadier general in the National Guard Reserves. John Bianchi is secure in himself.

He told me this story: "You may not believe this, but some thirty-eight years ago, as a kid, I was working in a coffee shop. I'd see company presidents come in. I'd watch them and ask myself, What makes them different? What do they do? Maybe I should study that. I discovered a big thing for me— their predominant trait: Those people appeared secure in themselves. They didn't have fear. They seemed confident. I've since learned over and over, fear is the root of so many problems. You have to be secure in yourself. No one else will have confidence in you unless you do."

Near-perfect CEOs are marked by confidence in themselves. An uncertain, apprehensive person will not make it to the top of anything.

> *I've always been self-sufficient. I have a lot of confidence in myself. There's no question I have faults. I'm super critical of myself. But I believe in myself. I have since I was a child.*
>
> —JULIE DONAHUE
> CEO and President,
> BBN Hark Systems Corporation

Top CEOs want to deal with self-assured people over any other type. For some that might seem like a statement of the obvious, but remember, people tend to choose people like themselves to work with. A less-than-perfect chief with his own set of insecurities tends to draw to himself other insecure people, thus making his own insecurities show less by allowing himself to be surrounded by people who are not a threat. But the near-perfect, and secure, CEO knows individuals who lack confidence cause more problems for themselves and their company than do ignorance, laziness, or arrogance.

John Wilson is the president of USC, a consulting company that specializes in change management, where operations, processes, procedures, and human resources are studied and changed to improve a client's operating effectiveness. I asked him if it makes any difference if an intelligent, hardworking, and competent individual has low self-esteem. Wilson responded, "[It is] virtually impossible to be a highly effective manager without it. You manage things and lead people. Management is to a large extent effective delegation. Leadership, of course, is the ability of inspiring and motivating people to worthwhile achievement. Both require respect. If you don't have it for yourself you're not likely to get it from others. In my opinion, many companies are too hung up on degrees and pedigrees. We look for PSM (poor, smart, and motivated) with some people skills." Then he enthusiastically added, "When we find them, we hire them and ask if they have any brothers or sisters too!"

Herb Pinder oversees one of Canada's most successful oil corporations (Saskoil) in addition to his business of acting as an agent to professional Canadian hockey players (Goal Management Corporation). He told me that after a certain ability level the difference between a good hockey player and a great player has little to do with his competence and everything to do with his confidence. And he added that the individual's confidence affects the entire team. "In the beginning of my career I was hurt a lot by not recognizing the effect others were having on myself and even my company," he says. "I've learned to accept the fact that people with poor self-images can negatively affect my endeavors. I don't let that happen anymore. Now I look for secure people, both in my players and my employees."

CEOs tell me that the effort it takes to convince

others to be confident is exhaustive, and lots of times it isn't worth their while.

Powerlessness is a state of mind more than anything else, and by occupying it you're doing such a disservice to yourself. You end up undermining everyone you are associated with: family, friends, their company, co-workers, other chiefs. Remember: No one can make you feel inferior without your consent.

> *I'm not sure if I'm getting better at acting or if the base is changing. I have just determined to have fun and I've concluded where I end up isn't all that matters . . . how I feel about myself does matter.*
>
> *It would be nice if we could put a quarter into a slot and pull out eight measures of self-confidence, but that's hard to accomplish. You need to act.*
> —CAROLYN DUFF
> President, WomenWorks, Inc.

Being secure in yourself absolutely rates near the top of the list of essential equipment for any climber. If a CEO wavers and shows signs of not being confident of which way he wants to go, it sends shudders from the top echelon all the way down the mountain. When the CEO of Philips (the world's third largest consumer electronics company) spoke to his shareholders about the company's struggle to turn research into hit products, he said in a secure tone of voice, "There are obstacles. We will conquer them."

Some insecurity is expected even at the top. Chiefs are not always totally secure in themselves.

> *If there was some way of measuring it, CEOs would have more self-confidence than most other workers. But that doesn't mean they have it all of the time. In fact, self-confidence might come from success they achieved by overcompensating for some insecurity. Fear of failure is an effective driving force. CEOs think a lot about tomorrow and next week in very specific terms; both in what they want to achieve and what they want to avoid failing at.*
>
> —GREGG MILLER
> President, RACOM Corporation

Regardless of whether you are talking to shareholders, customers, or your banker, you might feel some level of stage fright about your effectiveness. Choke that feeling down. Hold it inside, out of public view. Concentrate on your *goal* and *objective*, not your uncertainties. Put others at ease first rather than striving to put yourself at ease. There are times that everyone needs to swallow fears and insecurities long enough to take charge. Presidents Clinton, Bush, Reagan, Carter, and as far back as you want to go have all been scared, even terrified, sometimes. The fear feelings have to be conquered. Leaders have to be secure enough to just go ahead and do what is required of them. As do you.

Take a deep breath. Put a relaxed smile on your face. Act like you are secure.

Confidence for everyone unfolds over time and experience. Successes do help, of course. The first time you succeed in some arena your self-esteem may make you say, Well, that was just pure luck on my part. The second time you succeed in that same arena you will likely modestly conclude, Well, I guess luck struck twice. Finally, when you succeed three times, you realize, It must be due to me. Which is likely the truth.

Earlier I said act like you are secure. That is often the first step to actually becoming secure in yourself. Curt Carter, CEO of Mission Bay Investments, believes you have to act secure as well as be secure. (Surprisingly there are self-confident people out there who do not *act* self-confident.) Carter says, "Smile. Simply have a relaxed smile. If you are not smiling your competition will step on your neck." And he added, "Think of how wimps are portrayed on television—hunched over, no smile, shifty eyes. You can't look like that in business at any level."

The other extreme of being secure in self is people who act *over*confident. They aren't. Those people are probably the most insecure and they overcompensate with bluster.

Sometimes people who are insecure make it to the ranks of CEO because they overcompensate so fiercely. "A lot of people who make it to the top lack confidence. They succeed because they work so hard overcompensating for their insecurity," says Dennis

Wu, a partner at Deloitte Touche, L.L.P. But usually they don't last.

Duane Pearsall is an extremely mild-mannered, soft-spoken, self-assured person. He's largely given credit for the introduction of the first battery-powered smoke detector and development of the home smoke alarm industry. Some twelve years after founding Statitrol Corporation and expanding it to one thousand employees, he merged it with a major corporation. Since the use of venture capital contributed to his company's success and he did not enjoy the large corporate environment, he resigned to cofound Columbine Venture Funds, an institutional venture capital firm. He told me this story: "At one time in my career I reported to a very demanding executive who overcompensated for his lack of confidence with volatile arrogance. When performance figures slipped, the decibel level of his voice would increase and he would pound the table, sending the wrong message to many good, productive employees. After a particularly bad display I invited him into my office, reviewed the effects of his tirades, and told him I would not continue under this kind of management. He promptly apologized and promised to stop. The next month it happened again and I left. One week later he was fired."

You may question the need to emphasize being secure in yourself. You may ask, Isn't that a given if you're trying to climb the corporation mountain? You would think so, but you would also be surprised at how much of my time as a consultant is spent talking to managers, executives, and CEOs about their lack of self-confidence.

I'll never forget the first meeting I had with one CEO who founded an industry that he captains. He is known worldwide in top business circles, is the author of several books, and is philanthropic with his company's resources and his personal money. Almost every CEO in his industry admires the man's creativity, vision, and business savvy. Yet the first time we met, I walked into his office, closed the door, and, after we exchanged some pleasantries, out of his mouth came these words: "I'm rife with insecurities." I can assure you, I was taken aback by his candor and his comment. No one would suspect that of the man. He's only one example.

Daily I talk on the phone or meet with very accomplished people to discuss their professional effectiveness, and the conversations frequently steer toward something like, "Debra, I'm very comfortable and I deal well with people who work for me and with me. I have no problem. But people I report to and my boss's boss and his boss intimidate me. I just am insecure in dealing with those types."

If you aren't secure in yourself in dealing with anyone, anywhere, under any circumstances, *you won't be able to deal with anyone, anywhere, under any circumstances.* People have reason (or assume they have a reason) to believe in you if you truly believe in yourself.

Children are not born with self-doubt, they learn it. Wouldn't it be nice if as adults we operated like we did as children before we learned self-doubt? Remember: We wanted to do something and we tried it. If we failed, we tried something else. If we failed again, we tried something else. We didn't stop and think, I can't do this. We just tried something else. *Until* one day, when a parent, friend, sibling, teacher, etc., told us, "Well, you can't do that. You're a [pick one: girl, boy, black, Catholic, youngster, oldster, and on and on]." So we began to doubt ourselves.

Effective chiefs have found the way back to that "child" in themselves. They go on without self-doubt to face new challenges with enthusiasm and a secure feeling of adequacy.

Too many people have learned, either from dysfunctional family environments, counselors, teachers, ministers, bosses, or elsewhere, to have self-doubt and question themselves unnecessarily and unjustifiably. *You* have a choice to *stop* self-sabotaging thoughts or you have a choice to continue to sabotage yourself. You're in control of your attitude.

2ND VITAL TRAIT:
IN CONTROL OF ATTITUDE

If you lose control, you lose. Period.

Herb Kelleher, CEO of Southwest Airlines, says, "We hire attitude." Kelleher oversees what is considered by some to be the most admired airline in the country, a discount passenger carrier that has been profitable for twenty-one straight years. He says, "The best company slogan we ever had is, 'We smile because we want to, not because we have to.'"

People striving for executive status start by mastering their outlook—because they want to, first, and know they have to, second.

In life, there is so little you have control over. You can't control the government, the economy, the spouse, the kids—or anyone else! Fortunately, attitude is *one* area where you do have control.

Your success in business and in life is based more on your mental attitude than your mental capabilities. You will learn, if you haven't already, that you make yourself with your disposition. *Until, and unless, you're in command of your outlook, everyone and anyone can control you.* Only people who manage their attitude avoid being managed by others.

> *At top levels the impact of the person who gets recruited is dramatic. You can't be wrong. Too often emphasis is put on the functional perspective, but mindset and management style are more critical.*
> —NANCY ALBERTINI
> CEO, Taylor-Winfield

Attitude management is simple. Instead of lying awake at three in the morning, worrying whether or not you are capable of doing some project, switch your self-talk from "Can I do this?" to "I can do this." You're using the same four words, but by changing the order you totally change their meaning, your own attitude and perspective, and the likely outcome. As elementary as that advice is many of us don't do it consistently. The trick is to do it consistently—especially when they don't feel like it! That's control.

In the above example, none of the circumstances surrounding your project have changed except your attitude. But immediately you start working from a stronger foundation with the goal-achieving, positive words "I can" instead of the self-questioning "Can I?" People who are more successful than you don't have an easier life. They just have more persistently and consistently *controlled* their perspective about things.

Controlling your attitude can be as easy as telling yourself what you want to have happen. Curt Carter, CEO of Mission Bay Investments and an avid golfer, told me, "I decided to be a better golfer, and my last three games I have been!"

I witnessed a man in control of his disposition in a different way. At a restaurant popular with business-people, I happened to sit next to three men talking shop. A man who appeared to be the junior person started jumping on a decision the senior person had made in front of the customer. The senior person said nothing in defense or retaliation. After the client had left for a few minutes, the senior individual turned to the junior and said, "Don't ever talk to me like that again. What you did was unacceptable. I didn't do anything about your actions this time, but next time I will." That boss was in control of his disposition.

Now I know this next example of a controlled out-look may seem out of the norm, but it works for William Perry Pendley, president and chief legal offi-cer of the Mountain States Legal Foundation. When he faces a trying situation, instead of reacting on his first impulse he thinks to himself, "How would Jesus handle this situation?" Then he attempts to act that way. He takes the time to think how such a "good" person would behave, then does that. (Many success-ful people remember their Christian lessons but not as literally as Pendley does.) I asked him to give a re-cent example.

"Just last week at the car rental counter in Dallas I discovered they had lost my reservation and I was stuck at the airport without a car. I was so frustrated and beginning to get really irate, so I walked away from the counter. I gained my composure, then walked back to the counter to address the problem as I imagined Jesus would. I didn't get a car but I did feel better!" He laughed as he spoke.

What he was doing with his attitude control is re-laxing anxieties and thinking through situations rather than simply *reacting*. It's so uncomplicated, yet so few people do it consistently.

Attitude is conveyed in your facial expression, tone of voice, posture, handshake, handwriting, voice-mail message, decision making, delegating, manag-ing, leading, and on and on. Any time you have any contact with anyone, you broadcast your disposition. Your theatrical skills (which we will discuss later) help you control "leakage" of bad attitudes, but gen-erally your outlook always seeps through.

- Remind yourself to stay in control of your attitude.
- Select the outlook most effective for the situation and people involved.
- Stick with the attitude even when you don't feel like it or others try to dissuade you.
- Change outlooks when you need to and want to.
- Keep aware and in control of your bearing at all times through your physical and mental demeanor.

The higher up you go, the more critical it is to control your disposition. Co-workers, bosses, subordinates, and customers check you every day. They watch and study your inclinations and then frequently match theirs to yours. By controlling your disposition, you can literally affect their performance as much as your own. People often emulate their boss. (But don't naively assume their behavior matches yours. Check, watch, and study them as they are doing you, and if they happen to have a poor or out-of-control attitude, definitely do not let them affect you.)

Being in control of your attitude is choosing a perspective that fits the situation. Near-perfects aren't always in good moods, but that doesn't mean they freely show their bad moods. Near-perfect CEOs accept the fact that everyone in the organization looks to the leader to decide how to act and feel, and therefore they are accountable to employees in that manner.

Subordinates read the leader all *of the time.*
—TAMMY TIERNEY
Editor, *Kansas City Business Journal*

I want to reiterate that being in control of your attitude does not necessarily mean you are always utilizing a *positive* attitude. It means choosing your attitude versus leaving it to chance or human nature. But if you are uncertain how to handle a specific situation you can seldom go wrong by choosing a positive outlook. As Lodwrick M. Cook, CEO of ARCO, told me, "There are very few negative, sour people who pull success off."

Optimism is a dominant trait in the most successful people in business. For instance, the ability to see the best in people becomes a self-fulfilling prophecy.
—TAMMY TIERNEY
Editor, *Kansas City Business Journal*

It is true with some chiefs that what they mean by a "good attitude" is simply one that supports their position regardless of what it is.

A near-perfect chief has to be able to objectively look at herself and how she's feeling and realize her attitude is or isn't productive for managing people at this time. Good ones choose to remove themselves from the situation where they'll adversely affect people only to return when back in control of their disposition. Or they feign a beneficial outlook for the good of the company. (You've heard the expression

It's better to fake a good attitude rather than have a
sincere bad one.)

> *I want to see realistic attitudes but I also
> know stinkin' thinkin' makes you a stinkin'
> person. As the CEO, I know to deter
> stinkin' thinkin' I have to be unrealistically
> positive—almost overstate the positive to
> counter the negative people. . . . I wonder
> how, why, and where people pick up nega-
> tive attitudes. It floors me. I wonder what
> their life is like?*
> —PERRY DYE
> President, Dye Designs International

Mind you, it's a lot easier to abandon control of
your attitude than maintain it. It's indulgent to dislike, react, and tear down yourself, others, and their
work. You can't choose that direction if you want to
move up the mountain.

If you think you're currently at a level where you
are the "exception to the rule" in being concerned
about controlling your attitude, you're wrong. Every
climber needs to control his or her mood.

Again, a reminder: Any attitude not managed by
you can easily be managed by others (a situation you
can't afford at any level in the organization).

3RD VITAL TRAIT: TENACIOUS

Keep going until something stops you, then keep going.

If there was one quality that nearly 100 percent of CEOs have, it is tenacity. There has never been another group that carries the marks of persistence, determination, and resolution more than do the top chiefs.

> *The most required aspects necessary to succeed as a CEO are: one, tenacity; two, perseverance; three, the ability to come back on your own behalf; four, the conviction you know you are right no matter what; and five, the commitment to make things happen.*
> —LEONARD ABRAMSON
> CEO and President,
> U.S. Healthcare

Tenacity is not giving up when everybody else says you should. It is keeping on your path, even if you feel in your heart you might get pushed back or your journey goes slower than you thought. Accomplishing things worthwhile takes time.

> *You'll receive many setbacks and much discouragement and it will continue throughout life.* But that is life—you have to be tenacious.
> —BILL REAGAN
> CEO, Reagan Companies

Every group you deal with craves the unyielding person. Employees, customers, shareholders, board members all want determined leaders. Only your competition (and sometimes the media) wants you to break. Hold firmly to your aspirations; tenacity breeds tenacity as success breeds success.

Harold Sperlich was a product engineer at Ford who pushed tenaciously for the minivan product. His persistence was not rewarded immediately, because Henry Ford II remembered the Edsel bomb of years earlier and Ford didn't want a repeat with a minivan bomb. (Unfortunately, as in all of life, good traits are not *always* rewarded. Fortunately, they are most of the time.) Sperlich was fired and headed to Chrysler. At Chrysler, Lee Iacocca supported Sperlich's belief in the new product. Iacocca's tenacity kicked in when developing the product: "Everyone fought me . . . but that's what makes horse races." The perseverance of the two men produced one of the most profitable products of the decade. Tenacity is appreciated by the near-perfect CEO as well as being a necessary quality in that CEO.

Tenacity is not stubbornness elevated to the level of stupidity. It is commitment to the result regardless of what has to be endured along the way.

Nothing ever happens with one letter, one telephone call, one request. (Nothing worthwhile anyway!) If you were forced to give up all your qualities but one, the one you should keep is tenacity. You would be astonished at just how much you could accomplish with this one unyielding manner.

Salesmen are taught they need to hear three no's before it might really mean no for a customer. Consider the simple "rule of three" for everything you do. Try it three times, three different ways before you even consider giving up. Then, for good measure, try a fourth time.

The pages of *Forbes* magazine are loaded with stories of people who never gave up. As Josh Feigenbaum, CEO of MJI Broadcasting (and former salesperson at *Rolling Stone* and Arista Records who started a radio variety show that didn't go, developed a sports talk show that didn't go, and now has a series of interactive radio products with revenues of $11 million), says, "It doesn't take a rocket scientist to succeed. . . . You just have to work harder at it than anyone else," and, as *Forbes* adds, "be damned persistent."

Work through the constant challenge of tough situations that knock you down. Then get up. If you get knocked down again, get up. If you get knocked down again, get up again. Occasionally you may slow down, but don't stop.

If you slack off, waver, vacillate, and fizzle you deserve to fall short of your destination.

Persevere through disappointments, setbacks, frustrations, and inequities. Those who persevere will succeed.

As long as you stick to it, you can do anything you want: walk around the world, swim around Australia, climb every fourteen-thousand-foot mountain in the country, become a CEO.

There are exceptions to perseverance:

Give up if you are in a business situation that is throwing good money or resources after bad or putting good people into bad projects. Stop. Walk away. Cut losses, for you and others. Don't let ego, pride, fear of admitting mistakes cause you not to quit. One of the traits of the successful chiefs is a coupling of tenacity and the ability to know when to walk away. As they say, "Know when to hold them and know when to fold them."

Stop if you are wrong but your pride hates to admit it. Tenacity in that situation isn't a strength, it's a sickness.

4TH VITAL TRAIT:
CONTINUOUSLY IMPROVING

James Burke, CEO of Johnson and Johnson, tells Thomas R. Horton (CEO of America Management Association) in his interview for *What Works for Me*, "Business has become much more competitive on a world-wide basis. The answer to that challenge is no different than it's ever been: you've got to get better and better, and if you don't, you will be left behind."

Although longtime performer Mel Torme is not a CEO, he has created a business with his performing career, and he says, "Don't laugh, but I'm still learning to sing. I think of my singing career as a work in progress . . . [and] I'll keep on doing it until I get it right." After *forty* years of performing, he's continuously improving.

Martina Navratilova still gets coaching, as does Olympic medal winner Picabo Street, or any other athlete who stays at the top of his or her profession.

Continuously improving means learning. Just as kids who drop out of school are more likely to get into trouble, employees who drop out of continuing education are more likely to get into career trouble. Near-perfect chiefs always seem to be in an improvement mode where they are continuously watching, talking, and listening to do things better and then *doing* things better.

John Moore, president of Electro-Test, Inc., describes his company as "a continuously learning organization. We have to learn faster than our competitors. If we don't, we become technically obsolete and lose the game. The same is true of our management development. We are continuously improving."

Learning begins with birth and ends with death. Effective chiefs are always trying to improve.

With a heightened commitment to improvement, what should you be improving in?

- What you need to know to do your job well.
- What would be useful to know.
- What would be fun to know.

Near-perfect chiefs try to improve on their executive presence, organization, financial skills, confi-

dence, excellence, time management, listening, delegation, public speaking, personal habits, confrontation, assertiveness, paper management, communication skills, and diplomacy, just to name a few areas.

Constant improvement holds many benefits:

- You become useful to more people because you
  know more and can do more.
- You fulfill your abilities to their full potential.
- Your mind and imagination are developed, mak-
  ing you a more original thinker.
- You are able to make better decisions and better
  judgments, again because you know more.
- Others perceive you as wise, which often is half
  the battle to accomplish one's goals.
- Your destiny is secure because of your *worth*.
- Entertains you while you enrich yourself.
  When isn't it valuable to improve?

Berry Fowler was a junior high school teacher who
saw parents pay for their children to receive coaching in areas like math and reading. In 1978 he
started Sylvan Learning to provide after-school tutor-
ing. He built the project into 118 franchises, and in
1985 Fowler sold Sylvan for $5.2 million. His retire-
ment at age forty took him into new areas: ocean
cruising and sailboat chartering; drawing and painting caricatures, which he sold in an art gallery; golfing at his Kaanapali, Hawaii, resort home; and
traveling in Europe. All that fun caused him to get
"cerebral atrophy," as Fowler called it. So in 1992 he
bought 75 percent of Little Gym International, a

children's fitness center, which he has expanded from one operation into a $3.1 million business with seventy-six franchises.

Climbers can't just go along on a day-to-day basis without personal challenge and growth; they need to be constantly improving.

So how does a person on the way to the top with an exhaustive schedule learn? You devote time to learning. It doesn't *come* to you; you have to make it happen, and there are lots of ways to achieve that.

> *The day I graduated from school is when I really started learning. For example, to this day, I read biographies. What I like about biographies is that some great mind documented in a few hundred pages what took years to learn. Life insights are extremely valuable as well as fascinating, and I get to read and learn them in three hours!*
>
> *My advice to people who want to improve:* read. *You don't have to read everything. I read three key pages of the* Wall Street Journal *and my local paper every day. I clip articles for a friend. The friend reads the* New York Times, *and does the same for me. Then we exchange the clippings. There is time for all to read and* think—*unless they are workaholics who manufacture work for themselves!*
>
> —JACK FALVEY
> author of five books
> and a regular contributor to
> the *Wall Street Journal*

One CEO's corporate jet is stocked with current issues of *Fortune, Forbes,* and *Business Week,* but also *Cosmopolitan.* Why *Cosmo*? "To learn what women are reading and thinking. They are my biggest customers!" he explains. To learn continuously:

- talk to people,
- learn from mistakes,
- learn from others' experiences,
- emulate effective leaders,
- learn something new every day.

Talk to people. A favorite expression of effective CEOs is "Manage by walking around." In other words get in among the employees, customers, suppliers, competitors, and community. Most likely each group has a different perspective on any issue discussed. You improve your knowledge by talking to them and asking questions. (A section on asking questions is in chapter 5.)

A cliche chiefs like to use is "Knowledge is power." Well it is! Talking *with a purpose* (not just chattering away) to various people adds to your power. "I can sit in a meeting for three days on the status of the client company and learn less than going to a 9:00 A.M. appointment at the clients *at 8:00 A.M.* and spend the hour talking to people I see in the hallway. If I really want to learn a lot I go at 7:00 A.M.!" explains Ed Shonsey, CEO of Northrup King.

Learn from mistakes. The best way to learn is through experience. To continue to improve, add to your experience, take small steps, and do it every day. You know that experience comes from mistakes. Mistakes provide the opportunity for some of your best learning. When you struggle you will more likely succeed.

James Burke discussed a meeting with General Johnson, founder of Johnson and Johnson: "One day the General's secretary called me. I went to his office and his desk seemed a mile and a half from the door. He asked me to sit down. He went on with his dictating as he always did, then he turned to me. I was certain that I was going to be fired. Still, I found this all pretty exciting. Here was a company where the chairman took the trouble to fire you personally. I decided I would defend myself and was mentally preparing for a good fight. He said, 'I understand that your product failed.' I said, 'Yes, sir, that's true.' Picking up a piece of blue paper, he said, 'Furthermore, I understand it cost this corporation $865,000.' I said, 'Yes, sir, that's right.' He stood up, held out his hand, and said, 'I just wanted to congratulate you. Nothing happens unless people are willing to make decisions, and you can't make decisions without making mistakes.' The first thing that flashed through my mind was that he was giving me a license to make mistakes. But he quickly added, 'If you make the same one again you're through, but that doesn't mean that you should stop making mistakes.'"

Learn from others' experience. Watch people you look up to. Take what you value most from them and do what they do. Some people improve more from observation than from using traditional tools of learning. Closely watch others in the spotlight. Look for what it is that you admire, then try to do those things.

Emulate near-perfect CEOs. Let (or make) your boss teach you every day. Make *sure* he does. That will make you a tenfold better manager than putting "improvement" on hold because you're too busy doing your job. Pick a good boss to learn from. Or at least don't learn from a bad boss—except what *not* to do. A good boss is the best business school in the country.

When Captain John E. Odegaard takes the missile frigate USS *Clark* out for routine maneuvers, he takes several steps to practice what could go wrong and helps his men to improve. "Every underway is a low-visibility drill. (Even when in actuality the sky is blue.) We take sightings and plot the course like it was dangerous conditions. Sometimes we hang sheets on the windows. The crew always has practice, even when they don't need it. The crew grumbles sometimes, but they'll be better prepared when they need it."

Learn something new every day. Make a point to be aware of something novel in your office, home, and city every day. You see the same things all the time, but you really haven't *seen* them. Be excruciatingly aware. Develop your senses. It will round you out and make you a more alert person. Knowledge is out there to be had. And it can be found in the most elementary places. Drive to the office via a different route. Walk to the restroom by way of a different hall. Ask a question of someone you meet about something he or she knows. (That is, someone you might not normally engage in conversation.)

Live and learn. Observe. Listen. Think. Discuss. Ask yourself who, what, when, where, and why about everything. Formulate, test, accept, or reject the new information. But do it all of the time, not sporadically. Not when the whim hits you.

You could ask, "With my heavy workload, how can I make time to improve?" *Take small steps.* Continuous application of effort over time is better than taking occasional giant steps. And when you take those steps seek out a difficult route, not an easy path.

Be aware of balanced and appropriate improvement but always, always, always be tenacious about continuously improving.

Some caution about improving. Yes, as odd as that might sound, there are some cautions to consider about improving.

If your CEO values continuous improvement for himself, you better understand he expects it in you. If he doesn't value it, keep your new know-how a little covered up. It may not be prized. It could even make people jealous. Those who do not put effort into improving themselves resent others who are improving. If you find yourself in that situation, for your own well-being work on getting out of the situation. Work simultaneously and discreetly on your improvement plan and a plan to continue your career advancement in another environment.

Do not learn if you're using knowledge as an opportunity to hurt someone.

Do not flaunt your improvement to show how "smart" you are.

Do not improve only your technical expertise. For example, improve in personality, honesty, awareness, and common sense.

5TH VITAL TRAIT:
HONEST AND ETHICAL

Lee Iacocca was one of the most admired CEOs in recent years, largely due to the fact he was the most visible CEO. But he was also admired because of the type of executive he appeared to be. Alex Taylor III writes in *Fortune* about Iacocca's honesty after his dismissal from Ford: "[Iacocca] took with him the customer research on the minivan. Unlike J. Ignacio Lopez de Arriortua of GM and Volkswagen notoriety, Iacocca *asked* William Clay Ford, Henry's younger brother, for permission to take the material, and Ford gave it."

Honesty is truth, integrity, being genuine, equitable, fair, and frank. It implies an absence of fraud, deceit, artifice, and deception.

*There is no situational honesty. Honesty is
honesty.*

—LEONARD ABRAMSON
President, U.S. Healthcare

The truth is, people can and do get away without
being honest in business. The same person who feels
he's upright isn't always so in the eyes of others. People
judge others' honesty based on their own standards.
And their standards are based on many factors: upbringing, culture, experience, age, value of the transac-
tion (e.g., an employee stealing a box of paper clips
from the jewelry store is viewed differently by some
than one stealing a diamond from the same store).
Honesty is different to people depending on timing, circumstance, extenuating circumstances, penalty level,
and who's talking to whom—e.g., salespeople to customers, CEO to Wall Street, public relations to media,
competitor to competitor. Obviously the standards can
vary measurably from person to person while at the
same time each individual *professes* high integrity.

In an article about honesty, Alan Greenberg, chairman of the Bear Stearns Companies, Inc., says, "Trying to change [associates'] ethical behavior is
hopeless. The only thing we can do is take them to
Sing Sing so they can see the calculated risk [of
breaking rules] isn't worth it." Robert Eaton, chairman and CEO of Chrysler Corporation, said in the
same article, "The nexus of all ethics is truth, and yet
a chief executive officer today is constantly being
told by his lawyers, his public relations people, and
others that 'You can't say that!'"

In his book *The Meaning of Revelation,* H. Richard Niebuhr wrote, "One's view of truth is always partial. . . . I'm male, I'm white, I'm middle class, I'm rural. That shapes my view of the world. That's going to be different from someone who is black, female, lives in Cuba, and is a Communist. We have to recognize that our view of the truth is partial."

In a globally competitive environment, you have to realize people play by different rules.

Be cautious when judging someone's honesty. Sometimes people verbalize as fact what they think, and if it differs from what *you* think, you might conclude they state mistruths. Many people simply have lazy memories or are habitually careless with facts. In business you see it all the time where someone forgets who was due the credit and they give it to someone else or keep it for themselves.

Dishonesty does occur among people in business who are vying for promotions, selling the company's services, bluffing competitors, trying not to be taken advantage of, elevating their status, or simply trying to make good impressions. According to Sid Cato, who publishes "Sid Cato's Newsletter on Annual Reports," nearly 15 percent of annual reports are deceptive. "Never before have CEOs stretched the truth to the limit the way they did in 1993. At best they are imprecise. In the middle ground you might say they are less than forthright. And in many instances they are downright deceptive liars."

Headhunters tell me that at least 80 percent of the time they discover lies on a résumé (regarding dates, degrees, job titles, majors, schools, responsibilities, and so on). "And when people lie, they lie big. An MBA from Wharton or Stanford, for example. They think no one will check, but we do. A lot of times I'm told 'We never heard of him,'" relays Nancy Albertini, CEO of Taylor-Winfield.

> *We're living in an age where honesty, integrity, and good business dealing do not lead to success. It's very difficult to have honesty and integrity in business. It's more than competitive, it's a cutthroat survival level. I'm concerned about my grandchildren. They are being taught honest, ethical behavior by their parents. I wonder will that work against them in this work environment?*
> —MARIE MCDONALD
> President, Access Disability
> Advisors/McDonald Elevator

But really that's a statement every generation makes. In *The Stone Age Present: How Evolution Has Shaped Modern Life—From Sex, Violence, and Language to Emotions, Morals, and Communities*, author William F. Allman writes, "Being skilled at deceit, it appears, is a prerequisite for high office. Given the importance of lying in human affairs, it is perhaps not surprising that men who emerge as the best leaders in a group setting are typically also the best liars." To explain his statement, Allman adds, "Lying . . . is also a gentlemen's obligation. A eulogy describing the deceased's thieving ways might set the record straight, but will not do much to soothe the grieving widow. Telling a job prospect that no matter how talented he is, the boss's nephew is getting the position will not do much for the lad's ambition and drive. Detailing to your co-worker exactly how you feel about the contours of his or her body may send you to court, not bed."

Do be on guard for people who blatantly fabricate. People don't lie just once. Once people invent something, they usually continue the lie to support the original untruth. Thus starts the parade of part truths, half-truths, white lies, fibs, and strategic omissions. A problem for people who are frequently careless with the truth is that their credibility is jeopardized for the future when they *are* telling the truth.

Near-perfect leaders espouse honesty and integrity. So what exactly do they recommend and try to practice according to their self-evaluation? Here's a composite checklist of their dos and don'ts:

- Don't intentionally mislead or misrepresent.
- Don't straddle the line.
- Don't break promises or go back on your word (despite the fact that it is the norm for many political leaders).
- Don't waltz around. Don't put a "spin" on it.
- Do be honest with yourself—internally and externally.
- Do remember that regardless of how carefully you disguise the truth, someone will find out. It will be embarrassing at least.

- Do remember that your distrust of others will often justify their distrust of you.
- Do be precise, crisp, then move on. Long-winded explanations get you in trouble.
- Do understand *mis*understanding.
- Do realize one person's honesty is another person's dishonesty.
- Do bring out into the open uncomfortable issues. (For the people you are associated with, it's better to hear bad news from you than to read it in the *Wall Street Journal*.)
- Do stop exaggeration. Say it like it is. That is good enough. Keep in touch with reality, then you won't get caught "believing your own press."
- Don't forget even for a moment, people go to jail for dishonesty.

Two company presidents who read *How to Think Like a CEO* in the early editing stages both wrote in the margin, "This list alone makes the book worth buying."

There are many trails in life. The one that matters most for yourself, not for potentially becoming a chief, is to be a truly good human. Without honesty, there is no way to truly be a good human. No prescription of honesty surpasses the little voice inside your head that reminds you when you are honest with yourself and what you are doing, or dishonest and rationalizing to justify to yourself.

Integrity goes along with honesty. Try to be positively consistent in what you say, think, and do. People will notice, distinguish you from those less consistent, believe you, want you to succeed, and maybe even help you.

> *You can't step off the corporate jet in Kansas City and tell the plant manager he has to cut staff and share a secretary. You have to be consistent.*
> —JACK LUNDBERG
> President, Denver Sala/Svedala Industries, Inc.

The most important thing a young career person can establish is a reputation of good character. Fortunately for the CEO of Poudre Valley Hospital, Karna Kruckenberg-Schofer, she says, "I can't make things up, my eyes and mouth won't do it."

If you are honest in your business dealings you will be one less deceptive player in the scheme of things and set yourself apart from others. Nothing is more frustrating to a duplicitous person than a person of integrity and straightforwardness. Consider the thought of using honesty to get ahead, to make money, to do a job. Radical, isn't it!

> *Take a look at how a CEO manages his family life. That shows his honesty. If it isn't*

satisfying, there is likely a shadowy side to his management capabilities.
—PERRY DYE
President, Dye Designs International

Note to readers: At this point in the book you could be thinking, "I already know everything Benton has been writing about." I know you know it, but do you *do* it? Unless you always, all of the time, in every situation, without exception do the things I'm writing about, you're limiting your potential. You see, there is a fine line between the competence and ability level of the people who "make it" in this world and those who don't. The difference between those two groups is not huge. It is a minute distinction. And that minuscule uniqueness comes from being in control of your attitude *all of the time*, and being secure in yourself *with everyone*, and being honest *even when no one will possibly know whether you are or not*.

I am not saying that all chiefs or even the majority of chiefs live all those traits *all* of the time. I do know the near-perfect ones use a lot of them a lot of the time; that is why I wrote about them here.

But the most important thing for you to understand is that your competence, hard work, intelligence, and ambition are necessary to get ahead, *but not sufficient*. The tiebreaker between you and other equally competent, hardworking, intelligent, and ambitious people will be a constant utilization of these basic (but not usually followed) simple, Vital Traits.

6TH VITAL TRAIT:
THINKING BEFORE TALKING

Near-perfects think before they talk. You could say, "That's obvious; everyone does." Wrong. In fact most people don't truly stop, prethink their comment, consider the consequence, alter the comment for the consequence and effect they want, and only then speak.

Why should you try extra diligently to think before you talk?

You are more responsible for your words and their result. When you pause and think through what you are going to say it gives you time to consider reactions. Many times, after thinking it through, you will change what, when, or how you planned to say something. Near-perfect chiefs are answerable for their words.

President Bush was known to give his speeches to his dinner-table guests before giving the same speech to an entire room of politicians and press. Why? To test the reaction! (I know what you are thinking: Presidents Reagan, Bush, and Clinton sometimes speak like they know what they mean when they hear what they say. This situation isn't restricted to the political offices. You will find it is even more prevalent in the executive suites.)

Thinking before you talk does not mean slow, ponderous, boring speech patterns or actions. It is actually more lively than spontaneous, nonsensical outbursts that cause regret in the aftermath. Think how much more quickly you can answer a question if you have thought about it ahead of time rather than having to start from scratch. Neither does thinking before you talk mean you can't think out loud. But I suggest that even your "thinking out loud" be done inside your head first, for these reasons:

- you appear more intelligent,
- you avoid repeating yourself,
- you minimize stuttering and stammering and unnecessary "uh"s and "and"s.

You appear more intelligent. Think of some well-spoken person you know. When speaking they likely sound like they have considered—thought out—what they are saying. Quick-witted people have usually thought about the situation, or similar ones, to form a thought and therefore appear spontaneous. True, some smart people speak in gibberish, but we are talking about effective people here. And you know from your own experience that when you've taken the time to ponder a situation you have a better approach.

When you've taken the opportunity to figure something out, you make a more intelligent choice of the words or actions you use. It's rather like Monday morning quarterbacking: After all the facts are in, you can see what the most brilliant approach would be. People who appear witty or perceptive often just prethought various situations they would likely encounter; they aren't caught off-guard and therefore sound more intelligent. As the Greek proverb states, "Act quickly, think slowly."

I am often asked to advise CEOs on the preparation of the annual "road-show" presentation. The road show is the name investor relations people have given to the presentation made by the CEO when he speaks to Wall Street, pension funds, and other large investors to get them to purchase the company's stock. I've rehearsed, role-played, and sometimes videotaped the CEO's formal presentation and the question-and-answer session he will likely experience afterward from the shareholders, the media, and his employees. Their goal of practicing what they'll say in front of the tough audiences is not to just make themselves and their company appear "on top of things" but gives them a chance to plan their responses and reason out the reaction and aftermath—before it happens to them!

That's a formal version of thinking before you talk.

It's necessary whether dealing with investors, employees, vendors, or family, and of course the media.

> *When you're dealing with the media, as one example, they won't give you a half hour to respond to their questions. If you aren't quick and sharp to the camera, people will wonder if that's how you run your business.*
> —JERRY McMORRIS
> COB, CEO and President,
> NW Transport;
> owner of the Colorado Rockies

You avoid repeating yourself. Reuben Mark, the COB, CEO, and president of Colgate-Palmolive, referred to a salesperson in his office some time back: "If [the individual] used the word *paradigm* once he must have used it eight times. If I can avoid it I won't talk to him again. He just didn't think." When you repeat yourself you sound nervous or dumb (for not remembering you already said it) or sloppy (in that you don't remember or don't care you already said it) or ignorant that you couldn't think of something else to say or a better way of saying it.

Some of my corporate clients have a company vernacular that is so entrenched among the employees that to an outsider it seems like a foreign language. In those cultures it is important to know and use the current acronym or buzzword. But I tell clients to use them only once per conversation. You'll let fellow climbers see you know the language of the mountain but you'll appear smarter if

you think before you talk and use other fresh words
as well.

***You minimize stuttering and stammering and un-
necessary "uh"s and "and"s.*** When you speak without thinking you will more likely insert filler words
and excess verbiage, making you appear nervous and
unclear in your thinking. You waste time and others
lose interest and respect for you.

Watch and carefully listen to a few of the numerous talk shows on the air. Pay attention to the speak-
ers who use "uh" repeatedly. After concentrating on
their filler words a little you'll be so distracted you'll
totally lose track of the point they are trying to
make. And that's what happens to your audience
when you use those filler words. By stopping, slow-
ing down, thinking before (and while) you're talking,
you'll get people to *want* to listen to you.

Thinking before you talk simply gives you new
ways out of awkward situations. I got the opportunity to practice with a demanding client. We were
meeting in his office and I was sitting in one of the
two chairs facing his desk. He was letting me have a
piece of his mind for reasons I won't go into here.
Anyway, he somewhat furiously repeated his criticism
beyond the necessary amount. I had apologized, corrected my mistake, done all I could to rectify the situation, and wanted to go on. Fortunately I had
prethought this situation and anticipated his fury and
planned my words and actions. After an appropriate
amount of self-flagellation I said, "Okay, we've thoroughly discussed my error. You've agreed I've satis-

factorily corrected the problem and made assurances to you that I will not do it again." As I said the last few words I stood up from the chair, the "hot seat" I was in, moved two steps to the side, and purposefully sat down in the other chair and continued: "Now let's discuss what we need to do next." He sat there for a moment, silently watching me make my move, then burst out laughing. He remains a client and friend to this day. Until he reads this paragraph he won't realize I practiced my movement of getting out of the "hot seat" in front of a mirror seven times the night before to test the timing, pacing, and likely result.

Thinking before you speak can be as simple as one CEO who I noticed frequently referred to people as "compadre." When people met him on the street, stopped him in the halls, and even spoke to him on the telephone, his greeting was always "Hey, compadre." I asked him why that expression. He explained, "I can't remember people's names even though I know them, so I call them all compadre—or 'my friend.' It's the same for my teenage daughter. She has so many boyfriends that I can't remember their names, so I call them all 'son.'" That CEO has thought in advance of a recurring problem and come up with a workable solution.

Talking is much like eating. Most people eat too fast, gulping food, not tasting it, and endure indigestion later. The same is true for talking. Most people do it too freely and fast and suffer later. Health experts suggest chewing a bit of food twenty times to slow down. I suggest you chew on your thoughts before you verbalize them. Digest your words as you digest your food.

In our fast-paced never-have-enough-time lives, we blurt out words, not thinking. We simply do it too quickly.

So just how do we accomplish the task of thinking before talking? It only takes seconds to preview your thoughts and readjust your words before verbalizing them. The extra seconds, that silent pause, make what you say sound more important. It appears you've put *thought* into your words—which you have—and you don't choke on your words.

Take a blank piece of paper and draw one line vertically down the middle so you have two halves. Recall some recent conversations and write down on the left side of the paper what you said. Then on the right side of the paper write what you could or should have said had you taken a few moments to think about it in advance. Go through this experiment with a few past conversations. Then go through it with some situations that are coming up. After using the paper a few days you'll get into the habit of being able to do it in your head.

Try it. Tomorrow. Choose your first conversation in the morning to deliberately, consciously prethink everything you say. Later, reflect on the conversation. My guess is you'll be fairly pleased with the outcome.

There isn't a successful mountain climber out there who doesn't study how he's going to tackle the climb before tying on. He looks at the nature and height of the rockface, the length of climbing rope, he sets a top anchor, and discusses the approach and rescue plans with his climbing partner. The same is true in your daily corporate climb.

Because communicating a clear message is so important, always say first to yourself what you want to say out loud. It takes a microsecond of extra time, but it's worth it. When it's necessary to speak, calmly speak the words to yourself, think about your words and their meaning, then say the words you really intended out loud—and *purposefully*.

The intention is not to be overly cautious and nervously weigh words. But rather the objective is to think before you talk and choose the outcome you want to have.

Prethinking the possible responses to likely questions, for example, is not as cumbersome as you might think. If you think seriously about a topic, you'll probably come up with two or three sentences on the subject. Answers and opinions that are thought out show that you respect and have high regard for the people you're talking to. You're displaying disrespect and disregard when it appears you never thought about your listeners' interest long enough to take a position. And prethinking enables you to avoid saying something you wish you hadn't.

My thirteen years in Washington taught me everything you write, you should write as if you expect to see it in Jack Anderson's column.
— WILLIAM PERRY PENDLEY
President and Chief Legal Officer,
Mountain States Legal Foundation

As the near-perfect chiefs do, *practice* your delivery of thoughts on a subject. Write them down. Say them out loud. Videotape yourself if possible. Then reduce the time it takes to express a lengthy comment into a ten- to twenty-second sound bite.

The higher up you go, the more weight your words carry. It's a bit of a burden for the CEOs and those of you who are striving to be chief, but that's life at fourteen thousand feet. If you just slow down and prethink what you're about to say you'll avoid lots of problems. You'll set an example and maybe eventually get the same in return. You'll appear comfortable and, as one successful chief describes it, "appear to speak with the calm demeanor of a man who enjoys a low heart rate." What is most important, people value what you say more and will listen to you when you speak the next time.

You might ask what the value of spontaneity is. Spontaneity comes naturally to a person by reason of temperament and tendency. Too often that results in impulsive and involuntary behavior and comments. If you prethink things you improve the quality of your spontaneity.

By the way, it is a very effective communication tool to plan your spontaneous comments. For example, say a co-worker made an offhand, disparaging remark about you. You heard of it through the company grapevine. It bugs you. Instead of instantly putting the person on your hit list or attacking him back, plan some "nonpreparation." The next time you are talking to that person about some issue discuss the business with no hidden agenda on your mind. Settle the issue at hand. Start to leave, then in a relaxed but "Oh, I just thought of something else" tone of voice, ask about the rumor you heard. Let him respond. Ask again, in a nonthreatening but different way about the incident. Gently inquire until it is cleared up in your mind. The purpose is not to put him into a corner but to straighten out misunderstanding. You may find out you heard incorrectly (as is often the case) or you find out you heard correctly and you have now dealt with the issue by simply and "spontaneously" standing up to him.

Thinking before you talk is necessary whenever possible. But it isn't always possible. Many times you have to truly speak on your feet with no advance warning or preparation. But if you've practiced prethinking, when you're not on the hot seat your words will come more naturally when unprepared. Perhaps the best course of action is to cut to the heart of the matter when you do speak, in as few words as thinkable. Possibly an even better route is silence.

Silent

Ted Turner, president and chairman of the board of Turner Broadcasting, was talking about future business plans: "I have some little ideas in my head. But I can't talk about them too much because they're secret. . . . You can't show your hand. You didn't see Barry Diller saying 'I'm gonna do a deal with CBS' until he'd done the deal. You've got to keep your mouth shut and slip up on 'em when they're not expecting it."

Everyone, including near-perfect chiefs, needs to work at muzzling themselves sometimes. It takes an extra bit of self-control to remain silent, but it is often the perfect thing to say to have the effect you want. You might think that's a hard thing to do. Right. Not many do. You can, though.

> It's impossible to know everything, so I'm silent and listen. It gives me an ability to develop strategy. When I'm able to listen, I can envision how things fit together. I'm experiencing a need to be silent now with my children. They are grown up and on their own. Like a good boss I need to not jump in and tell them things they should be doing. As a dad, I want to save them. But I have to be quiet.
> —NEIL GEORGI
>   CEO, Neil Georgi & Associates, Inc.

There aren't many people who at the end of the day can't recall at least one comment they wish they hadn't made. If at the end of the day you can think of at least one flip, ill-timed, inappropriate remark you've purposefully held back—you'll feel justifiably pleased with yourself. Anything that should be said can still be said *at another time.*

Near-perfect chiefs can be quiet.

When silent you can plan what you need to say

and avoid babbling. Because you aren't chattering, you can listen and mentally convert and understand what something means. You avoid emotionally flashing. And you let possibly wiser people talk, and stupid people too. Some people talk because they have something to say; some because they have to say something. Quiet is associated with steadiness of character. Nervous, fast, and talkative behavior hides character.

It often takes more effort to physically do nothing and be silent than it does to go through the effort of talking. Also, silence

- lets you rest your mind and hear yourself,
- keeps secrets,
- avoids argument,
- allows you to observe others' weaknesses,
- suggests latent power, making it easier to look wise,
- can be done in any language,
- is the safest course to adopt sometimes.

When discussing the significance of silence, a business trainer I met told me, "I had a severe larynx problem this last year and I had to spend twenty-one days by the doctor's order without talking. Now I miss the silence. So I make one day of every week a quiet day when I don't talk. . . . The silence makes me serene, retrospective, and joyous. . . . I'm in the communication business and I learned more about communication from not being able to talk than I learned from years of talking. A side benefit of not being able to speak out loud was that I learned to stay in touch with people the old-fashioned way. I wrote letters."

Instead of waiting to be forced into silence, take it upon yourself to pick and choose the words that come out of your mouth. Some people think they look ignorant if they don't speak every thought that comes to mind. (It's usually just the opposite.)

How can you be effectively silent without making people uncomfortable?

- Initiate conversation, then be quiet and listen.
- After someone says something important, remain silent, ponder it, show you're listening and absorbing.
- Talk little but say a lot in the few words that you do say. (If you are able to do this, yours is the opinion that others will seek out.)
- Listen more than you talk; when you listen to others, *really* listen.

When discussing the value of silence it is important not to miss another aspect of speech. Consistent with the advice "Don't speak so *much*" is my recommendation "Don't speak too *quickly*." Slow down. Let others talk.

Sometimes enthusiasm, while good in itself, causes problems by letting you speak too much, too quickly, and not well-thought-out enough. Use the energy from enthusiasm to plan effective communication; avoid ineffective or destructive impulses.

I should have followed my own advice when I was

in Missouri giving a speech at a college leadership program. I was assigned to a dorm room for my two-night stay. Although I'm not a snob, the accommodations just weren't suitable. When traveling on business, I need a phone in my room (not one at the end of the dorm hall). In my work, I need to know what is happening and I need to be in touch. Hot water instead of cold in the shower is nice. I like a TV to watch and a bed already made (neither of which was available in the dorm room). Not wanting to be rude to my host, I quietly slipped out and checked into a local hotel. After my speech I simply returned to my hotel room instead of the assigned dorm room.

The morning of my departure, I was waiting in the lobby for the shuttle to the airport. En route another passenger asked where I was from and what business I was doing in Missouri (typical business small talk). I opened my mouth too quickly and told him. I chattered away about the college, the uncomfortable dorm room, and my going to a hotel instead. Then finally I stopped talking and asked him, "What do you do here?"

His response: "I am the president of the college."

Had I not spoken so quickly, I would have avoided the most uncomfortable feeling of having my foot in my mouth. Unfortunately he went back and spread the word, so my respect was diminished among the group. That was just an example of the problems we cause for ourselves when we talk too much.

As tough as it might be initially, a good thing about being silent is you get better at it as you get more experience. And this experience certainly helped me be better at being silent.

Speech is not some sort of proof of intelligence. Appropriate speech is powerful; silence is powerful, too. Listen. Observe. Evaluate. *Then* talk.

Do not, however, be silent about illegal, immoral, unethical activities. Contrary to the beliefs of many, morality is not dead in business; it just takes courage to not remain silent about it. You are guilty if you know something and do nothing. But think it through *thoroughly* before you speak up.

Postscript to Silence: **On the route to being a near-perfect CEO, try to limit your cursing.**

In this age of being politically correct, one of the important things to discontinue is cursing. A good time to purposefully practice a silence skill is when you feel like spewing forth some profanity.

> *If you listen to a tape recording of yourself using profanity, you'll regret it. Don't kid yourself into thinking it adds color. It adds nothing.*
> —JACK FALVEY, CEO, Intermark

Public cursing
• opens doors for others to lower their estimation of you,

- degrades the user,
- doesn't belong at all,
- limits you,
- may *really* offend in a diverse workplace,
- is unprofitable.

I realize plenty of business chiefs are ob-scene, abusive, vulgar, foul, and blasphe-mous, sometimes more than once a week! If you choose to do all you can to become a top climber and are working on that goal, use only a very light version of cursing for selected situations. Later you'll read a quote from Alex Mandl, and he used "deep yo-gurt" instead of "deep s—." I asked him about it. "Sure I cuss sometimes, but I choose not to now."

As with an overuse of buzzwords, an overuse of swearing limits your terminology and appearance of intelligence. Once you begin using swear words regularly they tend to become your entire vocabulary—particu-larly the adjectives. People who cuss a lot often are at a loss for words when they need to say something in a hurry—and without profanity. They literally get stuck for acceptable words!

Common swearing isn't interesting, clever, brave, polite, or wise. It's in the same school as table pounding and shouting. You may feel anger and frustration but should only choose to say swear words *silently*. If later you really feel it is the only way to express how you feel, you can go back tomorrow and give them an earful.

If you currently slip into the "profane lane" try to change the habit:

- Don't use profanity in public.
- Don't use it in private.
- Don't use it kiddingly.
- Don't use it because others do.
- Don't mistakenly think it makes you look "at ease" with yourself.
- Don't mutter it under your breath.
- And most important, *don't be bothered by those who use profanity.*

There are many factors that can knock you out of the chief's race at any time. Some of them you exert a little control over and others you do not have any control over. People above you, below you, and beside you are always looking for chinks in your armor—to hasten your defeat. The fewer faults you show them the better your chance of climbing one more ledge. Every trait I write about in this book, when developed, moves you a little closer to near-perfect status. Sometimes one gets there by adding to his abilities, sometimes by eliminating self-defeating habits. Liberal profanity is one of those self-sabotaging traits.

There are many potential irritating, tangible obstacles that you can't do anything about (e.g., sex, age, race, height). The ones you can do something about deserve attention (e.g., humor, courage, tenacity, ethics, profanity).

People may tolerate your profanity as long as you perform exceedingly well. But if you don't perform, and you cuss, you might be the first to go. If you do perform, and others perform equally well, you will likely find out firsthand that overt swearers don't get promoted as quickly. It's a small thing but one more eliminating factor from the top peak.

If you want further evidence, closely observe the people you truly admire and enjoy working with. Aside from the occasional humorous use of profanity, I'll bet they limit their cursing. If you want to be one whom others admire in a similar fashion, you should choose to limit your politically incorrect swearing.

7TH VITAL TRAIT: ORIGINAL

Mike Wilfley's office is handsomely decorated, neat, and organized. He's the fourth-generation CEO of the family business, A. R. Wilfley & Sons. They are an international manufacturer and supplier of industrial pumps used in the mining and chemical industries.

In his office there is a meeting area, sitting area, and work area, all with tidy stacks of files for ready access. It isn't cluttered or messy. It's elegantly and methodically organized. Over in one corner, on top of a four-by-four-foot sheet of heavy plastic, are laid the metal parts of a mechanical pump. Six or seven parts are laid out side by side. Except for the parts being clean, it's the same pile you'd expect to see in a corner of a mechanic's shop.

I curiously asked Wilfley why he keeps the pile of parts in this beautifully decorated office. Wilfley answered, "Those parts make up the product we sell. I look at them several times a day and constantly ask myself, How could we improve this equipment? Could we make it smaller? Could we use different material? The pieces are always on my mind because I always see them."

I said, "You're not an engineer, you're a lawyer by training—that sounds like an engineer thinking." His confident response: "No, I'm not an engineer, but I do run this company."

Wilfley is original in his thinking, and his company's continued success under his helm is a testimony to the value of his originality. He doesn't follow overworn paths.

One of the biggest perks a CEO has is his option to be original. More than anyone in the company, the CEO has the opportunity to act and think with imagination. The CEO

- has the liberty and freedom to be atypical,
- can *risk* being different,
- can afford to be unique,
- *has* to be original if he's going to set the standard for his people. People often wonder what the boss wants. A boss needs to show them by setting the example.

The good CEO takes full advantage of his position to be inventive, different, imaginative, and *original*.

> *Every thought has been thought of before.*
> *The difference is in the ability and willingness to take action behind it.*
> —BRAD WILLIAMS
>   President, Dakota Beverage Company Inc.

Mary Anne Jackson left Beatrice as a strategic planner to form My Own Meals, Inc., a company marketing shelf-stable meals for kids. Within three years her revenues hit $1 million and big competitors started to market to her audience niche, so she switched to supplying shelf-stable kosher rations for Jewish soldiers during the Gulf War.

David Miller solved seating problems in his restaurant in Jensen Beach, Florida, by providing patrons pagers that vibrated when their table was ready. It worked so well he now runs an $8 million paging system business providing pagers and supplies to twenty-five thousand restaurants, hotels, and country clubs nationwide. His success caused Motorola to get into the market.

Dr. Roy Vagelos, CEO of a $10.5 billion dollar pharmaceutical firm, formed a division to reinvent the process of selling drugs, joining forces with the Swedish company Astra AB to form Astra/Merck. The president of the new division says the reason for the new division was that "we [Merck] weren't being different enough." Vagelos displayed his originality by creating a new division.

You don't have to wait until you're CEO to develop fresh thinking. You don't have to be particularly brilliant to be original. You don't have to have an IQ so high you get a military deferment, as the CEO of Mission Bay Investment, Curt Carter, did. You simply have to take (or make) the time to think.

> *I take the time to think. Lightning strikes and fireworks go off and it becomes inspiration.*
>
> —JOHN BIANCHI, Ph.D.
> COB, Bianchi International

As the popular poster quoting Albert Einstein reads, "Imagination is more important than knowledge."

What's the simplest rule for being more original?

Watch, carefully observe what most people are doing in any situation, and don't do that. Unconsciously you're being led by others and do what they do. Stop it. Be original. Be fresh. Be unusual. Precede others. Show a marked departure from previous practice. That's how new leaders are discovered.

Find better ways of doing things. Attack with zeal. Be open and ready for change. The simple way to get ahead in business is to give top performance today and significantly improve the performance tomorrow.

We all want to think of ourselves as unique individuals. We all *dream* of being what no other is and doing what no other has done. That's what we envision for ourselves, so that's how we need to work.

You are a huge value to a company when you create—*usually*. It is true that some organizations and some bosses do not value creativity. If that is the case where you work, you have to decide whether to stay there or not. If you choose to remain there you may have to suppress your display of ingenuity. But whatever you do, do not lose your ability to be original. You'll need the trait when you get your chief's job.

Never be satisfied with simply maintaining the status quo. You lose originality if you are satisfied with the present condition. *Originality is the principal source of human improvement.* Effective chiefs aren't satisfied, regardless of how well things are going. *Things will change.* Original thinkers don't fear change, they look forward to it because they know it is where they thrive and shine.

We're all imaginative in one way or another. While the business world has its limits, the world of originality is boundless.

Being original, innovative, and creative isn't a one-time thing but a continuing process. Ongoing originality is more important than a single brilliant breakthrough.

Being original and imaginative isn't just dreaming up a new product or service, a new twist on doing business, or a new focus for traditional methods. It is utilizing a different way of expressing yourself, of dealing with an old people-problem in a new way, using physical presence, varying dress or travel patterns, etc. That type of creativity provides one small triumph after another, which sets a tone of innovation for an organization. You don't have to be the father of the newest idea for mankind. You can be original by simply doing simple things *differently*.

How to be more original:

- *Decide to be.* It starts with your attitude management. Tell and remind yourself you are innovative. The idea is not to be creative for creativity's sake but to keep the thinking, working, and improving going. It might be just saying things in an uncommon way. Whatever you do try not to imitate, repeat, regurgitate, or rehash.
- *Be easy on yourself.* Don't be hypercritical about why such and such doesn't work. Don't worry that you (or others) have tried it and failed and therefore you are off base or wrong. Ask your-

self, Is this helpful to me or someone else? Is it change? Does it improve anything?

- *Support others.* Recognize when others are also trying to come up with fresh ideas. Ask questions to stimulate their thinking as well as yours: What are your unmet needs? What do you think about this idea? How will that help you?

   Most people are negative and destructive when new ideas are presented. Don't do that to others; set the example for them. Pick out your (and their) good ideas rather than too quickly dismissing weak ideas.

- *Keep at it.* Keep the flow going. Don't stop, get frustrated, slough off, or discourage others. Tenaciously minding your mind can result in a breakthrough when you least expect it and probably most need it. Make time to be original.

Most job descriptions don't include the words *be original,* but that's what it takes to fulfill the favored top-level leadership requirement of "providing vision." If you aren't creative now you won't be later. Leadership vision is all about originality.

Every CEO has to have a clear vision of where the company should go and must sell that vision to lots of people. A lot of people must buy into it. The CEO has to communicate and keep it alive at all times—what his team is about, the values, and what he sees the organization becoming. And that has to be reiterated at every level. If you

don't establish your culture you get a hap-
hazard one.
                    —TIM DAY
          CEO and President, Bar-S Foods

Don't ever say you can't build a better mousetrap.
Some friends of mine were setting traps for some
mice that had invaded their garage. The instruction
on the mousetrap packages read, "Dispose of trap
along with the mouse." The company did not invent
a better trap but got the customer to buy another
one nonetheless. *That's being original.*

8TH VITAL TRAIT: PUBLICLY MODEST

Secure people can be publicly modest. Insecure people aren't.

Seasoned near-perfect chiefs show a high degree of
talent and ability but speak with moderate estimation of their talents, abilities, and value. They observe propriety in speech, behavior, and dress. Bill
Hewlett, cofounder of Hewlett-Packard, is never
flashy or pompous despite the fact he could afford to
be.

Near-perfect CEOs can go from a reserved position to being extravagant, grand, and bold as necessary. It's more difficult to go from excessive to
demure.

When Dr. William E. Morgan, retired president of

Colorado State University, accepted the position of president of Colorado A&M (now CSU), one of the directors gave him this advice: "The college is in need of you. You'll come in on a white horse. So come in and tackle a problem right away. Even a stranger will be able to see problems. Go after that problem with vigor. *But* every once in a while look over your shoulder. If they ain't coming with you, you ain't leading. Don't forget you're not an indispensable agent. Before you get too taken with yourself, go sit under a tree and remember your fortuitous circumstances are due to time, place, and friends. If that still doesn't keep you humble, remember there are twelve people who could do your job and one or two of them could do it better. Be modest."

Being publicly modest does not mean being shy, undervaluing yourself, or letting others do that either. Being publicly modest is avoiding pretentious, ostentatious, braggart behavior full of bluster and ego. Even a hint of self-boosterism can backfire. One CEO interviewed at age fifty-one has built a company from zero to $1.9 billion in less than twenty years. The company commands a leading 40 percent market share in his industry. He could be considered a *very* successful CEO. Yet in an unforgiving business world, examples of seemingly immodest behavior seem to be remembered forever. For example, when a weekly business magazine wrote about him they repeated business activities from five years earlier and reported that the CEO, "who once appeared in TV ads to pitch his product . . . is the irrepressible dealmaker."

You need to get your position—and your victories—across, but in a palatable way. In fact, a boss must understand what you are actually doing to earn your pay. He's busy managing your climbing partners as well as you. Someone has to effectively let him know what his people are doing. It may be necessary he hear about you from you because no one else may tell him. The key is that just as you readily take credit for the good work you've done, you readily take responsibility for bad work. You can be direct about your capabilities. It's okay to make declared statements: "I am good at . . ." or "I know I'm right on . . ." or "My approach was . . ."

Too much self-praise alienates the people who helped make it happen. Overexposure sets up resentment and contempt.

You will get closer to near-perfect status if you control the uncontrollable urge to over-self-promote. You can resist the urge if you remind yourself that everything that can be said about you can be better said and done by someone else. Donald Trump, who is the opposite of being publicly modest, has learned exposure in media builds people up *and* tears them down.

By using self-effacing humor, being lighthearted (versus heavy-handed) about success and power, turning attention from yourself, and pointing to the contributions of others you promote yourself in a palatable way.

Graciously accept nice things someone has to say about you but don't believe it. As CEO you get more credit than you deserve when things are going well. And when things aren't going well, you'll get more blame than you deserve.
                    —HAL KRAUSE
                    CEO, Crestcom International

This happens at all levels of responsibility, by the way.

In his book *Thoughts*, Malcolm Forbes quotes Baltasar Gracian: "Don't show off every day, or you'll stop surprising people. There must always be some novelty left over. The person who displays a little more of it each day keeps up expectations, and no one ever discovers the limits of his talent."

Viacom's Sumner Redstone is described by an acquaintance: "He was not given to self-puffery but he was skillful with anecdotes that managed to drop names."

Being publicly modest means simultaneously avoiding being arrogant while still getting recognition for contributions. How? Prethink conversations before they happen. Control your attitude toward the situation and people involved. Be honest with yourself. Take credit that is deserved but share credit more than deserved.

Again, being publicly modest does not mean staying in the background, being a shrinking violet, sheepish, living afraid to speak, or looking like you lack self-esteem. Being publicly modest is being persistent in your efforts toward living an effective life. It also means being patient that others will acknowledge your abilities before you have to point these out to them (which certainly dilutes any thrill you might get from being recognized by others!).

Not one chief I interviewed felt he or she always got credit as deserved. Probably no one in life feels they get due recognition. That's life.

APPROACHING THE CLIMB SUMMARY

Be secure in yourself: No one makes you feel inferior without your consent.

Be in control of your attitude: Success in business is based more on mental attitude than mental capabilities.

Be tenacious: Nothing ever happens with one letter, one telephone call, one request.

Be continuously improving: Take risks. Mistakes provide some of your best learning.

Be honest and ethical: If you are careless with the truth your credibility will be jeopardized when you are telling the truth.

Be sure to think before you talk: Think fast, pause, then speak purposefully.

Be silent: Listen much more than you talk. Talk little, but say a lot in the few words that you do say.

Be original: Watch, carefully observe what most people are doing in any situation, and don't do that.

Be publicly modest: It's more of a thrill to have others recognize your ability rather than your pointing it out first. Be patient but be persistent. As Franklin D. Roosevelt said, "Never underestimate a man who overestimates himself."

Think: The higher you go up the mountain, the more treacherous the climb, the more important it is to slow down and think things through. You'll enjoy the view a lot more also!

CHAPTER 4

Putting It into Practice

How near-perfect chiefs enjoy the climb

NEAR-PERFECT CHIEFS ARE:

---

9. Aware of style

10. Gutsy/a little wild

11. Humorous

12. A tad theatrical

13. Detail oriented

9TH VITAL TRAIT: Aware of Style

One week *Forbes* praises the CEO who "accomplishes the mission without the dedication and enthusiastic participation of those being led," and the next week it praises the CEO who "instead of acting dictatorially, tries to place himself in his employees' shoes . . . giving workers plenty of flexibility and discretion." Which style is best? The one that fits the situation.

One CEO told me, "In today's leadership training seminars you will hear fourteen different lectures and they will be stating tomorrow's leaders will be twelve different ways. Every three months a new management style trend comes across my desk. I promised myself early in my career if I ever become CEO I wouldn't chase the latest whiz bang program. Not just because it's supposedly new."

An accomplished climber needs to know who around him needs information; what, when, and how. He needs to be able to supply it. He needs to know who needs motivation; what, when, and how. He needs to supply it. And he needs to be able to stop supplying what he's providing when it is no longer needed. Then he needs to know when to restart supplying as needed. The near-perfect simply finds out what is needed when for that particular situation and is able to provide it.

Curt Carter, CEO of Mission Bay Investments, told me this story: "I try to meet every new employee on their first day regardless of their level. We recently hired a maintenance man. So we met, chatted, and I pointed out that the west parking lot needed attention. When he said good-bye, I said, 'Go to it!' An hour and a half later, I was passing through the lot and saw him standing there. He'd gotten a broom and pan together, but that was all he'd done. I walked over to him and said, 'Go to that corner and start there. Sweep the leaves first. Sweep a line along one side, sweep it to the center, bag it at that point.'

"'I got it, boss,' he said with an enthusiastic grin. He did the job identical to my instructions. I learned the employee needed specific direction. He liked it and wanted it. So I gave it to him and directed his boss to do so also.

"Sometime later a new man was hired to do the job. After we had our introductory chat, I asked him to sweep the west lot. I went out to the parking lot with him and said, 'Go to the corner and start there. Sweep the leaves first. Sweep a line along one side—'

"'That isn't the best way to sweep,' he interrupted me. 'You want it swept. I can figure out how.'

"He did and he did it well. Some people like to be told what to do. Some don't."

Effective style is best defined as proper behavior at a given time. An ineffective style is being one way all the time with everyone.

> *You can get things done with different styles. One isn't the best. Compare Jack Welch (GE) to Bob Allen (AT&T). They are very different but both very effective.*
> —ALEX MANDL
>   CEO, Communications
>   Services Group/AT&T

You likely got hired because of a demonstration of some predominant style that was needed by the company at that time. Great. But if you don't constantly work to add other styles to your repertoire you might eventually get fired. If you are unable to project an ability to fulfill the company's currently needed style, management will find someone who can. CEOs are grateful when they find someone who can balance and utilize many style traits. It helps with their ultimate goals to maintain balance and growth in the company.

Clearly there are styles that do not work: being abrasive, unwilling to listen, antagonistic with people, having no empathy toward others, etc. And styles that usually do work: being decisive, collaborative, candid, and straightforward, and listening to the team.

Be aware of your type. But don't use it as an excuse for your behavior, blame it on your parents, your first-grade teacher, or your first spouse. Your style is determined by your behavior. Change your behavior and you change your style. It's that simple. If you can give an excuse for yourself—"I'm *this* way and that's it"—you will be right.

Be aware of others' styles. Adapt ones that are effective and learn to deal with those styles that aren't so effective. Every employee, customer, supplier, and boss will vary in what works best with them. Don't *assume* anyone is a specific type. Intelligently observe and then *ask* to confirm your assumptions.

Even if you are three or four levels down, you can still see what is going around in terms of operating style. Often the farther you are from the top the clearer you can see. Don't mistakenly think you are too insignificant to matter. You become significant by seeing what's needed in an organization and working to fill the gap.

Develop new ways of behavior and a new personal operating style. Test them out with various people and situations. Concentrate on different traits at different times. Fill in, blend in, and balance out. If you're uncomfortable in one area, concentrate on improving in that one. Good managers hire people to correct their own weak areas. They surround themselves with people who make them look good. Look for the chief's weakest areas in the company and judiciously work on those areas yourself. The goal is not to attempt to outshine but to supplement those areas.

Don't guess another's predominant style. Ask. Understand. Remember, when you ask others about their style, they may not be able to honestly or clearly answer. Or they may not choose to reveal anything about themselves. But asking is better than guessing, and you'll get *some* clues. You can ask questions like the following:

- How do you like to have things happen?
- How would you approach this?
- What do you think would work best here?
- What have you seen works well in this situation?

People fundamentally have a dominant style acquired through genes, upbringing, and work experience, but they can still modify

*it, work on it, or tone it down. It's difficult
to switch totally, but it is possible to adapt.
Style can be thought out, planned, and exe-
cuted.*

—TIM DAY
CEO and President,
Bar-S Foods

Sometime during your career, you will undoubtedly be tested by a "specialist" to determine whether
you fit a currently popular label. The following are
some possible labels:

- mediator, boss, perfectionist, giver, performer,
  romantic, observer,
- driver, analytical, expressive, amiable,
- dominate, extrovert, patient, conformist,
- loyalist, returnee, believer, seeker,
- general, ambassador, governor, senator,
- empty suit, stiff suit, suitless.

This testing is just one part of your style to determine primary and secondary personality tendencies.
Once you know your type theoretically you can better understand yourself, better understand others,
change yourself where change is needed, build on
personality traits that will help you succeed, and attempt to redirect others. Like most information,
awareness of current popular labels is valuable. It's a
gift to learn something new about yourself. It holds
some importance, but taken to the extreme it inhibits
a more real-world discovery about yourself.

The problem with the examination is explained by one chief: "I know the purpose of the test and I can easily sabotage them with my experience."

Regardless, some chiefs feel more comfortable if they can put a label on subordinates. (It seems to make them more manageable, perhaps.) You should try to avoid getting labeled. Labels are limiting. You want to be effective *across* label boundaries.

> *Style testing is often a gimmick. I hate labeling. I've seen labelers liken people to dogs. People could say, "I'm just a collie. That's just the way I am!" Then they have an excuse to not change the way they operate. It can make you lazy. However, everyone has styles they can learn to enhance. And whether you are fresh out of college or somewhere at the top, you can use a lot of different styles. You don't have to be one way all of the time.*
> —PAULA ANCONA, Scripps Howard News Service columnist and author of *Success Abilities!: 1003 Practical Ways to Keep Up, Stand Out and Move Ahead at Work*

An aspect of your visual style is your physical appearance. The *San Francisco Examiner* writes that "Americans pick their political candidates, in part, the same way they shop for cars, cosmetics, and cantaloupes—by appearance. . . . Voters are judging candidates by the one trait in which they all have experience: looks."

Referring to the California gubernatorial race with candidate Kathleen Brown, daughter of the former governor of California, Shawn Rosenburg, professor at University of California-Irvine's department of political psychology, says, "What is happening is that people aren't paying attention to issues, except the salient ones. And the salient issues are the ones politicians shy away from. . . . So people are relying on their own sense of who a candidate is, based on what he looks like. . . . People think they have a sense of what 'competence' and 'trustworthiness' look like, based on images that are pervasive in our culture."

Physical image affects electoral outcomes as it affects corporate career outcomes. Unfair as it may be, tall, white, nonbalding, nonobese men with thin eyebrows and lips, short hair (combed to the side or back) framing a broad or round face, and almond-shaped eyes—but no trait *too* perfect—are favored.

Forbes, Fortune, Business Week, and the *Wall Street Journal* are filled with page after page of descriptions like the following:

> "*A stout man with a commanding presence.*"
> —*Forbes* on the CEO of Philips Electronics

> "*A flamboyant black sheep [of his family] . . . who has scrubbed pink skin, round tortoiseshell glasses, and a sonorous*

*voice calling to mind a feisty Garrison Keil-
lor."*
  —*Vanity Fair* on William Koch, sponsor of
    all-female crew America's Cup contender

*"He retains his boyish haircut and oversized
glasses; the smallish [Bill] Gates walks purposefully with long, fluid strides."*
                         —*Forbes ASAP*

Naturally there are CEOs who don't fit the ideal
physical prescription. The reason for pointing out
the ideal physical image of people who look
"trusted and competent" is to (one) suggest you
take on those qualities that can fit you, (two) choose
the qualities you could develop to compensate for
those you don't naturally have, and (three) keep you
from being fooled by someone else's "smooth,
pretty-boy style."

To develop your physical style here's a synopsis
from my book *Lions Don't Need to Roar* (Warner
Books, 1992):

MAKE A FAVORABLE FIRST IMPRESSION

1. Use your entire physical being to express
    yourself. (Your physical presence is the
    foundation on which you build your credi-
    bility. Act in a slow, controlled, purposeful
    manner.)
2. Have a physical game plan. (Physically set
    the stage to accomplish a purpose you have
    decided upon ahead of time.)

3. Show people what you mean with coordinated words and actions.
4. Don't respond to distractions.
5. Develop by subtraction. (Retire your sabotaging actions, the ineffective things you say or do.)
6. Do the opposite of what most people do.
7. Be flexible.
8. Be willing to merely "go through the motions" for a while.
9. Remember the four-minute rule. (Be aware of and consciously control your actions for at least the first four minutes of any encounter.)

GIVE A GOOD HANDSHAKE

1. Respect people's preferences for space and distance.
2. Clasp palm to palm, not palm to fingers.
3. Talk to the person whose hand you're shaking.
4. Hold on for a split second longer than duty requires.
5. Be firm but not so forceful that you cause discomfort.
6. If you wish to convey additional warmth, use two hands.
7. Briefly and in a purposeful manner, pause again as you retrieve your hand.

REMEMBER PEOPLE'S NAMES

1. Relax; memory improves when you are at ease.

2. Immediately repeat the name aloud, using it in the very next comment you make to that person.

3. If possible and appropriate, use the name again within a few minutes.

4. At the first available opportunity, write the name down somewhere.

TOUCH IN A BUSINESS SETTING

1. Touch males and females the same way. Be consistent.

2. Be supportive, encouraging, or caring—whatever fits the situation. (Being condescending or sexually seductive is not the appropriate attitude for touching in any business situation.)

3. Be sensitive to the reactions of people you touch.

4. Don't sneak up from behind. Make sure that the other person is aware of your presence.

5. Plant your hand firmly on a hand, arm, or shoulder. (Touching an elbow seems most universally acceptable.)

6. Maintain physical contact for a split second.

7. Keep your hand still and steady. Do not stroke or pat.

8. Place your hand and remove it in an equally purposeful and definite manner.

9. Smile, relax, and look as if you expect the other person to accept the touch in the manner you gave it.

10. If you simply cannot bring yourself to touch physically, at least make an extra effort to convey what a touch would through your facial expression, tone of voice, and words.
11. Practice, practice, practice.

RECEIVE A BUSINESS TOUCH GRACEFULLY

(Assuming it is appropriate and not an act of sexual harassment)

1. Don't act as if you've been zapped by an electric shock from a cattle prod and grimace, glare, jump, or abruptly pull back as if you're having a repulsion convulsion.
2. Allow the touch. Be aware of it. Accept it. Or merely withstand it if you are, for some reason, repulsed or offended by it.
3. Don't read excess meaning into a touch (unless the person reaches for your wallet or worse).
4. Lean into it.
5. If possible (and comfortable for you), reciprocate.

THE BUSINESS HUG

1. Expect acceptance, but if in doubt, the first time you hug, say something along the lines of "You've been so supportive, I'd like to give you a hug."
2. Grasp right hands and place your left hand around the person's shoulder, then lean your upper body toward him.

3. Turn your head so that your lips don't brush against the other person's cheek, collar, or lapel.
4. Hold the embrace a second or two longer than a typical handshake.
5. Don't touch pelvises.
6. Release the person from your embrace, look the person in the eye, smile, and step back. Pause briefly and then resumé your conversation, exit, or do whatever else you were planning to do after the hug.

STAND WITH PROFESSIONAL PRESENCE

1. Maintain a relaxed, energetic posture with eyes and head level.
2. Assume a neutral or "ready" position with your arms loose at your sides so they are free to gesture.
3. Stand close enough to the other person to be personal, but not so close as to be intrusive.
4. Stand upright rather than leaning against a door, wall, lectern, or furniture.
5. Don't touch yourself or: pick real or imaginary lint off your sleeves; smooth your clothing; tug at your waistband; straighten your tie; fuss with your hair; rub your hands (like Lady Macbeth attempting to scrub the "damn spot" from her hand).

SIT IN A CONTROLLED MANNER

1. Approach the chair.
2. Pause.

3. Keep your upper and lower body in alignment to stay balanced.
4. Maintaining good posture, bend your knees and purposefully lower your body.
5. Sit on the edge of the chair first.
6. Use your thigh muscles or hands to push yourself toward the front of the chair.
7. To stand up in a controlled manner, follow the same sequence in reverse.

GESTURE TO ENHANCE YOUR PRESENCE

1. Always get gestures that are appropriate for and acceptable in a specific situation. Also keep in mind that gestures which mean one thing (and have a positive impact) in the good ole USA may have a different meaning and effect in other countries.
2. When using your hands and arms, keep them away from the rib cage.
3. Hold each gesture for a split second and try to make each motion as smooth as possible.
4. Synchronize your words and actions: think of what you will say; show it; and say it. DON'T: think of what you will say; say it; and after the fact remember to show it.

It's your choice. Michael Eisner, CEO of Disney, has this to say about tackling any obstacle such as changing your style: "You've got to either paddle your canoe faster than the water or slower. You just can't let the water take you where it wants."

Near-perfects develop more than one style while

they retain a prevalent tendency toward one. Just as they change clothes for the office, the golf course, a camping trip, a party, or a funeral, and on and on, they change the way they deal with situations. Whether it's appearance or personality, near-perfect chiefs work on appropriate styles. As Ernest Howell, retired president of Packaging Systems International, says, "I have to come into a staff meeting and try to enjoy it. I'm a good example of someone who doesn't come into a charismatic style easily. I have to really work on it. But I do work on it!"

Near-perfect chiefs are aware of their predominant mode of operation and appearance but aren't stuck in it!

10TH VITAL TRAIT: GUTSY/A LITTLE WILD

Paul Cook, the founder of Reychem Corporation, retired and gave his successor a baton and this advice: "Take risks, be bold, take chances."

Being gutsy means taking risks—with money, strategies, plans, operations, and people. Climbers who become mountaineers brave the remote heights.

"I was transferred to a new boss who was described as 'no one can get along with him.' Two days into the job we tangled. I went into his office and said, 'If I'm not doing the job satisfactorily, get yourself another boy!' He chuckled. And I never had a problem again," relates Jim Rupp, who later became a competitor of the difficult boss after changing companies.

Rupp added, "A person is as good as his courage. I do the thing I fear most to test myself. I love uncertainty. You never know what will happen. I'm always happy finishing one job so I have the unknown to look forward to."

Guts, pluck, and courage are used interchangeably when describing near-perfect chiefs. Gutsy is a spirit able to face danger with a firm resolve despite the criticism, attacks, and ridicule of people important to the chief, whose efforts these people will battle all the way. There is no substitute for fortitude. And *you* know in your heart the courage it takes to do and say what needs to be done and said. As the saying goes, "No guts, no glory."

> *What I like to see in people [who are liable to take my job] is they don't let themselves be limited by what they don't know. That means they step up and plant a stake—even if they don't know the details of how to get it done. Then they figure out how. In other words they say they will accomplish something—and they get it done. They have courage.*
>
> —RICHARD MCCORMICK
> Chairman and CEO,
> US West

You develop courage by not worrying, generating unnecessary internal stress, or procrastinating. You develop it by doing things others are afraid to do. You get it by just being tenacious, sticking to your point of view. You just face problems. Bring them out into the open. Do something and keep at it until you have changed things.

I'm not promoting gutsiness without effective strategy. Kari Kairamo, former CEO at Nokia (a company second only to Motorola in production of cellular phones), was noted for his fearlessness in making dozens of acquisitions, including some real money-losers. Boldness without focus and purpose is not gutsy, it is reckless. Kairamo committed suicide.

To be gutsier, first *think*. When you think, you'll discover alternatives. Take time to be alone and think even if it is just a few seconds, depending on the circumstance. You will likely come up with a way to handle the situation. *True courage comes from reasoning as well as instinct.* Don't settle for either *thoughtless* cowardice or *thoughtless* recklessness.

Second, *be honest*. Honesty with yourself gives you direction to take risk. When you honestly weigh cost and benefits of actions you more likely take responsibility for outcomes and make better choices.

Third, to get better at gutsiness *get the right input from the right people about your decision*. You need the right people to advise you, people you can trust. (Read the section on mentoring in chapter 8.)

Fourth, *have fun*. Seldom is the job situation life or death. When you are able to see the lighter side, often you open your mind to fresh alternatives. The alternative to being gutsier is to be a business coward. And business cowards miss out on all the fun.

Many businesses are changing drastically and are increasingly willing to accept significant risk. If you are risk averse you won't make decisions that drive the company forward. I recommended we buy McCaw. It was an $18 billion acquisition. Fortunately it turned out to be a good decision but that could have been a career breaker. When Business Week *ran a story on the deal the cover photograph was of a telephone with the number 1-800-GUTS. . . . Many people thought I was taking a big risk moving from CEO and president of Sealand to joining a company twenty times the size, in a complex industry, in a new industry for me, as the CFO. It was another potential career breaker.*

—ALEX MANDL
CEO, Communications
Services Group/AT&T

Corporate life—like life in general—is about doing things you previously never thought you could. Top people are always taking on some new challenge. The climb to any top takes backbone, not wishbone. You *do* have a choice, so you might as well choose courage, in small ways, on a day-to-day basis.

When I talk about being gutsy most everyone says to himself, "Well, I am gutsy. I use common sense of course. I'm not stupid." That is great. That makes me very happy. That is what will make you more successful. I'd also like to say that whatever level you are on the Gutsy Scale, try to go up a notch. Let me give an example of what I mean by going up on the Gutsy Scale.

Say you are a midlevel manager in a company that has a policy that allows you to take a three-week vacation after three years of employment. For the last six months you and your family have been planning a fishing and canoeing trip to Canada. You have cleared it with your boss, made all the necessary commitments and arrangements, and are set to go. Your boss calls you into his office two days before your departure and informs you that some important, but not critical, work schedules have changed and you have to be back in two weeks instead of three weeks. He adds, "You have to be back in two weeks or you are fired."

You can choose one of the following reactions:

Gutsy Level 1: Bend over backward to the point of total pliability. "Oh, I'm sorry, I didn't consider a schedule change when I made my plans. Of course I'll change my vacation. Would you like me to just cancel it altogether? I can do that if you want."

Gutsy Level 2: Be accommodating without challenge. "Sure I can cut off a week. Anything you need."

Gutsy Level 3: Express your concern and offer alternatives. "Let's talk about the scheduling problem. Is there any way around it without changing my plans?"

Gutsy Level 4: Hold your ground like a pleasant bull terrier and don't bend. "I'm going on the trip as

planned and approved. If you are going to fire me, do it now, and I won't be back at all."
Gutsy Levels 5, 6, and 7: Depend on you and the situation you face.

Whatever level you'd likely choose, go to a higher level next time. You might be pleasantly surprised if you go all the way to level 4. You might just call his bluff, he backs down, and a problem is averted. On the other hand, you might get fired. A boss who threatens subordinates like that isn't a good boss. You might be doing yourself a favor to get out of the organization. I can assure you, if he intimidates you once in this manner he will do it again on a bigger scale.

Going up your *own* gutsy scale in other situations might mean volunteering to present a speech, initiating a conversation with the CEO in the company cafeteria, asking for a raise, confronting a co-worker who has misrepresented your work, challenging another department to some friendly competition, changing your dominant style, offering to deliver the bad news to the customer, and on and on. There isn't one gutsy level that fits everyone. Each person has his or her own scale. But wherever you are on it, you need to go up.

I'm sure you noticed that my suggested gutsy level 4 is not unreasonable or outlandish. It is, in reality, very acceptable interpersonal behavior when done with a pleasant but certain tone of voice. But most people's reaction is still "I could never do that." Yes you can, and to empower yourself, you should.

Often you lose nothing and gain everything from going up the Gutsy Scale. "No" is usually the most you'll ever get.

I'm not promoting a stupid, all-out, devil-may-care level of "You jerk, I'm out of here. I'll sue you and then you can go to h—." That is not being gutsy. I am promoting a more reasonable assertion of yourself than you'd typically undertake. Why is that so important? So you will grow, get stronger, hold your own, gain respect from others, increase self-esteem, and be able to take the lead when your time comes.

A few years ago I entered an elevator on the first floor of a Denver high-rise to attend a fund-raising event on the twenty-sixth floor. On the third floor a local politician entered, pushing the button for floor 26. On the fifth floor another community leader entered and pressed floor 26. On the tenth floor Jim Baldwin entered the elevator and pressed 26. Baldwin was the president of a major grocery store chain. He was highly visible through the press and respected in his business and community activities. The other two men immediately recognized him and eagerly introduced themselves, shaking his hand. Neither of them had gone out of their way to introduce themselves to me. And I could have easily stayed in my comfortable elevator corner, but *if one wants to be counted among the big boys one has to do what they do.* So wanting to go up my own gutsy scale, I introduced myself, shaking Baldwin's hand like the two men had. He held my hand for an extra long shake, turned his back to the men, and said,

"Debra, it *is* a pleasure to meet you. I've been reading so many good articles about you. Do you have a moment to talk? I'd like to discuss you doing some work for my company." This as we all four traveled to the twenty-sixth floor where Baldwin escorted me off the elevator and spent the next ten minutes in conversation.

That situation was part luck and timing, but also *guts*. You create your own destiny.

When asked what is more important, luck, timing, or guts, the overwhelming near-perfect chief voice confirmed that luck and timing without guts won't do you much good. Once you utilize your bravery skills you'll laugh inside how easy it is—and how worthwhile.

Now sometimes you may look at people with guts and wonder if they have brains. I recall one division head who wanted to try skydiving. He had no instruction. But his pull got him a ride on a plane. He literally jumped to try it. A broken collar bone later he said, "Next time I'll get some instruction." Physical courage makes you brave in one way. But you need judgment too!

Another parachutist (one with proper instruction), John Krebbs, president of the Parker Company, is nearly fifty years old. He skydives. Why? "Not too many people my age do. It's a thrill, a visceral feeling. You feel yourself riding on air. It's an accomplishment few get to experience." Two years ago he had a malfunction, hit a wind shear, and didn't open properly until seventy-five feet off the ground. Despite a broken ankle and a number of other broken bones in his feet, back, and rib cage, and hand damage, he is "physical therapying" (as he puts it) himself back into the parachute harness.

Wild is a strong word in business. In the dictionary it's defined as "not domesticated or tamed." The thesaurus suggests "unbridled" and "abandoned." And all those words are exactly what you need to do *occasionally*. It takes guts to shake things up in a traditional, staid business environment. But it is the chief who is willing to do it that reaches the tallest peak.

Being gutsy, and a little wild, is about the willingness to take risk—the willingness to expand your comfort zones by pushing at the boundaries. When Ross Perot organized the rescue of two of his EDS employees from an Iranian prison, that was outlandish.

When Glenn Armbruster let his employees put a pie of whipped cream in his face because they met a production schedule, that was a little unusual. (True, we aren't talking apples and apples here, but both of the above situations are out of the norm and to the different people involved a little wild.)

In your everyday life, and in business, there are boundaries, restrictions, precedents, regulations, and expected behaviors. Every once in a while go outside of them. Some of the most successful chiefs told me they *always* go against what the textbook says. Wild isn't so "wild" once it's been done. It simply sets the *new* precedent, boundary, or expected behavior.

Imagine if you were the CEO. Who would stand out among the crowd to you? Most likely it's the individual who does things a little differently from the rest. This does not mean one who exhibits weird, stupid, or extreme behavior. You want to use your common sense. But the fact is the leader of any group always stands out. Conversely the one who stands out looks like a leader. If you are look-alike, act-alike, people conclude you lack creativity and are uninspiring. If you aren't a little wild and shake things up, you will get cozy and set in your ways, which stymies your change and thwarts your growth.

Being a little unbridled is easy to do. Just carefully observe what most people do, and *don't* do what they do. (It's very similar to being original with some extra flair!)

One CEO gave me a for instance: "My banker came to us and said they were raising our rates from three quarters over prime to 5 percent over prime. After getting irritated, my first thought was responding with all the reasons and pleas why they shouldn't be raising my rate. Instead I surprised them with a relaxed and sincere tone of voice and said, 'You can have the keys [to the company].' Plus I indicated the meeting was over. They didn't say a lot to that, and in a short while they excused themselves and left. I met with my team and we discussed bankruptcy. I left town for a few days of golf. Next day the banker called desperately trying to track me down and set up a conference to say no changes would be made." The man successfully handled a potentially bad situation by simply responding to the banker's demands differently than he expected. It was a little gutsy—a little wild to offer the "keys" to the company—but it was incredibly savvy and original too.

Remember, just doing something a little differently can be considered a tad wild to you. "Wild" is an individual and relative thing. My good parochial school training (respect authority, obey the law, honor thy father and mother) taught me to be nice, polite, humble, and not to question. It wasn't my original nature to do what I did in the following story. But I know to grow I have to do things differently.

I had an appointment to meet a cable company CEO. It was difficult to find a time to meet with him because of his work load. But we finally scheduled to meet for lunch on Wednesday three weeks away. At 10:00 A.M. on that Wednesday his secretary called to reschedule the meeting for 2:00 P.M. "He wants to go jogging at noon, instead of lunch," she plaintively explained.

"Fine," I agreed, "2:00 P.M." (What else could I do?)

I showed up at 2:00 P.M. and was shown to the reception area where another person was sitting comfortably, waiting. Finally, at 2:20 P.M., the secretary came into the reception area to escort someone into the CEO's office. The CEO had mistakenly scheduled *two* people at 2:00 P.M. Since I was standing while waiting versus sitting like the other person (a small example of doing things a little differently), I was on my way into the CEO's office before the other man got out of his chair.

I walked into the CEO's office and held a relaxed smile on my face but did not immediately shake hands and sit down. With a friendly, challenging tone of voice I said, "I don't think this appointment is very important to you, is it?"

"Oh yes. It's important. Definitely. I apologize for this mix-up. I'm really sorry. What can I do to correct the situation?" he responded earnestly.

"No problem," was my response, and I meant it. The *gentle* chastisement was a little wild for me (relatively speaking), but it let him know he couldn't just dismiss my effort in making the meeting. I continued by explaining why I wanted to meet with him, and he hired my consulting firm for an assignment. Months later he said, "That mix-up the day we met, that happens to me a lot. But you're the first person to call me on my behavior. I respected that."

I realize this example isn't as barbaric as, let's say, throwing a rock through his window to express displeasure. But it was daring for my proper, polite, don't-challenge-people training. (It was a step up on my Gutsy Scale!)

Having courage, guts, and pluck isn't a luxury. It's a necessity.

> *Some people can never be fearless; maybe it's part of their personality. As a CEO, I can't let those people go very far in the organization. We demote them down to their level of competence and decision-making ability.*
> —TIM DAY
> CEO and President,
> Bar-S Foods

11TH VITAL TRAIT: HUMOROUS

John R. Stanley, CEO of TransTexas Gas Corporation, was in charge of GHR Energy Corporation when it almost went bankrupt twice. Sometime later, the former CEO was trying to sell $500 million of bonds to a group of California investors, and he was asked the uncomfortable question in front of a large group, "Why should anyone invest with someone who has almost ended up in bankruptcy court twice in ten years? How could you do that?" Stanley's response: "It wasn't easy, I had to work at it."

You have to have (and use) a sense of humor. Near-perfects understand they can and should use good cheer almost all of the time, with anyone, under any circumstances. Secure people can laugh at themselves. Scared people don't (except out of nervousness).

To be genuine, humor has to be a constant way of life. An occasional sparkle of joviality isn't sufficient. If you understand (and listen to) human nature, its pleasures and tragedies, you *have* to be amused.

According to *The Gate Book of Average*, the typical child laughs four hundred times a day, but an adult laughs only fifteen. (Contemplate that for a while!)

Everyone can perceive, enjoy, or express humor when things are amusing if they choose to. Top CEOs are able to do it when things aren't so entertaining. You can have a basic serious nature and still have a great deal of humor. You can be upbeat while still being earnest about consequences, behavior, and values.

Lee Iacocca was advising President Clinton on

NAFTA and Iacocca needed a commitment of time from the president. Iacocca asked Clinton for a third time for the schedule, whereupon Clinton put his arm around Iacocca and said, "I told you three times you could see the schedule. You know, Lee, you're okay, but you just don't know when to take yes for an answer." Not rip-roaringly funny, but it brought a smile to the faces of people around. We like a president with a sense of humor (remember Reagan). We like a CEO with a sense of humor.

Most chiefs want to be happy. And the happiness and well-being of their employees is usually important to them. Happy people are pleasant, good-natured, and jest, joke, and quip with each other. It makes for a productive workforce *if not taken to the extreme*. Morose, slow, depressed, sullen, gloomy, in-the-dumps people make up a lousy workforce.

Lawrence Land is an attorney and head of his own law practice in Norfolk, Virginia. He has a terrific sense of humor that he uses in and out of court. Recently an important assistant of his explained she was going to quit her job because she wanted to spend time with her children. A disappointed Land talked with her to learn about her motivation. When he clearly understood her decision was not based on job dissatisfaction but was purely family motivated, he offered to change her five days a week to four. He put it this way: "Your kids called me last night and told me the situation [the children are only two and four years old and they obviously hadn't called]. I told them I would give you Fridays off. And listen, tell your husband to tell his boss, I said he could have Fridays off too!"

You do not have to have the repartee of David Letterman. You do not have to have the "joke recall" ability that some people have. You simply need to have a willingness to inject levity into somber situations. You have to be willing to try it.

Think about it. A professional comedian, Phyllis Diller, strives for twelve punch lines per every minute of her routine. Bob Hope goes for six jokes a minute. All you have to strive for is one every fifteen or thirty minutes!

Americans are afraid to laugh, partly because of political correctness. We need to see the humor in the intolerance of intolerant people! Fortunately there is a humorous spirit that lies within most everyone. We need to be brave and let it out.

It's okay to plan levity. Yap Lim Sen is the managing director of an international commercial construction company based in Kuala Lumpur. His name is difficult to say and spell, so he helps his American clients, saying with a friendly wink, "My first name is Yap—*pay* spelled backward." The comment doesn't qualify him for a job as a stand-up comedian, but it brings a smile while making a business point.

Good humor is more important than

- a perfect business suit and tie,
- the car you drive,
- hair on your head,
- weight on your body.

Humor is the great equalizer, cutting across bound-ary lines of culture, rank, and other seeming limita-tions. You bond with people you use humor with. People like people with whom they can laugh. Get them to laugh (or at least smile) and they'll like you and choose to be around you over others. Having the courage to inject some levity drives your competition crazy. They wonder, "Why isn't she acting scared?" Most important, by maintaining an attitude of good cheer (especially when you don't feel like it), you will set an example for your co-workers, subordinates, boss, and friends. You don't have to make them laugh, but you should make them at least smile.

> *Making people feel at ease with humor puts*
> *you in control.*
> —JEFF BARENS
> President, The Barens Group

Since near-perfects are flexible, they can devise a va-riety of ways to demonstrate good cheer. Ironic (and funny) sayings, quotes, cartoons, jokes, facial expres-sions, verbal expressions, sight gags, amusing stories, mischievous pranks, and jesting remarks can all be used at various times. You won't find a chief doing all of them in one meeting, but you will see many of them used by one individual over a period of time.

I've seen CEOs throw pies in the faces of employ-ees, sign off on chain letters, give gifts of underwear in public, dance on public dining tables in their long underwear, moon an audience, place a fake bomb be-hind a friend's toilet seat, wear a disguise and go to a social dinner as an unknown, answer their business phones and identify themselves as an assistant while saying to the person talking, "My boss left clear instructions that under no circumstances would he accept a call from you," send cartoons via the fax, call overseas to tell a ribald joke on company time and money—to name just a little of the levity that goes on in business.

Just as you develop a decision-making comfort zone over time and experience, you should develop a humor comfort zone as well. The basic requirement of a humor comfort zone is that it is compatible with your personality and puts others at ease.

There are people out there who say they have trouble respecting and following lighthearted people. There are always *some* people who apparently have no sense of humor. You might temper your use of humor with them, but do not discontinue injecting levity altogether. Who knows, you might get them converted, but more importantly you stay in practice and are consistent. Remember, attempting to use good cheer selectively makes you appear insincere, or trying too hard.

As with any good trait, if taken to the extreme it becomes bad. Indiscriminate levity can reduce your credibility and your serious, strong, focused leadership.

It's true bankers and shareholders don't want you to joke about your earnings. But bankers and shareholders are humans who want to get the job done right and also *enjoy* getting the job done. That only happens in an environment of good cheer. You can get the job done without fun. And *sometimes* that is the only way. But most of the time there is the additional option with fun as a prime component.

There are some cautions about humor: Laugh. Don't giggle. Laughter is "ha, ha, ha." Laughter is good-natured; it comes from deep within. Giggles are "te he he" (a high-pitched, spasmodic, repeated sound). Giggles are giddy; they are a superficial surface response. Laughter reduces tension, relaxes you and others. Giggles increase tension because they are nervous fillers to ingratiate and seek acceptance.

We've all seen and heard humor that was inappropriate, ill-timed, misunderstood, or hurtful. Just because some people utilize humor poorly does not mean you shouldn't attempt to use it well. Obviously, use good judgment in your levity. If the little voice inside your head says, "You shouldn't make that comment, it isn't appropriate"—well, don't say the comment under the guise of a jest! Think up a different and more appropriate quip, or be quiet. You will have plenty more opportunity for good cheer, if you have the guts to keep at it.

Remember, even if you say the perfect humorous comment at the perfect time and you break the ice, relax others, reduce your tension, and ease communication, you may not get much positive reinforcement. Don't expect guffaws, applause, or thanks for the humor. Most people are so surprised to see any glee spoken that they are out of practice to respond favorably. Some are afraid to respond out of their own insecurities. Too often people don't know how to respond to good humor because it is such a shock to hear effective humor. At most a listener may crack a smile for a nanosecond.

> *I use humor a lot. I kid at very serious mo-*
> *ments. It takes people a while to get used to*
> *it. And it doesn't always work, but most of*
> *the time it does.*
> —ALEX MANDL
> CEO, Communications
> Services Group/AT&T

It's like the time I was speaking to a group of accounting firm partners. I said something humorous and I caught the senior partner breaking out with a smile in reaction to my comment. In half a second he caught himself and immediately held his hand to cover his mouth so no one would see that he slipped and almost laughed.

It should go without saying that if co-workers around you courageously attempt levity in your business dealings, acknowledge them. It would be okay to even laugh out loud. Reinforce their effort. You may need them to do the same for you sometime.

If you don't seek out the comical, initiate humor, or respond well to amusing things, you will likely not become a mountaineer. And if by some strange event you do become one, no one will want to climb with you.

12TH VITAL TRAIT: A TAD THEATRICAL

I watched a Fortune 500 CEO at a social business function where chairmen and presidents of major corporations, sports heroes, politicians, and entertainers were in attendance. After a couple of hours watching the CEO make small talk (and big talk) from table to table with everyone from the governor of Kentucky to country music star Waylon Jennings, *USA Today* columnist Dan Dorfman to NFL quarterback Bo Schlesman, I asked somewhat kiddingly, "Ever consider acting?" He calmly responded, "I am."

Everyone at the top uses theatrics to some degree. Even when CEOs don't admit it—they are acting like they don't! CEOs are very intense and they work overtime to not look intense.

Near-perfect chiefs admit to acting. "There is a bit of theatrics at the top for sure. There are times you need to be an inspirational leader," explains Tim Day, CEO and president of Bar-S Foods. "For example, twice a year I talk to everybody in every plant in every location. I have to appear confident, positive, and that I know what I'm doing even though I might have doubts. Maybe the word should be *presenter* instead of *actor* because you can definitely tell when someone isn't genuine. As the CEO, you do have to be able to give your message power, capture their attention, and make it memorable."

The reality is that the "acting" part of an effective chief is one of his most closely guarded trade secrets.

John Bianchi, CEO of Bianchi International, told me about his visit to the White House: "When I walked into President Bush's office, he acted happy to meet me. And I had to act happy to be there!"

Sometimes near-perfect CEOs simply *act* like good CEOs! CEOs do not have the option to admit they are uncomfortable, they must appear comfortable at all times—that's acting. Even the most confident climber needs to work to feel comfortable with the uncomfortable while appearing totally untroubled—that's acting. Sometimes they have to be cool and calm. Lots of times that takes acting. Near-perfect CEOs must look comfortable, confident, and competent to their competition, customers, employees, banker, board of directors, and media—even when they don't feel it. Acting is the polite term; bluffing may be the more accurate one.

I can assure you, all CEOs don't enjoy corporate socializing, media interviews, stockholders' meetings, selling, or even managing 100 percent, but to be effective they need to look like they do. That might mean smiling more than they are inclined to, shaking hands with people they don't want to meet, or working with people they don't like. That's acting.

> *Sometimes you have to act positive and up-beat even if you aren't feeling great. You cannot let that show. A leader cannot lead an organization into battle with an attitude of "we're in deep yogurt here."*
>   —ALEX MANDL
>   CEO, Communication
>   Services Group/AT&T

Remember the man I described earlier as mild-mannered, Duane Pearsall, cofounder of Columbine Venture Funds? He told me, "I *act* angry in front of the board, and sometimes in front of employees. I jump from flashes of anger to self-deprecating humor. They call it my deliberate drama. But sometimes it's the best way to get a lesson across. I force myself to do it. It takes a lot of energy, but it is necessary."

Sometimes it's necessary to get a "fire" built under people to get them going. A CEO might have to turn up the drama to demonstrate his fervor.

A problem for subordinates is that effective chiefs, who are good at being theatrical, make themselves difficult to read. For example, I would caution you about attempting to read your chief's body language or attempting to send your boss a message through your body language. Chiefs are probably the best in the company at being expressionless and controlling their thoughts and actions. (That's also acting.)

The near-perfect chief's CIA/poker face disguises his true thoughts. You will likely guess incorrectly what his state of mind is. More than ever, you need to *ask* what it is. Don't guess. Don't assume. Ask. You must not let another's theatrics overpower you, regardless of whether or not that person is the boss.

These are just a few questions you can ask to avoid guessing, second-guessing, reading into, assuming, and any other ineffective reactions:

- How do you read this situation?
- What do you see happening here?

- What sort of action do you think we need to take?
- How do you think most people feel about this?
- What would you prefer to happen here?

Just as I caution you not to read others, I want to remind you that others *are* reading you. You might want to make sure they read what you want them to, and that might require some acting on your part.

Try some of these actions:

- If you want to look like you're a level-headed businessperson, keep your head level instead of letting it relax into a tilt toward one shoulder.
- If you want to look certain about what you're saying, don't speak in a high, squeaky voice like a scared animal. Speak out loud while driving your car alone to practice a more commanding voice.
- Shake hands and hold on a second and a half longer to appear more sincere.
- Stand with good posture to look energetic, youthful, and taller.
- Sit with your upper body and arms asymmetrically positioned to look at ease, and relax.
- Walk into Mr. Big's office purposefully, deliberately, and calmly, like you belong there. You'll be acting more comfortable, self-assured, and confident.
- To appear comfortable when "getting down to business" in their office, pull the chair you're sitting in closer to their desk.

- Maintain eye contact when you meet a boss in the hallway. Smile. Say, "Good morning, Joe" (assuming that's his name). Don't nervously divert your eyes. It makes you appear scared, uncertain, guilty, or something else negative.
- If you want to look mad, pound on the table like General Motors' CEO Roger Smith allegedly does.

Or if you want to combine "a little wild" with dramatic you could

- greet your Monday morning meeting partners with a deep bow,
- strike a match to an article or report you didn't like in front of everyone,
- or let go with a whistle blast when someone does something special.

Try these suggestions on people you're having trouble with. Break out of old patterns of behavior—that might be what's causing the problem! Any single step may not solve the problems, but repeated, fresh approaches just might.

You and I "act" all of the time now. We do it unconsciously. For example, we talk and behave one way to our parents versus our boss, a college friend, a collection agency, a minister, and on and on. We just have to learn to be a tad theatrical purposefully when in the tough spots.

When in need of a reminder, remember what President John F. Kennedy used to say (and live by): "Appearances contribute to reality."

During my book promotion tour for *Lions Don't Need to Roar*, I was being interviewed by a well-known national television reporter (I'd prefer to keep her name confidential because revealing her style to the public would not increase my popularity with her). When she asked me a question and the camera was on her, she looked at me. But when I answered, looking at her with the camera on me, she was looking at her notes on her lap. When the camera was off her, her attention was off me and on her notes and the next question. (I later observed she did that with every guest.) I had to act like we were having a conversation when the camera was on me when in fact we weren't. In reality, we were not talking to each other at all as the viewing audience thought. Being prepared and willing to act helps you exert some control in situations like this.

Being a tad theatrical is not an affection. Nothing is more ridiculous than acting like you have qualities you don't have. Near-perfects don't *act* when conveying concern, care, sympathy, or interest. That would only compound the misunderstanding and negative attitude toward situations in the workplace. Instead, first-rate chiefs develop their ability to be dramatic to enhance the workplace. They make the effort to walk the talk. They look like what you expect in a leader even when they don't feel like it. Theatrics is taking on the responsibility to do all one can to effectively influence people around one. It might mean the chief acts enthused when he isn't, act certain when he isn't, acts displeased when he isn't, and acts pleased when he isn't.

Half of being a CEO is looking like you know what you're doing. The other half is being able to do it.

Wolfgang Puck, owner of Spagos in Los Angeles, described catering the Governor's Ball dinner at the Academy Awards: "Sure I'm nervous, but I can't show it. The 350 people attending would get nervous. And the whole thing would go downhill."

13TH VITAL TRAIT: DETAIL ORIENTED

The higher you go, the more exposure to the big picture you have, the more you might think being detail oriented is unnecessary. Wrong. It's just the opposite. According to near-perfect chiefs, the higher you go, the more critical it is to be aware of details, both the ones you put out as well as what others do. Unless you are alert at all times to as much as possible about what is going on around you, you will miss important signals and lack focus. These signals can be found in the details—the details most ignored too frequently.

John Bianchi, Ph.D., chairman of the board at Bianchi International, tells this story: "Before I had my own company, every day I used to drive by the company C. F. Braun International, in Alhambra, California. At first I thought it was an Ivy League university. Later I learned it was an industrial company. It left an indelible impression. It looked perfect to me, the buildings, the landscape. I told myself, If I ever had control of a company, I'll use Braun as a

model. Years later a friend of mine became CEO—
Gordan Anderson—so he invited me in for an in-
depth tour.

"Braun was founded by two German men with
rigid rules of conduct, dress, and performance.
Everything measurable was controlled. And morale
and productivity were high because of it.

"At night when executives left, all that was permit-
ted on their desk was their telephone, not one piece of
paper. Based on their level, two pens, three pencils,
one dozen paper clips, a certain thickness of corporate
paper was all that was allowed. No clutter or garbage.

"A retired navy admiral was in charge of the effi-
ciency effort. His job was to maintain the standards set
by the board. Attention to details was preeminent."

Near-perfect chiefs are detail oriented. They are
aware of as many aspects of what's going on as possible. A former editor of *Cosmopolitan* told me
about her boss, Helen Gurley Brown: "She knows
exactly what she wants in everything. You don't have
to support her or not support her, she doesn't care
because she has a very clear vision of what she
wants. It took me a year to get to understand her
mind-set. But once you do, you never have to guess
about what's right or not to her. She taught me, unless you're highly involved in detail, it won't turn out
like you want."

Bianchi was impressed by the attention to details
that he observed at Braun. Another CEO told me the
story of joining his current company as a young engineer where he wasn't so impressed, at least initially.
"I had a headhunter convince me to interview with

this company. I was comfortably employed but I went as a lark. Driving home the day before the interview I decided to drive by the plant. The grass was waist high, the buildings were rusty. I thought to myself, There's no way I'd join this company. I called the recruiter to cancel and he said that plant had been closed for four years and that the facility I'd be working at was brand new with a beautiful view of Manhattan across the Hudson River. That turned out to be the best career move in my life, but I almost didn't even try for it based on the details."

Being detail oriented does not mean nit-picking. It means being specific, taking full responsibility for outcomes. It does not mean being so immersed in minutiae that you lose the big scene.

- Nabuo Ishibashi (a Japanese CEO I will tell you more about later) writes about the day he registered his company: "It was a beautiful, warm, spring day." That's detail oriented.
- One CEO I know establishes a relationship with a new doctor with a "letter of understanding." It specifies billing, insurance, and medical history. Then it goes on to lay out late-appointment practice: "If the doctor is running more than fifteen minutes late the assistant is to call and change the appointment time. If I arrive for the appointment and I am kept waiting more than fifteen minutes, I will start billing the doctor my rate of $500 an hour. . . ." If hospitalized, he requests a sample of each exact pill he is to receive pasted on a piece of paper alongside the time

the pills should be taken and their dosages, "to allow no mistakes from hospital staff." That's detail oriented.

Near-perfect CEOs know that paying attention to detail saves you time that would be lost in going down the wrong path because you are missing out on specifics. It sets a good example for others to be aware of and to follow.

Details keep you accurate. Accuracy keeps you honest. Inaccuracy, lacking the details, invites dishonesty.

Tom Peters writes in his syndicated column, "On Excellence," "Think small. It's the details you're after."

The number-two reason for job terminations, according to the CEOs I interviewed, is lack of attention to detail. (Poor chemistry is the number-one reason.) Your attention to detail about their attention to detail is critical for your success. If you don't notice, you lose out. If you ignore, you lose. Diagnose by observing. Get an idea of the organization before you get involved with it. Also, if it's important to them, it should be important to you.

Say you're interviewing with a company for a position.

Pay attention to the parking lot. How convenient is it for employee access? Is it clean? Where do employees park? Is the lot in need of repair? What are the surrounding grounds like? Do they have any security? (A vehicle is a big investment that is usually not fully paid for. Does the company care? Paying attention to such details tells you a lot.)

I check out how employees handle the company equipment. They don't own it so how they care for it is an important sign of their attitude toward the company. Have you noticed the difference between the inside of a privately owned cab compared to a company-owned cab? The owner doesn't have fourteen used coffee lids on the dashboard.
> —BILL BLOUNT
> President, Power Motive Corp.

Pay attention to the entrance. Are these doors you'll be happy to walk through every day? My friend Shelley Monfor told me about her interview with Burlington Resources: "I walked through the double-glass doors approaching the descending staircase and said to myself 'This is where I want to work.'" Does the receptionist truly welcome you or do you feel your presence is an imposition? Why is the area laid out the way it is? What's the atmosphere?

Pay attention to the interviewer. How are you greeted? On time? What is his office like? Does he have frequent interruptions? Notice how his secretary acts around you versus him. What does he say to warm up the conversation? Does he answer *your* questions? What is he wearing?

Continue paying attention from that first meeting at the company on, in a job interview as well as any other encounter you're in.

Not paying attention to details more often than

not gets you in trouble. The IRS descended on an old partner of Jim Rupp's for not paying taxes on $100,000 income. He hadn't avoided paying, he'd just misplaced the checks. Jim's partner's clients had filed 1099 forms showing their payments to him. Jim was in trouble because of his legal association, so he helped search through piles of paper. Jim searched the chairs facing his partner's desk, which were covered with piles of papers. The partner explained the mess, saying, "I don't like people coming into my office and sitting down, so I keep the chair covered." Their joint search discovered one unopened letter after another with checks for $10,000, $20,000, etc., eventually totalling the $100,000.

The opposite extreme of Jim's partner's carelessness is John Bianchi's neatness (remember he was the fan of C. F. Braun). "The green shirts in my closet hang in descending shades. When I buy a new pair of shoes, I give away an old pair. For example I have ten pairs of footwear: two boots, two tennis shoes, two leisure shoes, two dress blacks, and two dress brown shoes. Anything additional is clutter. Being detail minded provides peace of mind to me."

How CEOs act is just that—how they act. Obviously the person has to be able to do the CEO job, but they have to act like they are the person who should be doing the job.

To achieve near-perfect status you have to be aware of your style, its impact on others, and be willing to change as necessary. You have to go out on a limb, try gutsy things, risk. If you don't you may be safe and comfortable but you will not advance to the top levels. Humor helps you recover from faux pas you might commit through taking risks. Using some theatrics creates the charisma people want in their leader. And being detail oriented on the small things helps you achieve the focus necessary for the big things.

PUTTING IT INTO PRACTICE SUMMARY

Be aware of your style: Style does not pertain to clothes. It's about what you do in your clothes.

Be gutsy: List the things that scare you the most—then tackle your to-do list.

Be humorous: It takes guts to inject levity into serious business situations—but somebody has to do it, so it might as well be you.

Be a tad theatrical: Get comfortable with the uncomfortable. That's life at fourteen thousand feet.

Be detail oriented: The small things will always make the biggest difference.

Act like a chief to become a chief.

CHAPTER 5

Bridging Gaps

How near-perfect chiefs interrelate, lead, and learn

NEAR-PERFECT CHIEFS ARE:

14. GOOD AT THEIR JOB AND WILLING TO LEAD

15. FIGHTERS FOR THEIR PEOPLE

16. WILLING TO ADMIT MISTAKES, YET ARE UNAPOLOGETIC

17. STRAIGHTFORWARD

18. NICE

19. INQUISITIVE

20. COMPETITIVE

21. FLEXIBLE

22. GOOD STORYTELLERS

14TH VITAL TRAIT:
GOOD AT THEIR JOB AND WILLING TO LEAD

It should go without saying that, above anything else, a near-perfect CEO should execute his job with technical excellence. That is a tough expectation.

One day the top dog is manipulating capital structures and the next day, talking to lenders, sizing up a new business situation, or planning a restructuring, or terminating an employee, or hiring a successor, or reforming the sales reps compensation, or gathering ammunition for expansion, or dealing with dropping net income and net margins and return on equity, or developing a foreign business, or rejuvenating an old division, or myriad other decisions that are constantly on the CEO's desk.

Few people will be expert in every aspect of the technical side of the job until they've had many, many, many years on the job. What enables them to effectively and successfully do the job earlier on, is the soft side—how they think, act, and interrelate with people—that ability enables them to successfully decrease debt, trim costs, raise operating margins, and increase earnings with the business.

How you think, act, and interrelate is the people side of business. A sterling education and brilliant strategic ability will not take the place of being able to talk and bond with people, plain and simple. The key to success in business is information—not information from computers but from people. To get the needed information from people you have to understand and be able to effectively influence them. Philosopher Don Marquis wrote, "The chief obstacle to the progress of the human race is the human race."

Individuals want to know the status of the organization, the company's ranking, the di-

rection, mission, and the standards of the game. That comes from the communicating CEO. A CEO is a coach, counselor, consultant, and referee. He has to provide resources and tools to his people so they can do their job. And he has to provide the appropriate goals, objectives, and motivation to facilitate getting the job done.
            —FRED FLORJANCIC
                President, Brunswick Bowling
                and Billiards

Being good at your job involves being both a specialist and a generalist.

Being a specialist means you are extremely competent in one or two areas that are important to your company, such as finance, marketing, legal, engineering, or technology. If you don't know the critical areas needed in your company, *find out*. Observe, ask, and double-check what you learn. If possible select and develop a specialty route that (one) you enjoy and (two) the company needs. "If you don't have an anchor in a specialty you'll be lost at sea," said a CEO who likens running a company to sailing. Know everything possible about something to be a specialist.

Being a generalist means knowing your specialty and knowing something about all other specialties. The higher up you go, the more decisions have to be made every day involving areas other than your niche. If you don't know something about everything you won't be able to asks questions to learn more about general areas.

> *Most CEOs have an understanding of two specialties. The age and size of the company determine which two are needed at the top. But all areas are discernible and understandable by the CEO.*
>
> *A large number of people who are really generalists think they could do the CEO job, but the trouble is they don't have a specialist background. First, you have to be a specialist in engineering, or marketing, or business law, or accounting, or personnel administration—and do an exemplary job in the specialty.*
>
> *The main difference in the CEO perspective versus vice president of engineering (the generalists in training) perspective is that you have to be able to step out of that specialty. You need to be able to see marketing's point of view and production's point of view and personnel's point of view even when in conflict with engineering. And you must see all functions much more broadly than when you were an engineer.*
>
> —CURT CARTER
> CEO, Mission Bay Investments

There is only one generalist job in the company, and that's the top boss. But there is no generalist path to that job. On your path to the CEO job, you will find it is a balance between realizing you must develop generalist talent while vigorously pursuing the goal of excellence in your specialty. The fact is that people have to take a specialist path to get the generalist's job! The combination of being good at your job and be willing to lead is where you will set yourself apart.

Somewhere along that specialist path you may be forced, or choose, to lead others. That's the turning point for the generalist's job. You see few chiefs set out to be the mountaineer at the top. They didn't go to CEO school or even envision themselves at that lofty height. But somewhere along the line, being good at their specialty broadened their decision-making realm, and not only were they working for themselves but for the team, the organization. Near-perfects soon found out someone had to step out from the crowd to lead. The ones who end up at the top made that step.

You also need to make those steps, when you can, in your career. You evolve from being good at your job to leading others in their jobs.

Be willing to lead. Neil Georgi, CEO of Neil Georgi and Associates, Inc., describes leading: "When it comes time to pull the wagon, a good CEO gets everyone to pull in the same direction."

Businesses strive to develop leadership. Companies look for it in their people. People claim it on their résumés. Politicians make it their platform. Near-perfect CEOs have it. Just what is leadership and how do you get it are the key questions people have asked for generations. For the near-perfect CEO, leadership is simply taking a company or person from where they are to where they ought to be.

Some say leaders are born, some say leaders learn to be leaders. Either way you need to be willing to do it. Willing to step out front, to take risks like the near-perfect chiefs do.

> *People leap from the ranks of vice president to president when they clearly demonstrate the ability to lead instead of the ability to just manage. By the time you begin to reach the higher echelons of your industry, everybody learns how to "talk" a good game. But rhetoric and B.S. are just that. You must demonstrate in an unmistakable fashion that you have the heart, the desire, and the ability to help lead the organization to higher ground. You simply must perform. All the people in your organization need to see, feel, and touch that intense desire to make a better world—a better world for them, your customers, and your shareholders. You must do tangible things that consistently demonstrate your commitment. Send a thank you note to a secretary who stepped in to help yours. Find ways to offer relevant training and development opportunities to all employees. Get the heat repaired in your people's offices. Put on paper your beliefs and "Guiding Principles" so people know where you stand. Then act on those beliefs—never deviate. As*

J. L. Kraft, the founder of Kraft, once said, "What we say we do, we do do." A successful leader will clearly declare himself and deliver.
    —DOUGLAS R. CONANT
       Group Executive Vice President,
       Nabisco, Inc.

A chief isn't automatically a leader—but he has a prime opportunity to be! That is, a chief may be chief because of an uncanny business sense, or his total knowledge of a company, not because of his ability to inspire people. But by virtue of his position he has an opportunity to lead like few other people have. Even the CEO who was not a born leader can lead if he is willing to and understands that leadership is never completely learned or totally developed—that it's always evolving.

The important thing is that you keep working on developing your leadership skills. The goal is to get *more* people to seek your lead *more* of the time. To do that you have to be someone who is

- worth listening to,
- worth believing,
- worth following.

Leadership isn't just learned, it's *earned*—and sometimes returned.

Brad Williams, president of Dakota Beverage Company, uses what he calls "peer leadership, where you accept a little extra responsibility for setting an example for the rest of the workforce. You set the tone for the rest of the team."

Think about the individuals you currently allow to influence you most. Do they live up to your expectations? If not, don't continue to let them have a hold on you.

One CEO who was new at the job proclaimed to me, "I intend to give the group leadership."

I asked, "What if they don't want it?"

He paused and said, "I never thought of that."

The fact is, most people want it. What varies is how you do it successfully for different groups.

Some leadership skills are never totally "gotten" and you're never sure if you totally "have it." The best you can do is *act* like leaders act. When I interviewed CEOs, I'd ask how they attempt to lead. What exact actions do they take to be a leader. The CEOs could describe some actions that they take and qualities they seek to develop, but to be exceptional the actions had to be used in combination with the 22 Vital Traits.

The following are the actions and qualities CEOs seek to develop:

- Set clear expectations for people.
- Use physical presence.
- Be an obvious presence in the company.
- Don't communicate your "ownership" of an idea too early into the problem-solving session.
- Check up on yourself periodically (even CEOs need to do this).

- Decide and plan four to five things you want done.
- Ask your key people key questions to help keep them on target.

Set clear expectations for people. Leaders look like they know where they are going, which inspires confidence in those below. Be clear: Say, "I want (or I don't want) you to do this now." There is no confusion. Who? You. What? This. When? Now. Setting clear standards of expectations limits what does or doesn't happen under your watch, and it takes excuses away from people.

Since near-perfect chiefs know what they need from their subordinates they can point out and explain when those expectations are not being met. Correct and critique constructively, one on one. "Part their hair" when necessary but avoid blame and personal attack. People wither and die (or counterattack behind your back) if you tear down their self-esteem.

Of course, effective leaders praise people when they meet expectations. (A wise leader lets subordinates "overhear" praise from a third party.)

Near-perfect CEOs particularly like and are impressed by the subordinate who asks what he can do to exceed expectations.

You might ask, "How can I ask this without sounding like or acting like I'm bootlicking?"

You have to earnestly want to know, then actively move on what you discover. If you ask to curry favor and ingratiate yourself you will quickly be seen through and pushed aside. But if you don't ask you'll never clearly understand the expectations.

Steve Silk, president and CEO of the Estee Corporation, rewards people who've met expectations with his Wall of Fame. Silk is an avid photographer, so he takes photos of employees. "We have four interior walls at our executive offices and one of those is an Estee Wall of Fame where we hang eleven-by-fourteen-inch framed pictures of employees. They change from time to time to show different individual successes and company milestones."

Use physical presence. Leaders utilize their nonverbal communication skills. They maintain a relaxed, slightly smiling facial expression when delivering good news and bad. A comfortable, confident, competent expression says, "I have the lead and I want you to climb with me. You matter. Be assured, things are under my control." The effective boss will sustain the relaxed, confident smile especially when he doesn't feel like it because he knows it is necessary to guide.

The person willing to lead is willing to touch. Literally and figuratively, the top chief gives pats on the back about as often as kicks in the pants. That would be, of course, literally for pats on the back and figuratively for kicks in the pants. Appropriate laying on of hands, by the leader, is the most empowering physical action a chief can take.

I watched Captain Odegaard of the USS *Clark* missile frigate as his men snapped salutes at him and he returned salutes to them, a very strong indication of just who was in charge. I also watched the captain approach an officer and lay his hand on the man's shoulder as Odegaard praised some action. The officer appeared to grow three inches taller before my eyes because of the positive acknowledgment of his good job by the touch of his commanding officer. Every CEO I have observed for any length of time appropriately touches men and women around him. Touch has gotten such a bad reputation because too many people selectively touch. If you are going to use touch as a leadership trait, you can*not* just touch the ones you are attracted to, you have to touch the ones unattractive to you also. Touch is *not* a sexual move when done in a suitable manner. (A suitable manner is with the right attitude of support, not a lecherous attitude, and with proper placement of the hand to the shoulder, upper back, or forearm.) To lead you must be willing to effectively touch, up and down the ladder.

Be an obvious presence in the company. Walk around the building talking with the people you encounter. Don't just sit at your desk. Be hands-on. Walk around and talk with people outside of the company as well. Don't count on your past leadership to carry into the future. Consultants like to say you are only as good as your last assignment. The same can be said of a chief; he's only as good as his last success. Let the casual (and casual-appearing) conversations guide you to wherever a crisis is unfolding. Get close to people.

Tim Stack, president and CEO of Borgess Health

Alliance, will work in the cafeteria one day "stirring the huge pots of food with boat paddles." Another day he'll put on the janitor's uniform or work at the admissions desk. He wants to be among his people both to lead and to learn from. "It's amazing what people will tell me that I'd never find out otherwise," Stack says.

Brad Williams, president of the Dakota Beverage Company, goes on the route with his truck drivers periodically.

Herb Kelleher is famous for serving beverages on his Southwest Airlines flights. He shows appreciation for people (employees and customers) when walking, talking, and listening to their comments.

When with other climbers (and hikers), quality chiefs query about management, and simultaneously share company problems or goals. These two steps make subordinates feel they have access to management. They don't feel so far down the chain or that they aren't important enough to be kept abreast of where the business is going.

Don't communicate your "ownership" of an idea too early into the problem-solving session. It is better for empowerment, team building, consensus building, and so forth if the chief asks carefully directed questions to get staff to supply ideas and suggestions. The leader offers a suggested direction, and then another later, rather than earlier. Subordinates view that kind of leader as a colleague, not just a boss; as a facilitator, not a dictatorial administrator.

Check up on yourself periodically. The CEO (and you) should ask yourself, "How could I have handled that problem differently and better?" Then ask a business coach, counterpart, or mentor the same question. Take note of your thoughts and others' observations toward your approach. Decide what and if to change next time, but at least check up monthly on yourself. Occasionally share your conclusions with subordinates. It demonstrates your humanness, modesty, honesty, and willingness to improve. If, as the chief, you set a precedent of assessing your own effectiveness you can more readily rate others, too.

Decide and plan four to five things you want done (today, this month, this year). Assign someone to do them. Let them do it. Support their efforts while checking on their progress. When noteworthy events take place, follow up with your satisfaction or dissatisfaction, then and there, before it goes further.

Ask your key people key questions to help keep them on target. On a quarterly basis, ask each of your key people the following questions:

- What are your objectives for the new_____ (period of time)?
- What are your plans, priorities, and hopes?
- How do you intend to go about achieving them?

Agree (or disagree) and write down the conclusions of the conversation in a journal. Use a journal to evaluate the person on whether or not objectives were met. Have managers do this down the line with everyone. A CEO of ITT methodically follows similar steps and sets the requirement for his subordinates to use the steps as well. (I realize this may be a hard habit to form, but your willingness to do it is just one more factor that differentiates you from other climbers.)

R. Carter Pate, CEO of Sun Coast Industries, gets weekly one-page reports on sales, backlog, order confirmations, dating of receivables and payables, overhead as a percentage of direct labor, and payroll. "These things sneak up on you."

Lee Iacocca regularly asked his key people these basic questions: What are your objectives for the next ninety days? What are your plans, priorities, and hopes? And how do you intend to go about achieving them?

Alex Mandl, CEO of Communications Services Group/AT&T and former CEO of SeaLand, tells me, "Leadership really boils down to an ability to work with peers, subordinates, and bosses. I'm candid, I tell them right away, 'John, this isn't right and this is why,' working with them on a real time basis. And this goes both ways. I'll tell someone who comes to me the only way this will work is if I'm absolutely certain he will tell me that my way is a bunch of baloney. That is enormously valuable to me, that people will tell me what they really think. I try to infuse this into the whole company, to encourage people to speak up."

You may respond, "Sure, *my* boss says that, but it is just untrue."

How do you know? Have you thought and strategized such an approach? Or have you heard of someone who heard of someone who tried it and it backfired? Unless you *responsibly* take the action, don't judge the reaction. For example, I know Alex Mandl and he means what he says.

To do a good job you have to be a specialist and a generalist who is willing and able to lead employees, lead the competition, lead the media to your message, lead customers to buy, lead bankers to lend money, lead the board to your thinking, lead your children to a happy, successful life.

Leadership isn't something superior chiefs began to display once they got to the top. They know, as you too should know, the more you look like a leader the better your chances of joining the leadership rank.

15TH VITAL TRAIT:
FIGHTERS FOR THEIR PEOPLE

If there is a list of dos for success, near-perfect CEOs know that being willing to fight for their people needs to be at the top.

If you want people to back you, back them, back them, back them. Be loyal downward; spread credit downward. Share the spirit and share the lead.

Every chief wants people to see his vision and follow his lead. He needs loyalty to make that happen. The chief needs to provide loyalty to get it. How can they complain about subordinates' lack of loyalty if chiefs don't give it to them first? You get what you give.

Buzz Taylor, the president of ProCounsel in Dallas, tells the story of meeting Herb Kelleher (CEO of Southwest Airlines) at a party. Taylor said to Kelleher, "I am a customer of Southwest and want to tell you that Southwest is not only the best airline I fly on, but also the best business I interface with." Mr. Kelleher guided Taylor's attention to a woman at his side and said, "Here is the reason why: Meet my executive vice president of customers, Colleen Barrett." This public display of appreciation and acknowledgment shows Kelleher stands behind his people.

In public the chief openly supports his people. Privately he might take them aside and try to "correct" their thinking, but he doesn't let them roast on the open fire. An average boss who consistently backs up his people can propel himself into near-perfect status with that trait alone.

When I worked in Washington for [Interior] Secretary Jim Watt, I asked him to approve a document I was going to release. I told him it would be controversial. He relied on me, trusted my judgment, and approved it without reading it.

When it was released some people were furious. Some top officials called Jim and demanded, "What's Pendley up to?" Jim calmly responded, "He's just doing what I told him to do. We're totally on top of the issue."

Jim backed me up. Then he called me into his office to get to the bottom of the situation. There could have been hell to pay in public, but he didn't blast me, he backed me up. I'll never forget the way he handled what could have been a tough situation for me.

—WILLIAM PERRY PENDLEY
President and Chief Legal Officer,
Mountain States Legal Foundation

I realize not all bosses are like Rod Friedman, publisher of the *Johns Hopkins Medical Letter*, when he says, "I have a great deal of faith in people, and if they say they'll perform, I assume they will, and I don't worry about it." Near-perfect chiefs challenge their people, but they also back their people. Bill Gates, of Microsoft, says his approach is to demand that employees be on top of their stuff. If they know all the angles and cover all the bases, Gates gives them full support to have their way.

The opposite of fighting for your people might be demonstrated in K Mart Corporation's CEO, Joseph Antonini, who reputedly called employees "stupid," "inept," and said "they are not worth the salary they were paid." Antonini explained his manner: "Remember, we're changing culture, and not everyone is happy with change." He admitted to being demanding and challenging of his people, but not abusive. (He has since been pushed off the K Mart mountain.)

If you want your boss to stick up for you, keep him informed of your activities *in advance*. Don't surprise him. You can't expect support unless he is informed on touchy situations. David M. Holland, retired senior vice president at DSC Communications, calls this form of communication his "hallways management technique." He advises, "Tell your position to the boss and others who can support your position in advance of possible difficulties, in the hallway if necessary. Even if it's last minute, let them know before you go forward. The key here is not to blindside the decision maker or influencers!"

Avoid surprising the boss. The following will keep you away from unexpected (and undesirable) reactions from the chief:

- Have a track record of good effort so that the boss has developed trust in your decisions.
- Clearly and simply state what you're planning to do. Don't skip the sensitive stuff. "I've done the following for the following reason. . . . Here's what I'm recommending. . . . Here's why. . . ." (If your chief okays the recommendation, you may not need to go to "why.")
- Lay out all the possible reactions that you've considered. Tell your chief what he's likely to hear *before* he hears it.
- Tell him what you'd like him to do. The boss may or may not see things your way, of course, but at least you've made a good effort.

• If, despite these steps, a huge blunder occurs, follow the advice in the next Vital Trait section, on admitting mistakes.

As Jack Falvey, the CEO of Intermark, says, "Management requires great patience while others screw up."

The most telling example of the benefit of standing behind your people was explained by Nabuo Ishibashi, chairman of the board of Daiwa House Industry Co., Ltd., in Osaka, Japan. In his book *Business Battles*, Ishibashi writes,

I asked [General Truman, cousin of President Truman], "Why did Japan lose the war?"

"In Japan, when a Japanese soldier was captured by the enemy, no matter what the reason, he was punished for becoming a prisoner of war. In the United States, it is considered an honor to be captured while carrying out combat duties. This can be the difference between victory and defeat." [Whereas] the United States used an entire airborne division and a tank division to rescue just seven U.S. prisoners of war . . . the [Japanese military] punished their own prisoners of war. Not just the Japanese soldiers themselves but the parents, brothers, sisters, and other relatives were all subjected to cold-shoulder treatment. . . . Since returning was in practice impossible, the prisoners of war became bitter and were prone to reveal military secrets and other information to the enemy. Classified information and secret codes were therefore leaked to the enemy by these prisoners of war. The American took advantage of this situation, and won the war. Japan treated her own prisoners of war poorly and lost. It is the same in the case of an enterprise.

Ishibashi goes on to advise that when criticizing an employee "scold, but stop short by 20 percent. . . . Later compliment them with 'You did a good job.' " This demonstrates a willingness to work with and develop your people, key components in the total quality of being able to fight for them.

When I talked to top chiefs about open and direct communication such as that promoted by Ishibashi, I asked them how they would hope their staff would respond. Following are three answers:

- Listen to what the boss has to say.
- Question the thinking of the person giving the critique if necessary for clarification, not a smart-aleck challenge.
- Disagree then and there if you're going to. Redirect their reasoning at the time by asking, "Have you considered . . . ?" Don't let anything slide by.

Again, before you challenge with "But that won't work with my boss!" try it. Honestly, give it a good try.

With clear and open communication in business like we have been discussing, the amount of surprises the CEO receives is greatly reduced, that being his obvious preference. However, when the near-perfect chief does get that occasional surprise, he takes a neutral position rather than a negative one in public. He will take great effort to show support of his employees' decisions to be sure his people don't have to look over their shoulders in fear.

Obviously, near-perfect CEOs don't back up questionable, immoral, unethical, illegal behavior. It shows bad judgment, a spineless character, and it is an open invitation for unpleasant legal intervention.

With the exception of the immoral, unethical, and illegal, fight for your people publicly and behind the scenes. *Do it more than they even realize.*

And when you make a mistake in this area, show support of your people by admitting the transgression.

16TH VITAL TRAIT:
WILLING TO ADMIT MISTAKES, YET ARE UNAPOLOGETIC

"I say oops, you're right, I was wrong," claims one manufacturing CEO in California. "Not so," whispers his secretary, who added, "Don't tell anyone I said that."

Near-perfect CEOs admit mistakes. Experienced mountaineers know most missteps aren't fatal rockslides for a career climb. If the rockslide creates a landslide endangering others, well, that's a different situation.

John Sculley, the former CEO of Apple, admits he made mistakes heading the personal computer company. He says it took him fifteen years to learn the soft drink business at Pepsi-Co and he just hadn't had enough time at Apple to learn the new business before taking the leadership role. He feels he was running the business but didn't fully understand it.

The CEO of Ford, Alex Trotman, readily concedes his company didn't have the courage to put the money into competing with the extremely successful Chrysler minivan and therefore missed a huge market.

Pete Coors, CEO of Coors Brewing Company, ran a full-page ad in the *Rocky Mountain News* with a two-inch-high bold headline, "We goofed." Then he went on to explain about a batch of beer shipped with a harmless beer-spoiling bacteria that hadn't been filtered out and what customers can do to get a replacement.

Even Peter Drucker admitted he was wrong when he wrote in 1976 about giant investors questioning management. He was quoted in *Forbes* as saying, with good humor, "Don't rub it in."

Mistakes take place. What happens next is up to you.

Don't fear fessing up. It shows you are wiser today than yesterday to see your error, humble enough to admit it, and potentially able to correct it.

Are there mistakes we've made as a corpo-
ration? Sure I can think of three or four. I

*admit it all the time—in real estate, finan-
cial services, and one international partner-
ship for example. I cite those continuously,
but I don't dwell on them. I cut losses and
get on with it. That's the CEO's responsibility. Admit where you made mistakes and
take corrective action. If you've made mistakes that can't be corrected, step aside.*
                                    —RICHARD MCCORMICK
                                    CEO, US West

A mistake is an error, fault, misconception, misunderstanding, blunder, blooper, slipup, flaw, or faux
pas. With a list that long, you'll likely stumble into
some of the behaviors on a daily basis. When it happens, *admit it.* Stop it, correct it, and, most important, don't repeat it. But don't fear it and don't
constantly try to rectify it. Mistakes are nothing but
education and the first step to something better.

Dead people are the only ones who don't make
mistakes. If you are error free you're likely effort
free. Risk and mistakes are close together.

Make the same mistake only once though. Repetition of similar mess-ups shows lack of attention to
detail, sloppiness, poor attitude, thoughtlessness, and
one in dire need of improvement. Nicholas St.
George is the CEO of Oakwood Homes (a $42+ mil-
lion mobile-home manufacturer). He made the mistake of relying on banks to finance mobile-home sales
during the aggressive 1980s, which almost took his
company down. Now he finances the home sales
through the company. He admitted the costly mistake,

paid the price of absorbing the bad debts, changed the system, and won't let financing get out of control again. (That's a big example, but smaller ones occur every day in our own lives.)

All the mistakes that can be made in existence have already been made millions of times over. Unfortunately, we don't always learn from the mistakes of others. We need to make them ourselves. Then we get *experience*, then we learn.

I'm not saying celebrate mistakes, just admit them, correct them, and go on. A near-perfect does not have to let mistakes slide by, but he can't let people fear their career is out the door by making them either.

A near-perfect manager encourages risks that result in mistakes. It promotes growth, creativity, and loyalty. Rarely can an honest mistake not be fixed.

Michael Maples, the executive vice president for Microsoft, explains the company's recruiting: "We look for somebody who learns, adapts, and is active in the process of learning from mistakes. We always ask, [in a job interview] what was a major failure you had? What did you learn from it?"

What separates effective, successful people from the pack is their ability to handle the inevitable mistakes that occur in all lives. Many times an error goes undetected by everyone except the maker of the mistake. The near-perfect, nonetheless, acknowledges it, corrects it, and rectifies it. Not-so-near-perfects make others pay for their mistakes—something that happens way too often in the business world.

If you approach mistakes thinking no one noticed,

you are likely incorrect and on your way to making another mistake by not admitting the first one (and losing your job).

Think about the error and deliberately decide not to repeat it and devise a plan to make sure you don't. Stick to the plan, revising as needed, but stay well centered on a course that keeps you from repeating the same mistake. I met Anthony O'Reilly, CEO at H. J. Heinz, at a business conference in Cannes, France, where we both were speaking before a company of insurance executives and I had the opportunity to observe and talk with him. When I read the following quote from the book *What Works for Me*, I was reminded of our meeting and his personality. "I like to analyze a situation very thoroughly before I make my move. As a football player that is one thing I did: I always hung back. While this has surely caused me to miss some opportunities, I have made very few major mistakes. By taking this approach, I think that I have kept the mistake factor at a tolerable level and have made a few touchdowns as well." O'Reilly simply stops and thinks before he acts to balance the risk and reward.

I also remember talking to one of O'Reilly's executives, who confidentially explained that to work well with O'Reilly he himself has learned to correct his mistakes before he makes them.

Good CEOs likely make more mistakes than the people they manage. That's probably how they got to become CEOs, but they seldom make the same mistake twice!

CEOs make many of the same mistakes the general

population makes—mistakes in choosing the companies they join, stock they buy, wine they select, and spouses they marry. It is the way they handle them and maybe optimize them that sets them apart from the general population.

"I'm not fearless but I will take risks. I'm very good at forgiving myself when I make a mistake. It's too bad people don't bounce back. I've seen really talented people let an organization dictate how they should feel about themselves," explains Julie Donahue, CEO and president of BBN Hark Systems Corporation.

New York artist Robert Freiman proudly showed me his latest work and explained his unique technique. It seems he'd had a frustrating day with pieces not coming out as he wanted. Being a perfectionist (and a bit temperamental) he tore them up and tossed them onto the floor along with crumbled paper towels used to blot excess paint. He looked at his "waste" on the floor and liked the look. He glued the torn and crumbled pieces onto artist board and added a few brush strokes. He produced a new, impressive, and very original piece of abstract art. Out of failure came newfound success.

You may look at your CEO idol and think she never made mistakes, she got it right in advance. Wrong. Some did, some didn't. The difference between the good and not-so-good is how they handle mistakes and how they avoid repeating them.

I admit mistakes to get employee support in the new direction we need to take. I do not

admit them [to get] understanding from
them. I'll tell them when I'm going down the
wrong course, but I want them to feel I
make few slipups. Sometimes I correct my
mistakes without them knowing so they end
up thinking that was the direction I wanted
to go anyway.

—BILL REAGAN
CEO, Reagan Companies

If you haven't had any mistakes lately from which
to learn, create a hypothetical one. Try conjuring up
a situation. Select some crazy option. Then play out
the results in your mind to see what might have happened, what you could have done about it, and, most
important, what you learned from it. Work the mistake out in your head. Then perhaps you won't make
it in real life.

Admitting mistakes is *not* being apologetic.

Be unapologetic. I was talking to a CEO friend who
buys and sells real estate (properties in the million-
dollar-plus range). I was seeking his opinion on a
Colorado mountain condo I was considering. "It's
not much compared to what you deal with. It's only
a—" My friend cut me off: "Don't apologize. It's
distasteful and unnecessary. Avoid it. Just tell me
about the condo without comparing to me or anyone else."

Apologizing *unnecessarily* is unflattering. (That is
not what I mean by admitting mistakes.) Near-perfect
CEOs do not engage in the apology game, prefixing

statements with "I'm sorry," "Excuse my intrusion," "Please pardon me." Constantly expressing regret or asking pardon indicates insecurity and begs for affirmation. When you apologize, the other person feels compelled to make you feel good. Most of the time people are apologetic upward—that is, they tend to apologize more readily to people with higher positions than they would to subordinates. Regardless of who you're apologizing to, you put them in a position to have to apologize to you for having to apologize to them!

If you honestly think about it, the thing you might apologize for is something you've consciously let yourself do: "Oh, I'm so sorry for being late" or "I shouldn't have eaten so much" or "I apologize for not getting back to your earlier," and on and on. It's ineffective and vain to make excuses for yourself. Many times the first your fellow climbers will know of your shortcomings is when you apologize for them. If you or the situation you've caused is truly bad, you do little to help by begging for forgiveness. It would be better to control yourself from letting the situation happen again.

People usually apologize for the wrong things. The truly foolish behavior that one wants to justify continually gets ignored. Apologies are often vain attempts to vindicate oneself for something one doesn't plan to change anyway!

Just as near-perfect CEOs don't continually apologize to others they don't allow people to incessantly apologize to them. They generally cut you off to shut you up, or just don't give you the forum to apologize. Over time, the ones doing all the apologizing will only resent the ones they are apologizing to.

Occasionally when I interviewed a CEO he would say, "I don't know why you'd want to interview me after all those big-name people you've met." It served no purpose other than to make me say to myself, "Maybe he's right."

One computer service company CEO told me her story of apology but swore me to conceal her identity. "I was a consultant to George, a partner in a manufacturing operation. He was planning a plant inspection by a major prospective customer. He had the place painted and scrubbed to prepare for the big 'dog and pony show.' Most of the changes were for show, not substance. While he was doing his last-minute scurrying, he came to the department where I was working and proud as punch announced it was done and what did we think—was anything missed? I told him, 'It looks really nice, but just one thing— don't forget to wipe the brown off your nose.' He chuckled and left.

"The person I was with thought it was really funny and while she was laughing squeezed out an 'I can't believe you said that.' All of a sudden I was overwhelmed by what I had just said, thinking, 'Oh, no, this is it. I've finally gotten myself in trouble with my teasing.' People on the staff thought it was great because I had said what they wished they had the courage to say. But I was consumed by what I said—for over an hour I was unable to concentrate on anything else. Finally I had to go talk to

George. I told him I was sorry if what I said offended him. He had kind of a dumbfounded look on his face, as if to say, 'What did you say?' I continued, 'You know, the crack about brownnosing?' 'Oh that.' He laughed. 'You and I have talked enough, I know what I'm doing and I know you know what I'm doing too. But it's just business. I thought it was funny and just what I'd expect you'd say.' "

Sometimes an apology is *exactly* what is needed. In this case it was exactly what was needed. If George had been bothered by the comment, the work relationship would have been damaged without expressing regret for the remark. But in this case the uneasiness was in the person who made the apology. Apologizing was the only reasonable way for her to let go of the mistake.

Admitting mistakes is not the same as frequently apologizing. The first is necessary; the second is tedious. Justifiable apology is good manners, which is different from an apologetic attitude. And occasionally groveling is exactly what is needed. Apologies can break tension, ease communication, add some humor.

But be on guard that you don't fall into the biggest apology mistake: If someone compliments you, whatever you do, don't respond with an apology like "It was nothing." Instead say "Thanks."

17TH VITAL TRAIT: STRAIGHTFORWARD

CEOs have the least time and least patience for people who beat around the bush. The higher up you go the less tolerance you will have also. Top chiefs are generally straightforward, and they expect the same in others. You must be direct, honest, frank, and follow a straight course. Don't distort, twist, deviate, or trick.

Wick Simmons, CEO of Prudential Securities, writes, "It's my job to set the tone for this company. That starts with laying it on the line inside the company and out. We call that straight talk. Straight talk means our investors hear the upside and downside of every opportunity. It also means facing up to hard issues—admitting mistakes and fixing them. Straight talk means if we fall short, we'll hear about it. That's good. It makes us do better. . . . It's something we have to live by."

Although straightforward talk is the preference of the near-perfect chief, that does not mean it is necessarily the standard form of communication in the business world.

The corporate language largely spoken is beat-around-the-bush-to-see-what-reaction-you'll-get. It's common for the first twenty minutes of a meeting to be filled with "slip and slide" to test the water. It's a game of signals that separates the bright ones and

*the dull ones . . . to see who's smart enough
to detect what is required.*
> —JACK FALVEY
> CEO Intermark

I remember a seminar I attended early in my career. The leader wrote four huge letters on the overhead projector: CIPU. "That's how we communicate," he ranted, "*Clear If Previously Understood.*" Meaning, "I think I know what I think you want, and you think I know what you think I know and you want, and neither really knows exactly, but we go on like we do know." Know what I mean? The circle people talk in can be absolutely mind boggling, and the effect is always bad.

When you beat around the bush attempting to communicate

- you sound hesitant, sometimes devious, or at least dishonest,
- you miss or forget to relate key information,
- you set yourself up for attack because you look vulnerable,
- you dig a hole for yourself that is tough to climb out of,
- you usually forget what you said,
- you are (or appear) disorganized,
- you lose.

You must have people be straightforward in business. You don't always need consensus, but if they oppose you, you need to hear

about it. I'm not looking for people to
argue. But I want things resolved. Clear the
air.

—RICK HOLLEY
President and CEO,
Plum Creek Timber Company

James Burke, CEO of Johnson and Johnson, explains that his people can politely say to him, "You are wrong. You don't have the facts. I do. Here's evidence to prove it." The candid manner helps people to reach a workable, satisfactory solution.

When two or more are gathered together there is the possibility for misunderstanding. Fortunately, straightforward is pretty straightforward. Immediately clear up mutual mystification by asking the following:

- What are we trying to accomplish?
- What are the fastest steps?
- What is my role?

Then you might offer suggestions, beginning in the following ways:

- Here's what I need to achieve. . . .
- Here's what needs to be done. . . .
- Here's what I plan to do. . . .

More often than not the other person or people involved will deeply appreciate your being sincere and plainly outspoken. (Note: Outspoken does not mean obnoxious.)

If you get a reputation with the boss for pompous communication it will take inordinate effort to change that general estimation. On the other hand, if you communicate in a simple, unpretentious, but interesting way, you'll be sought out.

Everything you write or convey can be done in a plain, simple manner. Traditionally the best ad campaigns are brief and to a point. Employees follow clear instructions better. The media seeks five- to ten-second sound bites for the nightly news. As brilliant as Reuben Mark, COB, president, and CEO of Colgate-Palmolive, is, he says, "I like things presented in a simple A plus B plus C fashion."

Talking

Are there people you avoid talking to because they can't get to the point and conclude the conversation? Do you think there are people who avoid you because you can't get to the point or end the conversation?

If you don't take the seconds required to think through the conversation, meaning what you need to say, what the other party will likely say, how you'll both feel about what the other says, etc., one of two outcomes is possible.

1. You won't get the opportunity to be tested with significant work.

2. You will get the opportunity and you'll botch it.

Remember the earlier discussion on thinking before you talk? You are more to the point when you prethink every conversation and telephone call (even the routine ones). Before talking, ask yourself the following questions:

- Why are we talking?
- What do I want to accomplish?
- In what order?

Then to start the conversation you might say, "These are the things I want to cover now." And you can end with, "Did we cover everything we needed to?" If the people you are talking with are really pressed for time, your opening comment might be, "Do you have the time to talk about this right now, or should I contact you another time?"

In your communication strategy, it is also important to be prepared to be able to effectively end the discussion. To end the conversation you can simply say, "I've got to go" or "I wanted to take your call because it was important but I have other people waiting." (Somewhere!) An explanation may or not be given, and you can still be pleasant while ending the exchange.

Speak with a relaxed, well-modulated voice when happy, mad, or in between. Chiefs need to act in control, and their voice is the physical characteristic that gives them away when it is too harsh, breathy, high-pitched, low, choppy, or hesitant. Just as you should be straightforward in your communications your voice should be straight on, even when you are anxious, nervous, frustrated, or scared.

Relax your tongue to even your tone. Feel the loosening of your jaw when you relax your tongue? Your tongue is the carpet of your mouth—don't bundle it up. When you relax the tongue it de-stresses your throat and minimizes a tense, tight, forced voice. (Loose-tongued should not be confused with loose-lipped.)

Slow down. I ask CEO Mike Wilfley, of A. R. Wilfley & Sons, for advice on business issues from time to time. Because his ideas and time are valuable to me, I am mindful and respectful of them. In the beginning of our business friendship my concern caused me to speak rapidly and hurriedly, so he could go on to other things. After several conversations like this, he stopped me. "Debra, don't speak to me so hurriedly. You sound nervous to me. Also, don't rush me."

I protested, "I'm just trying to be respectful of your time."

"Don't worry, I control it. Slow down," he said.

When Wilfley and other CEOs speak to me, no matter how pressed for time, they very seldom appear harried, hurried, or out of control. (That cannot be said for most people.) Partially because they think before they talk, they come across as CEO-like. Because they think, they are more organized and throw in fewer filler phrases, thoughts, or words. Near-perfect chiefs say what they have to say, then are comfortable with the silence.

Important people are willing to talk with you if you speak in a way that indicates you are worth talking with. However, if top chiefs don't like the way you communicate, they won't communicate with you. It's that simple. You need to write and talk to them as they need and want to be written and spoken to. Otherwise you'll experience what Robert Half philosophizes—"Postponement: the sincerest form of rejection."

Straightforwardness is not only essential in oral communications but also written communications.

Writing

Many more letters and faxes are sent than necessary. And a great many more are sent than ever read. Less than five seconds is given to most general pieces of business correspondence. In that time you'd better get to a point. When writing, too many people don't think, they just type.

Near-perfect chiefs write clearly. In a sentence or two they bring the reader up to date, summarize, and set the scene. They take a sentence to state their recommendation/request, another sentence or two for reasoning and figures to help the reader understand the recommendation/request, and then give a specific time by which the reader should respond and indicate the manner of response. And that is it!

Irvine Hockaday Jr., CEO of Hallmark Cards, Inc., responded to a *Wall Street Journal* article about the rumor of the company going public in a letter to the editor: "Hallmark going public is not necessary, will not become necessary and is deemed not to be desirable." Pretty much to the point, right?

Writing with this style does not come easily. Paula Ancona, of Scripps Howard News Service, writes in her "WorkSmarter" column, "There's a tapping going on in thousands of offices right now. It's the tapping of pencils on desks and feet on floors . . . nervous people who are trying to write a report, letter or memo—but can't get started."

There are seven steps to writing a letter or memo:

1. Prethink your objective.
2. Write from the heart.
3. Start. Continue. Finish.
4. Put aside.
5. Edit. Read it out loud. Does it still sound like it's from the heart?
6. Reedit. Reread. Stop editing.
7. Send out.

Bill Daniels, chairman of Daniels and Associates, has an expensive, monogrammed stationery card, about 3 ½ by 6 inches in size. A typical Daniels note has a date, salutation, and message that may be no more than "Thanks," signed *Bill Daniels*. The one word delivers his message and follows the seven steps listed above.

As in other areas of your business style, don't be

afraid to see what others do and do something a little differently. Do not hesitate to write to someone you don't know and compliment or comment on something they've done. Nine out of ten times your note might be read and put aside, but that tenth time could lead to something you hadn't dreamed of.

The best chiefs occasionally send notes of compliment or congratulations to employees. Subordinates will save a handwritten acknowledgment from the CEO *forever*. One subordinate, talking about a note from his boss, told me, "I kept his note on my desk for weeks and read and reread it. That note was the nicest thing that happened to me all year."

With personal computers and word processors volumes can be pumped out. I suggest that you resist the impulse to write a dissertation and instead do something more personal, memorable, and impressive. *Handwrite* the letter.

The number-one excuse for not handwriting an occasional business letter is *time*, but in actuality it's probably poor handwriting. Your handwriting doesn't have to receive an A from Sister Agnes, but it does have to be legible. Just slow down when you write and make it readable. If it is truly awful, change it. (A client who learned Chinese lettering from her grandmother gave me a hint on improving my handwriting: Write in a straight up-and-down movement. Messiness comes from deviating from straight movement. *Try it*. You'll be surprised how quickly you'll see improvement.)

Sloppy writing is not a status symbol. People usually write poorly out of haste and laziness. (With the push of a button your computer or word processor checks your spelling and your grammar, for example.) Unfortunately in the business world people can get away with bad habits. They simply scribble words down. Because even they can't read them, they pass the message to a secretary, who has to decipher the code, type it, and in doing so remove the note's individuality. Frequently, typed correspondence is necessary, but even then you have to sign it. Write legibly. It takes deliberate effort every time you put pen in hand, but it's worth the effort to you and your reader.

If what you have to say is important enough to write, it's important that it can be easily read.

When you slow down and put effort into writing legibly you

- look neater,
- enable your reader to read *and* understand what you wrote,
- appear more organized in thought,
- improve your grammar,
- make fewer mistakes,
- *will be remembered.*

A drawback of handwriting selected correspondence is that it can be analyzed. I had a secretary once who analyzed handwriting in her spare time. Every letter I received she put through her analysis. Every once in a while she'd volunteer information on the writer, and it gave me insight on how I might respond to them. The things she told me about the writer, based only on the signature, made me aware of the reaction my own signature must be receiving. I changed my illegible writing to a style I could be a bit more proud of.

A European-based CEO I know sends outrageously expensive Christmas cards to business acquaintances around the world. One year the holiday greeting was a series of beautiful lithographed prints of holiday scenes. Another was a poem accompanied by an original autographed sketch for each recipient. The director makes a point to personalize each card with a message. One year my message was so illegible I had to call overseas to get it deciphered. I called and asked as graciously as possible what the note said. He laughed and answered, "My family will be in Colorado after the holidays, we hope we can get together with you." This man is a straightforward communicator, but you wouldn't know it because you can't read his writing!

Try using extra-legible handwriting yourself, then ask people like your secretary, co-workers, or spouse if they notice the difference. Get some positive feedback to reinforce your effort. Don't be like the army buddy who sent a long, handwritten letter to a friend after some forty years. The friend who received the letter told me, "I just cried when I received the letter from my old buddy." I asked if it was that emotional, and he explained, "No, I couldn't read his handwriting!"

18TH VITAL TRAIT:
NICE

Viacom's CEO, Sumner Redstone, fired the titan of
the publishing industry, Richard Snyder, because he
wanted someone *more benevolent*. The termination
rocked the publishing world because Snyder was
known in the industry as brilliant, the man who took
Simon and Schuster from a $40 million to a $2 bil-
lion company. But Snyder was also known for being
demanding, imperialistic, and mean, and for managing by fear and intimidation. As abrasive as he was,
he still had loyalty from his top people because he
was so good. But for all the good, at some point the
tolerance ran out; the situation was no longer acceptable.

Now, you could say it doesn't sound very "nice"
of Redstone to fire Snyder. Being pleasant does not
mean you can't get down to the tough decisions that
need to happen in business. The CEO often has the
reputation for being the least nice because of different judgments he has to make. Therefore even the
best chiefs aren't often considered nice. They deal
with many people with different opinions and different goals, and the chief has to be the decision maker,
which sometimes means the bad guy.

Being nice does not mean being concerned about
being liked. Near-perfect CEOs make a decision on
what's right, not what's popular. That gets them respect whether they are liked or not.

Being nice is based on a simple value system: Respect people (people who work for you and people you work for); what goes around comes around; and benevolence helps you enjoy your good work.

Near-perfect CEOs prove you can be an amiable guy with a warm, caring reputation and still be strong and get the job done. You can only be better by being nice. As Hugh Sullivan, president of Sullivan and Associates, put it, "People don't mind as much if you're a nice pain in the ass."

You can give explicit instructions and criticism to an employee with a sincere tone and caring smile and get effective results. You make yourself easy to listen to and understand, and people will meet your requirements. On the other hand, if you bark out those same instructions and criticism with a grim, flat, cold face, people will take offense and you will not get what you want.

The Cafaro family of shopping mall fame (worth around $600 million) built their fortune with the philosophy "If you make a friend today, you can always make a deal tomorrow."

> *The gentle way holds great value. Harmonious cooperation and understanding provide a reservoir of goodwill.*
> —GEORGE SCALIES
> CAO, National Semiconductor

Take pains not to appear superior or aloof. Being agreeable does not mean being "sucky" or going around saying "please" and "thank you" till it seems the syrup will begin to drip off of you. It means an attitude of "*I choose to be pleasant in our dealings and I expect pleasantness from you.* We won't avoid the tough issues, we will just address them with a mutual respect."

Chrysler Corporation spent $30 million *in one year* on training salesmen and mechanics to be polite and smile.

It's simple. You have a better chance of getting what you want out of people if you're nice first. Being coarse, unpleasant, boorish, or rude will not get you far.

> *I'm informal and try to be considerate of others. The other day, for example, as I was giving constructive criticism to an employee, I realized that I had devastated him because the criticism came from the chairman. So I went back and patched things up. It's important to talk about things with your employees, but an executive has got to be sensitive to the impact of his words.*
>
> —LODWRICK M. COOK
> Chairman and CEO, ARCO

But wait, you are thinking, you've seen a lot of people get their way who are rough, boorish, and unpleasant. True, a lot of times in the short run and even sometimes in the long run, those people win. But *most* of the time it does not work, particularly in this day and age when employees tolerate less and less abhorrent behavior from their bosses. If you are mean with people you will not last; someone with power from above or below will topple you, as Richard Snyder found out. Calamities more often than not start with what comes out of your mouth.

Start with a pleasantly assertive stance. You can always move toward a tougher position on things. It is nearly impossible to start as a boorish S.O.B. and later try for a benign, kind manner. Co-workers will never trust you.

But what about the extraordinarily tough tasks that sometimes fall on a CEO? How can a CEO lay off seven thousand people and maintain an image of "nice"? That can cause people to think he isn't even human, much less very pleasant! If his history is one of being arrogant and making people feel he really doesn't care what's going on, the employees and public will never forget it. Doing what has to be done as humanely as possible is the standard for near-perfect CEOs—which is the best anyone can do.

The lasting measure of success is: When it is all done, can those people on the losing end of your decisions admit the CEO was honorable, honest, and caring? That's being nice.

If you aren't amiable in the elevator or to the shoeshine boy, people will notice. Act collegial— support others—and you will get more success. My friend Michael P. Scott, international communications manager at Pioneer Hi-Bred International, Inc., has an army buddy who is the son of the former president and COO of McDonnell-Douglas. The two were talking about business success one day and Mike's buddy said, "I asked my dad,

'What did it take to get to be a CEO?' He told me,
'Be nice to the secretaries.' Meaning if you're nice
to the heart and soul of an operation, the less visible people, you don't have to worry about the big-
gies!"

From your own experience you know if you are in
the trenches, working hard, and a senior person asks
about your family by name, it makes an impression.
That's being nice.

Practice (if necessary) being nice:

Important note: This is a very short list
of opportunities to show mutual respect for
others. As with all traits I've discussed, you
must be consistent. If you must sporadically
remember to "be nice," you really aren't.

- When someone goes out of their way to meet
  your schedule, go out of your way three times
  for them.
- Open doors for men, women, bosses, subordinates.
- Step out of a meeting and personally tell your
  next appointment you'll be a little late, invite
  them to wait in your office or the boardroom
  (someplace with more prestige than the
  lobby).

- Remind your secretary to be pleasant with *everybody*, not just the ones *she* thinks you like.
- Whenever you encounter an ignorant, discourteous jerk, say a silent prayer of thanks that you aren't the same way.
- If you are the most well-known person at the office Christmas party, wear your name tag anyway. It helps you look approachable and not stuck on yourself.
- Say your name when introducing yourself rather than assuming they know you. Remember their name by being amiable enough to care about their name and pleasant enough to purposefully use it so you will remember it. (Unlike the CEO who said to me, "I can never remember their names when I meet them because I'm so busy looking at their face to see if I like them.")

It may seem that the more power and prestige you hold, the less you need to be agreeable. Wrong. The higher you go up the more people watch to see what you're about and follow your lead.

One department head describes her boss, Tim Stack, president and CEO of Borgess Health Alliance: "From as high a level as he is, he's still extremely aware and caring about the personal side of his employees."

It's easy to be congenial when there is happiness and success around. But effective chiefs will tell you that that is not sufficient. You need to be congenial when those about you aren't.

Tomorrow, not the next day or the next, go out of

your way to be benevolent to someone you normally would not go out of your way for. Try it, just for practice. Who knows what could happen. (I'll bet you it will be good!)

Two cautions about being nice:

1. This is not the time you use theatrics. Being nice can*not* be an act.
2. Don't be nice, pleasant, or amiable toward poor ethics or illegal activities. The slightest "soft touch" in that situation will be taken advantage of and ultimately resented by all.

The Arrogant Side of Success

The not so nice side of the CEO is the potential that's there for arrogance. Here is a person who works hard to achieve, sacrifices much, and if lucky gets lots of rewards in the way of money, power, prestige, and notoriety. That person can easily become arrogant. There isn't a trait much worse than arrogance, because too often people think they become "above the law"—the "law" meaning proper ethical, moral, and legal behavior.

The widow of publishing tycoon Robert Maxwell describes her late husband in a biography as "a monstrous man with megalomania tendencies." People who knew him would probably agree that it was his dangerous fantasies of wealth, power, and omnipotence that led to his downfall.

If you should get to the top of some mountain, or

are there now, please do your family, your constituents, and yourself a favor. Don't become arrogant.

- *Don't* treat your employees like personal servants, ready to jump at your every beck and call. An occasional unusual need or request is acceptable, but then pay back to them in kind. Respect is not homage.

  When the CEO is in a bind, asking his secretary to pick up his laundry during her lunch break before he heads out of town isn't outrageous. Insisting she take dictation while he sits on the head in his office's private toilet is.

- *Don't* try to bully or pull rank to get special privileges. If there is a waiting list for the restaurant, put your name on it like everybody else, or leave and go elsewhere. Demanding that you don't wait is arrogant.

- *Don't* take unearned money from innocent customers and investors. At the very least you'll go to jail. At the worst you'll disillusion millions of hardworking Americans trying to make a living and provide for their families. You will also set an example that will encourage others to attempt to try to get away with something.

  Unfortunately, daily in the newspaper, you'll read of executives literally faking sales, distributing harmful products to customers, paying themselves huge bonuses while running a business into the ground, and committing myriad other unethical, immoral, and sometimes illegal activities.

- *Don't* think your work is more important than your family. Most every CEO who is retired and looks back at his business experience regrets he didn't manage his personal life better. (If they had to do it over again they may not do anything differently but they wished the personal life had been more successful. What people want and what they'll actually put the effort into are two different things.) If you ask the ones who have been divorced three and four times, they will tell you they would have preferred not being divorced even once. Family members aren't employees; they don't have to jump at the CEO's request.

    One CEO's wife told me, "I get so tired of people saying how great he is. He didn't get there by being Mr. Wonderful. He's a bastard at home."

- *Don't* make public spectacles attacking or embarrassing people in your company or on your board. Feuds split employees, friends, and the business community. If it isn't something you'd tolerate in subordinates, don't feel you have a right to do it.

    The chairman and CEO of one company had such a personality rift they had to communicate through an intermediary who ended up resigning out of frustration.

- *Don't* take liberties with the opposite sex. You're in a powerful position. People are too often impressed with power and compromise themselves out of fear of losing their job or in hopes of personal gain. Some arrogant CEOs have stooped to making obscene phone calls, lasciviously grabbing employees and getting away with it, openly flaunting extramarital affairs, and using demeaning language about the opposite sex in jest. But it isn't in jest; there is a nugget of truth in all humor, and how a CEO is "kidding around" might indicate what he is actually thinking.

One CEO was asked how he was going to justify a year of severance he'd given to a employee he was having an affair with (but who didn't earn the money). "I'm the president," he said. "I don't need to explain."

- *Don't* think you don't need to be held accountable for your words. If you tell someone you were not responsible for some action when you actually were, you are arrogant. Then if you deny knowledge and pass blame to others when you are caught, you don't deserve to stay at the top. (This is a favorite tactic of arrogant politicians.)

  One CEO denied trying to sell off assets in a questionable manner in front of all the shareholders at the annual meeting. Within minutes he was confronted with evidence contrary to his claim. All he could do was admit that he had just lied.

Arrogance gets you fired while you are in the ranks and prevents you from getting to the top.

Sometimes at the top people forget how they got there and abuse their power. Sometimes they lose respect for others, stop listening to peers, treat people with disdain, and discount others' ideas and performance. It can happen in interpersonal or business relationships but usually carries over to both areas.

Humanity in general, and humanity at the top, is inherently good. At the top you will find tremendous energy, creativity, gumption, and conscience. You will also find faults and shortcomings, but you don't have to contribute to that behavior.

19TH VITAL TRAIT:
INQUISITIVE

One of the single most effective traits that good chiefs utilize is curiosity. To be successful in almost anything you have to be the one to initiate asking, getting answers, and really hearing answers. If you ever stop inquiring, you will stop growing.

One of the chiefs I interviewed was the former president of the San Francisco United Way. He told me he dealt with all situations by asking rather than assuming or guessing.

"When I took on the United Way job I flew to San Francisco and took a taxi into the city. I asked the driver, 'Do you know anything about how the United Way is doing in the city?'

" 'They are in deep trouble,' he told me. The outgoing executive hadn't told me that. The taxi driver was dead right."

If you are confused about anything, ask about it *right then and there.* If you conclude you will get clarity without asking, you are wrong. If you are overworked instead of moaning and complaining, ask for a solution to the problem. If you are angry, instead of getting angrier from misunderstanding, *ask* to get a better grasp of things. You will seldom see the seething thoughts of others (because they are probably acting) so ask to check out their feelings so there is less miscommunication. Needless to say, almost anyone prefers clearheaded, straightforward questions instead of dealing with muddled guessing.

If you don't ask you can end up in some pretty strange situations. A few years back I met a young couple at a community dining table in a ski lodge. I can't remember how the conversation got onto this subject, but the man started telling this story. He'd introduced himself as Clark and he volunteered his avid interest in soaring (piloting a sailplane).

He was soaring in his sailplane off the central coast of California one Saturday, enjoying particularly good conditions. It was time for him to land if he was to get to his hangar on time, but the conditions were so perfect he decided to soar awhile and risk not getting back to his hangar. Finally it was dusk and he had to get down. So he searched the countryside for a place to land safely. He found a road that looked safe and smooth enough and appeared relatively untraveled. So he landed. People in the surrounding area saw a plane come down on their property and rushed to the road. They arrived as Clark was climbing out of the cockpit checking himself and his plane. And they experienced a mutual surprise. They found there was indeed a plane on their private road, and the pilot realized he had landed in a nudist colony when he saw all of them naked.

Clark explained why he was there and they explained where he was. He couldn't make arrangements to get out until the next day, so the nudists invited him to stay the night. In exchange for room and board he agreed to be a dinner speaker on the sport of soaring. While in his room thinking about his speech, the expression "while in Rome, do as the Romans do" came to mind, so with some hesitation but without any inquiry he took off his clothes.

As he walked into the dining hall he was greeted with loud applause. Out of awareness for his possible discomfort, the nudists had all gotten dressed!

Clark got caught with his pants down—literally and figuratively—*because he didn't ask questions.* And that is what happens to people when they don't ask questions!

Consider how it feels to be asked questions. David Vogel, who runs a highly successful consulting firm that works with large health-care organizations, benefited from being the recipient of curiosity. Vogel told me, "I had been in an Atlanta hotel for nearly six weeks of business and consulting meetings. My bill was over twelve thousand dollars. As I checked out, the general manager made an effort to personally come out to meet me and asked, 'How was your stay?'

" 'Are you really interested, or is that just a routine question?' I asked.

" 'Yes, I am interested,' he answered.

" 'Let's go into your office.' We had a half-hour conversation about their phone service, room service, and front desk organization. I provided constructive comments on what I've seen elsewhere and suggestions that might work there. The general manager listened intensely and took notes. When I finished he asked, 'How much was your hotel bill?'

" 'Twelve thousand dollars.'

" 'I think I've just gotten twelve thousand dollars' worth of advice. Your bill is paid.'

"That hotel manager knew to *ask questions*. We both benefited from it."

If the person asking is not taking it as a license to pry, or a chance to paint you into a corner or interrogate, then you should welcome the query. Sometimes top CEOs challenge your reasoning by their questions and what they really want is for you to defend your thought process. They have to know you believe in yourself for them to believe in you. Just because they may be some Mr. Big, they do not know all the answers (even though they *act* like they do).

The key to being inquisitive is attitude and technique.

- You must want to learn new information or get old information clarified.

- You must find out the information in a manner that does not destroy the self-esteem of the person you are asking.

Say a chief wanted to know the status of a brochure his public relations department was producing. The chief could ask, "Did you do the brochure?" It's simple, straightforward, but implies, "Were you guys responsible enough to get that brochure completed? I seem to need to check up on you." His tone likely challenged them and suggested they might have forgotten. Now a top chief is more likely to ask, "Are you doing the brochure in color or black and white?" This question assumes they've done the brochure and reinforces the feeling they are on top of the job.

The more flamboyant and confident chief could even go to the extreme and ask, "Hey, dummy, did you remember to do the brochure?" Although risky, if done well, the extreme question generates humor and also implies "I *know* you did the job, I'm just curious how it turned out and I know I can kid with you as well."

You cannot selectively query only the co-workers you are comfortable with or feel you have some power over. You have to query any and all people, up and down the mountain. Too often people fear asking questions up the hillside because they don't want to look stupid or like they are seeking approval or asking permission. That is the wrong attitude. Near-perfect chiefs welcome your questions if they are well thought out and applicable. The very person who likely has the answer you need is probably one, two, or three ledges up. If you don't have the courage to ask the source, why bother asking anyone?

When Sam Sanderson, president and COO of the Canadian company Rogers Network Services, asks upward, he says, "I lay out my plan, tell them what I think we are facing, state our objective, list three or so options, explain the strategy, and ask if they have any questions."

Your well-thought-out questions should accomplish the following:

- Lay the groundwork for your thinking, e.g., "This is what we have come up with so far. . . ." "I wanted to ask you about . . ."
- Establish trust in your thinking, e.g., "Based on the information you provided and the objective we've agreed upon, this is the direction we are going. Is that in agreement with your thinking?"
- Shape the conversation: e.g., "The issues we need to discuss today are . . ."
- Open a door other employees can walk through, e.g., "If I've missed any issues you want to address, please tell me now." Or, "If I'm off target based on new information you have, now is the time we should discuss it. Anything come to mind?"
- Follow through as necessary, e.g., "So that is where we are currently. I'd like to have a few

moments to update you next week at this time. Can we set that up?"

Put yourself to the test. For a twenty-four-hour period try to communicate, direct, and manage *with questions only.* Don't make comments or demands in the normal statement form. Instead make them with questions tied to them. The purpose is to get you into a practice of asking more and to test the response and commitment you receive from others.

The opposite of asking questions is being a know-it-all. Even if you do know it all, you serve yourself better by asking questions. You learn something new. You bond with people better because you're making them a part of the conversation. You buy yourself time. And you set yourself apart from others.

In life, you need to know yourself, but you also need to know others. That only happens if you ask and ask and ask.

Two cautions.

First, think out your questions. Consider other peoples' feelings. People will think differently than you. The most innocent question on your part could be taken wrong by an insecure person. You must not make the question a setup or threatening. A poorly posed query can be menacing. If people aren't comfortable with your questioning approach, you won't get true and useful answers.

Second, don't ask questions to get the spotlight so you artificially stand out yourself, or detract from others. I watched an author discuss her book at Tattered Cover bookstore in Denver. The store frequently invites authors to read for the public and answer questions. One audience member who sat in the front row on the aisle interrupted the author eight minutes into her presentation with a question. Six minutes later there was another question. Within the next ten minutes, three more questions. These questions served no purpose but to bring attention to the person asking them.

20TH VITAL TRAIT:
COMPETITIVE

Life is, by its nature, a competitive environment, and certainly business life is a constant contest. You have to have a certain amount of competitive nature to thrive in it. The amount required will vary from industry to industry, but whatever business you are in, you have to have as much or more than others in that group.

Nabisco, Procter & Gamble, and Frito-Lay are engaged in a raging "snack food war." Chrysler uses fiberglass panels to camouflage the front, the rear, and the windshield of new model cars before they are taken onto their Auburn Hills, Michigan, test track, so the competition can't photograph them. The dogfights in the computer business are being repeated in the information superhighway business.

Even mild-mannered accountants aren't mild-mannered anymore. Hugh Sullivan, an accountant and company president, says, "I'm balls to the wall competitive and hard charging. I promote people because they are doers. . . . I just put it on kill and let it go. You get an opportunity to beat your opponent in the game and you do it. I don't know what keeps people going otherwise."

CEOs compete against other CEOs and wanna-be CEOs for jobs, promotions, assignments, sales, recognition, etc. Customers compete for suppliers, service, attention, and prices. It is the competition of life, and the stellar mountaineers don't just enjoy the game, they relish it (to some degree).

Competition is a good thing for personal and professional growth. The "positive hardship" that comes from struggling with a foe strengthens and sharpens your skills. Don't pray for an easy win in situations you are involved in. You don't learn much from success, *especially easy success;* you learn from the battle. If you look back on your successes in life, you probably savored the victory more when you had huge obstacles to overcome in achieving them. Victory is fleeting, but being effectively competitive gives you long-lasting business joy. The good thing about having a great antagonist (or problem) is that you will enjoy overcoming it more. Remember a competitor helps you get to the top, whereas easy winning makes you soft. You gain a healthy fighting spirit from continuous effort against contenders.

Jerry McMorris, owner of the Colorado Rockies baseball team, puts it like this: "If I lose I'm disappointed, but I reflect on what I did wrong and think what I can do to prevent a repeat."

Keep in mind the following when developing your competitive skills:

- Carefully choose among the potential battles that come your way. Not all are worth fighting.
- Seek out "test" battles if not enough come your way. You'll lose your competitive abilities if they aren't constantly tested. (This does not mean picking a fight to beat up on a weaker foe. It means constantly growing through self-challenge.)
- Maintain your sense of humor throughout winning and losing battles.
- Remember the competitive version of the golden rule: *They will do to you what you'd do to them, if you had thought of it first.*

Naturally there is competition among peers—sometimes very nasty competition. You likely have the same goals they have. Overly zealous, destructive combat where you're at each other's throats and prepared to kill is not what I'm promoting. You have to remember you may be in charge of your opponents someday, or worse—they may be in charge of you!

A female CEO who runs a consumer products company admitted to me, "I tolerate no fools. I'm intense, anxious, and impatient. I wouldn't work for me. I'm tough on people above or below me who do stupid things and disappoint me."

Although I praise the value of competition in life, I realize there can be a harmful side of it also. You will only be able to handle destructive combat if you practice on constructive contests. Don't shy away from a fight. It doesn't have to be a big deal with millions on the line; it can be something as simple as talking in a straightforward manner when others beat around the bush.

21ST VITAL TRAIT: FLEXIBLE

Near-perfect CEOs are flexible people. Flexible does not mean wishy-washy or undisciplined. Flexible means they aren't stubborn, ceremonious, rigid, unyielding, or unbending because they are the big bosses and can get away with it. People who can and will modify their response to new circumstances are better suited to deal with anything new.

> It's a global market where you have a constant group of new competitors and new products that obsolete old products. . . . You have to be fleet of feet. Quick. You can't be rigid. Necessity is the mother of invention and you must view things as dy-

namic and fast-moving. If you aren't flexi-
ble you are destined for failure.
               —FRED FLORJANCIC
                  President, Brunswick Bowling
                  and Billiards

To stay on course, you frequently have to go off course. You have to be willing to do things differently than what's been done before, or that others do. Warren Buffett, the chairman of Berkshire Hathaway and one of the five wealthiest men in the country, certainly is that way. Just one example. For years Buffett spoke against corporate jets, stating they were a waste of money. Yet a few years ago he bought a used jet for $6.7 million (according to *Fortune*), naming it *Indefensible*. He explained his purchase in the annual report with a note: "Whether Berkshire will get its money's worth from the plane is an open question, but I will work at achieving some business triumph that I can (no matter how dubiously) attribute to it." Even Buffett's friend Bill Gates, chairman of Microsoft, speaks out about the decadence of the corporate jet, then goes and repeatedly charters them. Mountaineers know you have to change your route, take a different path, or even abandon the climb if it's the wrong course.

We're all many things at different times. A key element of success is being flexible and adaptable as needed.
               —GREGG MILLER
                  President, RACOM

Near-perfect flexibility means being able to turn easily from one situation or subject to another. One CEO I interviewed rides a tractor Saturday and Sunday, checking fences, feeding cattle, and perhaps acting as midwife for the birth of a new calf. Monday he's lead man at a Senate hearing, arguing for government support of the national medical foundation he founded. He is flexible.

Flexibility is the ability to rub shoulders with workers on the shop floor as well as fellow community leaders at a social gathering.

A simple reason for bending and yielding as necessary is that you can white-out old decisions and attitudes. Duane Larson, president of Children's World Learning Centers, will continue to receive the participation he requires from his subordinates because they know he's adaptable to changing situations. "My managers asked me for a certain program completion date. I said no. One of them came up and in a coalition way gave the reasons why I should say yes. I agreed. He made a point to say to me later, 'It's nice to work for someone who will change their mind.' "

When I write about being flexible most of you will say, "Of course I am." Good. Nonetheless, think back to the last few confrontations that you have had and think through the scenario, had you been more bendable early on:

- Could you have reached a resolution sooner?
- Didn't you get a solution only after you did bend your position?
- Did it weaken your power? No.

- Did it demonstrate your willingness to change your mind as new information was provided? Yes.
- Did it show support of people? Yes.

When you are flexible you are able to admit mistakes, which can make you even more effective. Flexibility is strength.

22ND VITAL TRAIT:
GOOD STORYTELLERS

In my conversations with CEOs I'd often ask to what they attributed their success. Nearly 90 percent of them answered "luck" or "being in the right place at the right time" or "luck and timing."

CEO Bill Reagan answered, "Well, Debra, success is like leaning on a gate. Some people have all the traits and attitudes to succeed but they just picked the wrong gate to lean against. If you know for sure the gate will open in exactly three hours, you'll likely lean three hours. But what if it doesn't open? You decide to leave. At three hours and two minutes it swings open. You didn't know if the gate would ever open. Success is a combination of picking the right gate and judging how long to stick with it. I was lucky enough to pick the right gate. Some lean their whole lifetime and it never opens though."

He answered the question with the same basic answer as the others, but by telling a story he

- set himself apart from the rest,
- got me involved with his thought process,
- painted a picture,
- humanized his point,
- made himself more colorful.

Life is full of anecdotes. Near-perfect CEOs use them to describe, dramatize, and paint pictures to relentlessly communicate. Our lives are wrapped up in stories—novels we read, movies we watch, gossip we hear, jokes we laugh at, are all *stories*. With storytelling, the scenic route gets you there just like the direct one, but you and the audience enjoy it a lot more.

The purpose of telling stories is not to be evasive but to make information memorable, recallable, clear, useful, and appropriate. An example that recalls human experiences enables a larger group of people to understand what you are talking about.

As you listen to people talk, experience business, and read, you will learn the who, what, when, where, and why of situations—and in those details lies a story.

You can generate a story pool of your own. Reflect back on your daily life experiences. Think about events. Develop a story around them. Write the story down in an organized fashion: describe the situation, describe what you did about it, and show the results of your actions. Use the stories to illustrate your points in business conversations.

Several CEOs I interviewed had card files, three-ring binders, or computer databases of anecdotes categorized by different subject for easy reference. One man indicated where and when a specific story was last used.

Anecdotes are more interesting than just the plain facts while still being vehicles for the information. Stories should be

- true,
- appropriate,
- well-told,
- concise,
- new.

Near-perfect chiefs who are storytellers aren't story weavers, evasive, and without substance. Storytelling is not used to avoid issues, fill in, cloud over, or excuse the point. That happens if they are sloppily organized, inappropriate, or overused.

The key for successful storytelling is to fit stories into the conversation, have a good memory to recollect them for the proper occasion, and recall who has already heard them.

If in your zeal to use anecdotes you start rambling, losing your point, or digging a hole for yourself, *just stop*. Admit you are getting off the point, then get back on it quickly and concisely.

If you aren't sure if you've made a clear point, ask

if the example made your point clear. *Don't assume understanding.*

Like any good trait, taken to the far extreme it becomes ineffective. We've all been around people who have narrated to a nauseating level. Overuse of storytelling is as bad as underuse. So follow two cautions:

1. Avoid frequent repetition of stories.
2. Don't exhaust your story pool. In other words, constantly work to replenish your supply of fresh stories.

Think back to some of the stories in this book. You'll likely remember the consultant who got his twelve-thousand-dollar hotel bill paid by the hotel manager, or the lawyer who asked himself, "How would Jesus handle this problem?" or the sailplane pilot at the nudist colony, or the Japanese businessman explaining why Japan lost the war. Those were stories to illustrate points, involve you, humanize issues, and entertain. Diligently work on weaving your own anecdotes into your written and verbal communications.

When you look back at the last three chapters, you could say, "Benton sure paints an unreachable picture of a near-perfect." Keep in mind that every element of how chiefs think, act, and interrelate was taught to me *by* a near-perfect CEO. Not *all* top people are all of these things all of the time—but they strive to be.

If you don't have an ideal model to aim for, you

won't go far yourself. The difference between a good
and great CEO (or anything) is doing the basics well.

BRIDGING GAPS SUMMARY

Be willing to lead: Be worth listening to, worth
  believing, worth following.

Be sure to fight for your people: Be loyal downward: spread credit downward.

Be certain to admit mistakes: If you are error
  free you're likely effort free.

Be unapologetic: Apologies are often vain attempts people use to vindicate themselves for
  something they don't plan to change anyway.

Be straightforward: Everything you say or write
  can be done in a plain, simple manner. Just do
  it.

Be nice: The more power and prestige you hold
  the less it may seem you need to be nice.
  Wrong.

Be inquisitive: Ask, ask, ask, and then ask more.

Be competitive: Don't pray for an easy win in
  situations you are involved in. You don't learn
  much from success, especially easy success.
  You learn from the struggle.

Be flexible: Be able to stand out from the crowd
  while still fitting in with the crowd.

Be a good storyteller: People understand you
  better, remember what you say longer, find

you smarter and more interesting if you use
anecdotes to make your points.

*Be good at your job so you can effectively lead
others to be good at their jobs.*

CHAPTER 6

The Mountaineer

Every climber is different, and it's important for you to understand those differences

Mountaineers are the men and women who, by whatever route, make it to the top of some mountain. They come from the ranks of hikers and climbers in the organization. Although the top climbers have the 22 Vital Traits, that doesn't mean they are all alike.

I've met CEOs who are old, young, wealthy, poor, good, not so good, experienced, inexperienced, short, tall, balding, toupee'd, gay, straight, black, Hispanic, Asian, female, male, dumb, smart, and any other category you care to list.

I've seen office decor range from a wall of bowling trophies to a roomful of Kittinger furniture with a view of mountain lakes to a view of a city skyscape. Their office manner ranges from cowboy boots on the desk to silk handkerchief in the pocket with three corners showing. Where one CEO has photos of himself with Presidents Bush and Reagan, the next one has a reply note on the corner of his desk ready to be mailed to President Clinton: "Thanks for the invitation, but I can't come. I have too much to do right now. Invite me again."

CEOs' activities on and off the job take wide swings. A rendering plant president whose back building was piled twelve feet high with euthanized kittens and puppies from the humane society goes to weekly sensitivity training seminars. Another CEO who runs his family's billion-dollar philanthropic foundation spends weekends helping the vet artificially inseminate the cows on his ranch. A manufacturing CEO who spends twelve hours on Saturday personally repotting sixteen indoor plants collects a $2 million check for some personal investments on Monday. One of the wealthiest CEOs I wrote about doesn't like to spend money on himself, so when he needs clothes his wife has to *sneak* new ones into his closet without his finding out.

Some of the CEOs I spoke with created their company and went on to corporate fame and fortune, and some on to bankruptcy. Many started all over a second and third and fourth time. Some gave up and turned to alcoholism. The last time I heard about one of them I'd met he was delivering pizzas for a living.

Some of the CEOs went to the right schools and joined the right corporations in the right jobs and had the right mentors. Some became famous. Some got fired. Some became entrepreneurs. Some went to bigger corporations. Some became consultants.

CEOs vary in so many different ways, but they will always be one of two types:

1. An entrepreneur—the soloist climber.
2. A hired professional manager—the big-wall climber.

It is extremely important for you to comprehend the different types of CEOs. Misunderstanding or not caring are two of the best ways to lose your job. But if you know the patterns:

- You can identify how to work more effectively with your CEO.
- You can decide what style you *prefer* working with to aid you in job hunting and selecting a company.
- You can better determine your own natural inclination, as well as choose the type you want to develop into.

From my formal and informal conversations with CEOs I've seen distinct patterns that separate the entrepreneurial personality from the professional. The differences are not always along a clear-cut line of demarcation, but CEOs definitely tend toward one direction or another. Both types have their own nature, their own character, their own set of strengths and corresponding weaknesses. One type is not better than the other, just necessary for different kinds of companies, their stages of growth, and their future potential, although the more substantial the enterprise the less likely the top person is entrepreneurial. The trend into the late 1990s will be a CEO who can successfully and effectively wear both hats.

Anthony O'Reilly currently does that. He is the CEO of a large public corporation in the United States, H. J. Heinz, and also an independent entrepreneur in Ireland. His Irish job description includes being chairman of an oil company and holding the controlling share of the largest newspaper publishing business in his native country. He uses the best entrepreneurial traits at Heinz and the best professional management traits in his entrepreneurial ventures (and vice versa).

Executing the entrepreneurial CEO's role is as demanding as the professional CEO's role, but in slightly different ways. For your personal growth and development, you need to be aware of the tendencies and limitations of both so you can acquire abilities in both arenas. The CEO of the future, to be competitive, has to be flexible in going from one mode of operation to another.

ENTREPRENEURIAL TYPES (SOMETIMES CALLED HIRED GUNS) AS COMPARED TO PROFESSIONAL MANAGERS

The entrepreneur is an innovator. Almost like an imaginative garage tinkerer, he invents a product (as Bill Gates of Microsoft did), has a great idea, or takes on a cast-off business that others didn't see as worthwhile. The entrepreneur might have even learned the business from someone else and now wants to do it for himself.

The professional manager, on the other hand, is a perfecter. He takes what others have started, breaks former limitations, and is supposed to raise the thing to new heights. (Lou Gertsner was brought in to IBM to do that.) He is an overseer of others' creative processes.

> *Starting your own company versus being hired to run someone's company is like giving birth to a baby versus adopting one. You end up caring equally for it and giving both the same love and attention, but for one of them you were there at the conception and that's always special.*
> —MARK KIMMEL
> President, Paradigm Partners

The entrepreneur's personal money is often on the line. Or he secured additional financing from friends, family, banks, or venture capitalists. His subsequent compensation depends on his company's profitability and his ownership. (Down the road, if successful, he may be irked by the fact that he has to pay competitive salaries to a professional manager, someone who didn't put the same blood and sweat into the company.)

The private banking company J. P. Morgan runs

advertisements appealing to the entrepreneur, with a photo of a pair of boxing gloves alongside the advertising copy: "If you're like most entrepreneurs, it hasn't been easy making it. All the more reason not to lose it."

I was meeting three New York City entrepreneurs for lunch at a very expensive "white tablecloth" Italian restaurant. In response to something said, one of them jotted an idea down on a napkin—not a paper cocktail napkin but a *cloth* dinner napkin. When he saw his friend watching, he snapped, "It's okay [to write on the cloth] based on the price I'm paying for this meal!" Because company money is, in effect, coming out of his own pocket, he expects to get more from it.

On the other hand the professional manager is more frequently well financed (from the bond or stock market or some private ownership). Although his personal money isn't on the line, his personal skin is. Normally the CEO's compensation includes stock, options, or equity, which provide some "ownership."

For example, the top executives of Campbell's Soup Company have up to 75 percent of their total compensation tied directly to performance. Only if the company meets specific goals in terms of sales, earnings, cash returns on assets, and performance related to other food companies do the executives receive any bonus. And to ensure they feel like owners of the company they have to own stock valued at three times their base salary. They risk their own money (or gain) just like other shareholders.

Anthony O'Reilly, who spends the company's money as well as his own, says he is much more risk-aversive with Heinz money than his own. He feels a fiduciary responsibility as a trustee of Heinz's assets and much more willing to take real investment risks with his own.

The entrepreneur CEO doesn't like to, can't, or won't labor and sweat for someone else. Often he got where he is with an independent, "to hell with everyone" attitude. Or an "I'll show you" and "I'm not going to take it anymore" set of personal convictions. Maybe he was fired from a professional manager situation. But there is a good chance he had a major career displacement when he deliberately (or unintentionally) royally messed up. Sometimes he's called a maverick.

The founder of Gold Bond trading stamps, Curt Carlson, explains, "The minute I was out on my own, I knew I'd found my own element."

A different entrepreneur explained it this way to me: "I would never make it in a large company. I'm too irreverent. I tend not to play the corporate game by the rules. It's incredibly painful to work in corporate America—it's a career boot camp. I learned more from working with the biggest asses. I learned what I didn't want to be like! They interact and totally demotivate people. They advance from point A to B by walking on the heads of people."

His professional manager counterpart is much more likely to be able to deal with corporate politics

and the BS. This type of CEO has to work well as the "people-skilled" organization man, i.e., one who deals with politics and relationships among constituents (employees, government, corporate executives, media, boards, and customers).

As a generality, with fewer people in his required circle to please the maverick has developed fewer people skills. He has just enough to gain an acceptable presence. (Now this isn't always true. Some entrepreneurs have very effective people skills but have simply tired of dealing with the office politics and BS.) Whereas the hired gun, with his need to deal with hordes of employees and constituents, develops people skills foremost to deal with small, medium, and large diverse groups.

Having people skills is different from being people oriented. Small companies (say under $50 million) have to be people oriented. You have to worry: Joan matters to you; Sam matters to you. All processes are people oriented. One at a time. One on one. Big company CEOs have to worry about the process. You can't possibly be interested in Joan. There are thousands of Joans. You have to develop people skills but not on an individual basis.

The entrepreneur has more latitude to play by his own rules. He is frequently stereotyped as someone who is a nonconformist, a lone ranger who circumvents the system. Usually he has more freedom to go out and try new things. And possibly fail. *But the professional manager needs to play by corporate rules.* He is frequently stereotyped as a traditionalist. Tried and true. Stable. Experienced. Main-stream. Usually he has less freedom to mess up at any level.

Roudy Roudebush owns a trail riding operation outside of Telluride, Colorado. Like all chiefs he should be a "salesman" for his organization as well as the boss. Wearing his well-used spurs, chaps, jeans, bandanna, vest, and cowboy hat, he rides his horse into various bars in town—right through the front door, high in the saddle, to the bar, and orders a beer. "The Telluride tourists go wild with excitement, and they follow me right out the door to my barn to sign up for a trail ride," he says. Entrepreneurs can get away with that. You probably wouldn't see the chief at GM drive a new model car through the bar doors of Telluride or Detroit.

The entrepreneur gets to (and often has to) rely on himself and his own judgment. He answers to himself first and foremost, at least in the early stages of his company. (It's sort of like the Frank and Ernest cartoon characters who are walking out of the boss's office saying, "If I'm going to work for an idiot, I may as well go into business for myself!") He goes into the job with no In basket. He organizes and manages the endeavor, assumes all risks, and hopes for a big return.

Strong-willed people found companies or manage companies and they'll do well . . .

*as long as they don't fly the company into
the side of the mountain.*
—PAUL HOUSTON
President, Results, Incorporated

**The professional manager answers to lots more
legal constituents. So he relies on planning committees and teams more.** He must be aware of more
business goings-on than he could possible know
about personally, and he must be able to always defend decisions.

The professional manager has an In basket full and
waiting for him upon his arrival. He usually ends up
redoing or revamping work set in place by predeces-
sors. New management theories get tested in this organization because they have the time, resources, and
people to implement the latest trend.

*Entrepreneurs are more interested in what
are you doing to* grow *the business; professional managers are interested in what are
you doing to* run *the business.*
—SAM SANDERSON
President and COO,
Rogers Network Services

The entrepreneur thinks and acts fast. He frequently needs constant action and activity to keep
his venture afloat. And he can't understand why
everyone isn't as dedicated as he is. He's almost always the first one in the morning, last one out at
night. As one said to me, "I wish weekends were five

hours long. I could do that." A different CEO entrepreneur who went back to being a hired gun CEO
explained, "I gave up sleep for six years. It was hard
on me and my family." The entrepreneur usually has
a small staff and therefore wears many hats. He relies on himself. An entrepreneur gets his hands dirty.
He's more "in the trenches," although less so as his
company grows.

The professional manager has to be an executor
of well-thought-out plans. He's purposeful. Deliberate. And most important he knows to work within
hierarchies despite the excess time it consumes. The
hired gun generally has a large staff available to
him, but a large staff often requires a large staff to
support itself, thus building a lumbering machine
minimizing potential for individual entrepreneurial-
ship.

I asked a man why he left his executive position at
a big public corporation to start his own. He said,
"Don't quote me because of my contract with my
former employer, but I left because of the bullshit,
authoritative, chain of command of trying to get
things done. There wasn't enough money in it *and* it
didn't suit me because I didn't own it. Other than
that, it was a fine life."

The entrepreneur calculates risk against what he
wants to do. Results are very important. The professional manager has to be terribly careful about
what he says and does; careful how he positions
himself.

The professional frequently calculates risk against
his employment contract. Power is very important.

Big professionally managed companies often aren't as focused on results as rhetoric suggests. They are more focused on power.

You will seldom see a soloist hired to run a big public corporation, whereas professional managers are frequently recruited to manage an entrepreneurial organization. Many times you will hear of a company whose management requirements outgrew the founder/entrepreneur's capability.

One company and the founding entrepreneur I studied started with twenty-five people in the beginning and now they are so big their offices have more bathrooms than that. When the entrepreneur needed to develop into a professional manager, his financial backers pressed him to hire a pro. (This is often the point where many entrepreneurial companies get sold and go public.)

Campbell's Soup Company was managed by professional outside executives for decades. When the son of the founder (Jack Dorrance Jr.) died, it looked like Campbell's would be bought by a food conglomerate. Instead the family reasserted its business presence with the new vice chairman, Bennett Dorrance, being the first of the entrepreneur's kin to work at the helm since 1984.

> *Entrepreneurs are not made, they are born. You can't take Entrepreneur 101. They are a sum total of their life experiences from childhood on. . . . Entrepreneurs have a fire in the belly. A company started by an entrepreneur (through acquisition of other*

companies or through a new idea) often
turns to a professional manager once the
ship has been built. The entrepreneur needs
someone to maintain the ship and keep it
dry.

—LEONARD ABRAMSON
CEO and President,
U.S. Healthcare

It's a long haul to the top of most public or private organizations. The advantage of starting your
own company is that you get to the top right away!
(And as the expression sometimes goes: "Entrepreneurs are self-made men who worship their cre-
ator.") Being able to stay at the top of the heap is
the test for the entrepreneur as well as the professional manager.

By looking at the differences between entrepreneurs and hired guns you can see each has advan-
tages and disadvantages in their type. The strengths
of each are required at various stages of a company's
growth.

Whether an individual is an entrepreneur or professional manager, the CEO has to be secure in himself, competitive, straightforward, unapologetic, a
tad theatrical, and aware of his style. (Either way, entrepreneur or professional manager, he might be au-
tocratic. Neither group holds a title on that trait!)
Mistakes can ruin either type. And, of course, they
don't all succeed, regardless of their soloist or big-
wall climbing tendencies.

What Type of CEO Do You Work for?

If your CEO is the founder or owner, an independent, plays-by-his-own-rules, fast-acting, get-in-the-trenches type—you have an entrepreneur.

If your CEO was hired to do a specific job, oversees and manages various experts, operates with other people's money, deals with corporate politics and plays by corporate rules, executes well-thought-out plans through a sizable staff—you have a professional manager.

If your CEO wants innovation and creativity, has money to invest in new projects, encourages individual thinking, prizes people skills, expects people to follow the rules, acts purposefully but with energy, professes a willingness to get his hands dirty (but doesn't really)—*you have a professional manager who wants to utilize entrepreneurial traits.*

Entrepreneurial organizations generally strive to be bigger. And bigger organizations need to be more entrepreneurial.

Knowing the CEO type you are working with and may work with in the future enables you to see what he values, what his bosses expect of him, and what he looks for in those he hires and promotes. It's your choice to decide if that's the type you want to work for, but it's *your responsibility* to find out and understand the type.

Second-, Third-, Fourth-Generation Family Businesses (sometimes referred to as S.O.B.s—Sons of Bosses—though they can be daughters also)

There is a critical distinction between a second-, third-, and fourth-generation family business that is a public versus a private business, that is professionally managed or run by the family members. The public corporation with its legal requirements is closer to any other public corporation in makeup, the differences coming from whether "junior" is CEO or some hired gun. The culture and personality will vary vastly depending on who is at the top. A privately held second-, third-, or fourth-generation business is a totally different breed of business, particularly if it is run by junior or junior's junior.

Motorola is a publicly held third-generation operation where the son of the founder is passing his role on to his son. Campbell's Soup is privately held but professionally managed by an outsider with a third-generation family member overseeing as a vice chairman. Sauder Woodworking is a privately owned and family-managed $435 million furniture manufacturer, a mom-and-pop operation that grew big despite exclusively family leadership and being private.

I'm not being sarcastic when I say that. The reality is that despite the huge number of privately held family businesses in this country, few work successfully together to build a long-lasting, well-run, and well-managed organization. (Think about your own family! Honestly, how smoothly could you get along with and make important decisions regarding money with your parents, siblings, cousins, great-uncles, aunts, and so forth—on a daily basis? For a lot of people surviving even the smallest battle of who carves the turkey at Thanksgiving and in what order gifts are unwrapped at Christmas is a stress-filled, family-political problem, and an explosive situation!)

Sometimes business ventures end up successful but they tear families apart. One family in the South started out as manufacturers of ergonomically designed office chairs. The father developed the chair concept and enlisted his wife and two of their kids to help build a business. They did not succeed: manufacturing costs swelled, large potential customers were uninterested, and poor quality control caused the SBA to put them up for auction. An outsider bought the assets but problems were not contained and he told the family he wanted his money back. The family members allegedly removed sales literature, customer lists, prototypes, etc., from the offices in retaliation. One son decided that was wrong and went to the outside owner to fess up. The owner, in turn, made an offer to the son to run the business for a 25 percent equity. It grew to a $5 million company. Meanwhile the father, mother, sister, and sister's husband started a competing company that has subsequently grown to $7 million in sales. Today, although both are ongoing operations, each side bad-mouths the other. As the daughter is quoted as saying, "There is no chance for any merger." (How would you like to go to their family Christmas gathering?!)

Family businesses almost always start out entrepreneurial. With time and success many grow into huge corporate entities that often end up losing their entrepreneurial spirit. Sometimes the loss is aided by mergers and acquisitions with nonfamily business. But if there is a founding family member at the top, you still have a "family" business regardless of whether it is public or private.

An amazing story is that of the Homer Laughlin China Company, manufacturers of Fiesta dinnerware (you know the dishes that are making a big comeback in popularity with yellow pitchers; orange teapots; green, pink, and yellow plates). The current CEO and president respectively, Marcus Aaron II and Joseph Wells III, are running the company that three generations before was acquired by grandparents, Louis Aaron and his partner, William Wells. Not only did the families' successive generations successfully manage the business, but the original partners' families did as well.

Although almost every company had to be started by someone who was a family member, how it grew, who was involved, the money backing it, the type of business, the economy, and a whole list of other factors contribute to whether it is or isn't controlled by an S.O.B. (that is a Son of a Boss, so to speak). There are two things you can count on in any family-associated business when you are looking at the company to join or choose to move up in: How top management *gets* the job in that organization and how they *keep* the job.

One man who later became a CEO told me the

story of working in a family-owned business early on in his career. "I tried to work with the boss's son, but he wouldn't work. I told his dad. His dad sighed and said, 'I know, but he's my son. I have to give him work.' " And that's the way it goes sometimes.

Reality is that in an organization with strong family ties, the offspring are almost guaranteed to get the top jobs whether the company is privately or publicly held and whether they are qualified or not. The baton usually passes with a relatively smooth transfer of power from parent to child. The death of the parent frequently causes the timetable shift to the next generation to be sped up. Sometimes a power struggle among siblings squeezes out weak family members who don't have what it takes to run the business at that point in time.

"I guess you could say I was the strongest pup in the litter," explains a CEO who got appointed over two other brothers. (This same CEO subsequently placed his two brothers in executive positions in the company, later firing both of them.)

Blood is thicker than water. In general, it takes a lot of travesty for a family member to get fired. If you have a problem with the boss and he's a member of the family, you have a problem with the family. Loyalty usually goes with the family member; too often who is right and who is wrong is a secondary issue compared to who is family. Not that family members don't squabble. They do; as much as they love each other, they can hate each other. Husbands fire spouses. Sons push out fathers. Fathers choose one son or daughter over another. Siblings cheat each other. And on and on. But family is still *family* over outsiders!

It might sound wonderful to be born into the family business but it isn't always. An S.O.B. more than occasionally questions what he would have done if it wasn't for the family business. What could he have accomplished? Is he any good?

CEOs who inherit the business often feel they either have to prove something to everyone or they feel they don't have to prove anything to anyone—because they *own* the company! How the S.O.B. handles these feelings will vary. For most they accept their circumstances, try to bring professional management along with "new blood" and original ideas to the organization. For some there is a need to respond to the call of the wild before settling down with the family business.

> *My father and two uncles were in business together. I was the heir for the three. There was no choice, it was a done deal. I stepped into the family business and did well for two years. But I still wanted my own thing. I left to mine bat guano. It was great fun. I did well. I made enough to buy my wife a diamond. Then I went back to the family business and made a forty-year career. Now it's my son's turn. I hope he doesn't go mining for bat guano.*
> —MILAN "BABE" KNEZOVICH
> President, K & Z Distributing

If you work for a family business or a CEO who has family members in management in the company, there's a good possibility you'll never be number one in that company. There is also the reality that if you and someone in the lineage mess up equally, the "relative" will be less likely to get fired. But don't blame your problems on the fact (or feeling) family members are given special treatments or rights. Decide if this is the right situation for you because of the "family feel." That may be important to you. There is a lot to be learned working in a family enterprise as in any enterprise, but if your goal is a door with your name and the title CEO on it, learn what you can, then be ready to move on when the time is right.

As discussed earlier, a growing family business often needs a professional manager versus an offspring at the lead. At the company's conception, the founder gets the idea off the ground. It starts to blossom and get attention from the public and financial community. To grow more it frequently needs additional financing. Sometimes the personality and skill of the founder get that done but more often professionals get hired for specific jobs. Sometimes the family business needs venture capital money. Sometimes it goes public. With venture capitalist money or shareholder money, pressure is often put onto the founder to bring in a hired gun. And usually he does. That professional manager hopefully takes the developing family business to various levels of growth (while the founder's children are in some job inside the company or off at college). At some point an offspring of the founder himself often initiates moves to get the hired gun pushed aside and move in himself. That's the start of an S.O.B. And so it goes.

> *The best part of having my son in my company is that he brings new technologies. He knows a lot of stuff I never heard of or paid attention to. Things were a lot simpler when I started working. I bought things and I sold things. Another plus is he's extra security. Despite the fact I have good people, I've never left the place in others' hands. But I didn't force him to join the firm. My wife and I educated him and he chose the business. No, I can't think of anything bad about him in the company.*
> —MILAN "BABE" KNEZOVICH
> President, K & Z Distributing

Ideally the second generation has a blend of entrepreneurial drive and ability inherited from their parent; objective, professional, formal business training from some qualified source; along with common sense. The big advantage over competitors, beside blood line, is the gut instinct that comes with having grown up around the company.

As the owner of the largest block of stock in the Chronicle Publishing family business, Nan McEvoy says, "I grew up understanding that the company employed the family." Which is why family members continue to run the company.

FEMALE CEOs

When I was a young girl modeling, they taught us to pivot gracefully on the runway. I still do that today.

—LINDA CHAMBER
President and CEO,
Corporate Direct Air

Female CEOs make continuous decisions, give the nod or the ax to employees, evaluate businesses to buy, sell their company at road shows, talk up new ventures at corporate events, try to manage office politics—yes, I am describing the *same* day a male CEO would have.

CEOs know they can't do everything. But for the female CEO, in addition to the office requirements she is likely her family's cook, maid, nurse, tutor, and chauffeur. The female CEO may be able to afford nannies, housekeepers, cooks, and drivers, but many mothers (CEO or not) find it difficult to delegate such personal and critical tasks. They remember Jacqueline Kennedy Onassis's words: "If you bungle raising children, nothing else that you do matters much." The female chief knows it is an unrealistic expectation to try to do everything at home. But while the women's liberation movement helped women get to the top, it did little to alleviate their duties as mothers and wives. So the woman struggles to balance managing a profitable organization and making money with meeting everyone in her family's needs, often neglecting her own. The assertive-at-the-office often fail to take time to exercise, reduce stress, or get paid help. And with few women peers the female chief has a very limited support group, if any.

> *The most challenging time in my career was when I was pregnant. People write you off when you can't see your feet. I worked with eight executives. Not one called during my maternity leave. I found out they were all jockeying for my position. They tried to capitalize on my absence. Fortunately I took only two weeks' maternity leave.*
> —JULIE DONAHUE
> CEO and President,
> BBN Hark Systems Corporation

Female CEOs must strive particularly hard to balance their personal and professional lives. My friend Judy Marshall, president and CEO of the hugely successful Global Medical Review, Inc., in New York, admits, "I have absolutely no personal life whatsoever."

> *A big difference between being a female CEO as opposed to a male is that as the woman, you're generally the only one at the table. You don't have to worry about sitting boy, girl, boy, girl.*
> —SUSAN YAGER
> President, Domestications

Female CEOs are largely entrepreneurs. Of the companies headed by women, 70 percent were founded by them or inherited from the family. At the time of this writing, only one out of the *Fortune* 500 professional manager CEOs was a woman: Linda Wachner of Warnaco Groups, the menswear and intimate apparel company.

The segment of the population growing the fastest is female heads of business—entrepreneurial businesses. Women choose to start a business for the same reasons men start a business. They have a good idea, are willing to risk, have confidence, and don't want to put up with limitations imposed by an ongoing corporate entity.

As a female business owner/founder/entrepreneur for over twenty years I know women (and minorities) are discriminated against, stereotyped, sexually harassed, treated unfairly and even illegally in the workplace. But so are men! And sometimes women (and minorities) are hired or promoted *because* they are women or minorities. The pendulum swings both ways.

Not all white men who start a climb to the top make it by any means, just as not all women who attempt the climb make it. It's a combination of ambition, skill, focus, determination, will, ability, tenacity, luck, timing, and "numbers" in a company that gets one to the top. More women in the middle ranks put more women into the top ranks. Every year more women become CEOs of companies they didn't start and companies they did start. The numbers will grow, but they are still small.

The statistics show women are presently leaving the middle ranks of corporate America to start their own businesses. Some return home to raise children, and some simply stop working because they don't need to financially. When the numbers drop in the workforce, the potential number of female CEOs drops also.

Since there are many, many more male than female CEOs, I asked fifty male CEOs what advice they'd give to female wanna-be CEOs. The following is a composite of their answers:

- React like men to insignificant things, i.e., forget it. Don't be excessively emotional. Don't be defensive. Don't personalize. Don't be stubborn. Learn to deal with a certain "bullshit" quality men are used to dealing with and don't internalize it.
- Work at becoming a better leader, not a better team player.
- Work on being a better strategic planner rather than just a hard worker.
- Be more ambitious. Realize men are prepared to sacrifice family for business. Don't be afraid to take on something new and make family sacrifices.
- Have self-confidence, willingness, and the ability to promote yourself. Learn you don't get what you deserve, you get what you negotiate. But at the same time be patient for recognition.
- Use every tool available to you, including humanness, femininity, nurturing, relating, etc. But at the same time improve confrontation skills. Be assertive with a smile.

Now let's see what fifteen female CEOs gave as advice to female wanna-be CEOs:

- Don't overcompensate for being female, such as adopting male personality traits to compete with men. It's a mistake when women feel they have to act like a man to be tough in the business world.
- Don't be suspicious of other women; be helpful and supportive.
- Don't be unsophisticated in dealing with male counterparts. That is: Don't giggle. Don't have scattered thinking. Don't talk too much (petty or catty). Don't bring personal issues to the office. Don't be too social versus business oriented. Don't complain. Don't be overly emotional or overly nice.
- Don't put up with anything. Start early to keep control of yourself and keep at it. Don't limit yourself and settle for less than you're capable of.
- Don't personalize. You can't let it get to you. You need to strike a balance between being tough and having a sense of humor. Maybe you need to make some compromises. You need to ignore some injustice.

Then I asked the female CEOs what they wish their male counterparts would do in working with them:

- Don't feel superior. Don't feel women are on a lower level.
- Don't patronize, condescend, or be solicitous.
- Do listen to what women have to say.
- Don't speak support to a woman's face, then speak the opposite behind her back.
- Don't be threatened by women but do take us seriously.

I get respect from men, but there definitely is a difference. I point out an idea and it's passed over. Two minutes later a man says the same idea and everyone jumps on it. Prejudice is difficult to work against, so you have to go around it, or go beyond it.
—MARIE MCDONALD
President, Access Disability
Advisors/McDonald Elevator

The CEO slot is the only job where the job requirements are the same for men, women, or minorities. Few can successfully attack you, if you get the job done. There's no glass ceiling, cement walls, or any other descriptive limitation. The CEO could be a three-toed orangutan *if they get the job done—and get it done well.*

As Ruth Fertel (Ruth's Steak House) says regarding working in a business world more or less dominated by men, it's not a "man-woman-in-business kind of thing." Just do what you do: your job.

THE MOUNTAINEER SUMMARY

The entrepreneur versus the professional manager:

Innovator	Perfecter
Own money on line	Other people's money
Independent of people	Dependent on people

Innovator	**Perfecter**
Makes own rules	Follows rules
Answers to himself	Answers to constituents
Thinks and acts fast	Well thought out and deliberate
Seldom are hired to manage professional organization	Frequently are hired by entrepreneurial organization

Female climbers need the same qualities males do.

CHAPTER 7

Obstacles

A required scaling skill is overcoming the poor example set by not-so-near-perfect chiefs

I was sitting in a cafeteria with the CEO, executive vice president, two senior officers, and two department heads of a computer manufacturing company. We had just filled our plates at the buffet line, where the CEO had literally cut in front of two of his officers and myself to reach into fresh bowls of food first. Then he demanded of the waitress, "Ice tea. And I want some Equal [the artificial sweetener] too, right away." I had to chuckle quietly. From my day of close observation of him and his interaction with his team, the sweetener for his tea was the closest he got to anything being *equal*! But he's not a bad CEO; he's just *not-so-near-perfect*.

CEOs are everyday men and women, not universally gifted superhuman beings. When we are down on the flat land looking up at CEOs it's easy to find fault.

It's human nature to attempt to blame someone for

problems, and it might as well be the CEO. When in fact if we were in his shoes we might do the very thing we criticize him for doing. Occasionally a totally bad chief slips through, but most aren't bad despite what you might feel about yours.

At every level of workers, white collar, blue collar, executive, etc., there are good bosses and managers, and bad ones. The owner of one of New York's top modeling agencies was asked about the difficulty of dealing with pretty, but dumb, female models. He responded with the sentiment that there is the same percentage of dumb, pretty women as there are dumb lawyers, accountants, bankers, or politicians.

Just as there is a certain percentage of not-so-near-perfect employees, there is the same percentage of not-so-near-perfect CEOs.

The higher the corporate mountain you (or anyone else) climb, the more people will evaluate, judge, and criticize you. The more successful you become, the larger the pool of people who will potentially dislike you.

Chapters 3, 4, and 5 discussed the 22 Vital Traits of effective chiefs that I labeled as near-perfects. These recurring qualities enable the chiefs to utilize the right stuff in business actions that potentially enable them to do their job better: lead; strategize; create vision; increase sales, profits, assets, market value, productivity and stock prices; while decreasing overhead.

Although not all chiefs have all the traits all of the time, good ones do have them most of the time. If you want to join their ranks and work effectively with them, you have to work on the behaviors proven successful by those who have already made it. Learning from good people is necessary but not always easy. Unfortunately there are a lot of not-so-near-perfects out there that you have to constantly *fight against learning from*. One thing for certain in corporate life, you will have plenty of opportunity to learn the wrong thing. Bad bosses become obstacles to your climb. You must not follow their path!

What's good and bad often depends on in whose eyes and at what time! If you've just been promoted by a bad boss, is he good or bad in promoting you? If you've just been fired by a good boss, is he a good or bad boss? If a CEO owns a legal brothel as an investment where he improves the working conditions for the employees and increases profits, is he good or bad? If your CEO surpasses all profit to earnings ratios and develops radical new technologies, but sexually harasses employees, is he good or bad? If your CEO goes to Mass every day of the week, delivers food baskets to the poor, sponsors teamwork at every level, but has had earnings drop for the last eight quarters, is he good or bad?

Everyone can say at some time or another, "I have an awful CEO!" (That's one of the leading reasons people give to justify increased absences from work. According to a survey of 350 U.S. companies there was a 9 percent increase of unscheduled absences from work in 1993 over 1992.)

If you work for a boss you just don't agree with all the time, it doesn't mean he is not a good CEO. There are some people whose "nature" you will not like.

You may find him basically offensive. Seldom are you the first nor will you be the last offended by that person. But that does not necessarily make him a bad boss.

Not-so-near-perfect CEOs cause subordinates to suffer in various ways but the biggest way is that lousy bosses inhibit employees from doing good work for the company. Needless to say the employee, the company, and the community all suffer.

But who's to say who is a not-so-perfect CEO? Most every group goes on an attack of the top person at one time or another:

- *The media* makes, enhances, or breaks a reputation. For the last thirteen years the American press reviewed Jack Welch, CEO of General Electric, raving about the "management idol" as *Newsweek* described him. Then in the fourteenth year a bold headline in the same magazine read "Scratches in the Teflon: GE's Jack Welch is America's most venerated executive. Has he lost his Midas touch?" A headline that followed read: "Jack Welch's Nightmare on Wall Street: Like it or not, the scandals at Kidder Peabody were brought on by GE's management." Despite a record of endless profit increases for the $61 billion company and praise from top corporate headhunter recruiter Gerry Roche, who called Welch "absolutely one of the greatest CEOs of all time," the media was ready and eager to jump on the band wagon of criticism and critique.

When the press reported on allegations of tobacco company executives knowingly "spiking" the level of nicotine in cigarettes to addict smokers, the chairman of R.J. Reynolds Tobacco Company, James Johnston, had to respond in the media by buying a full-page advertisement in the *Wall Street Journal* denying the allegations.

I live in Ft. Collins, Colorado, at the base of the foothills of the Rocky Mountains. It's a pretty community that values the scenic beauty of this part of the country. One morning the town's paper had a big front-page article about the local Furr's restaurant. Seems the company president had visited a month prior and he thought trees were blocking the view of the Furr's sign from the street and ordered them to be cut down. Thanks to the media's headline everyone in town knew the story and the president's image was forever soiled. (By the way, the city managers required Furr's to replant the missing trees.)

The media is often the first to readily proclaim the shortcomings of business chiefs when the problems are isolated or have little to do with the top person. The press is very powerful and many CEOs avoid contact with the group as much as possible, fearing ending up on the critical side of press reports unfairly.

- *The governing authorities* bring CEOs under public scrutiny when the press reports a government investigation of a company. An example was CEO Tom Smith's Food Lion, Inc., grocery chain, studied by the Labor Department because of alleged violation of child safety laws following charges of unsanitary meat handling and false package-dating.

No matter how profitable, productive, and effective Smith was as a leader of the organization, people put him in the not-so-good category.

Same with William Lavin, who had to step down as CEO of Woolworth Company when the Securities and Exchange Commission began investigating allegations that executives sold the company's stock before they disclosed news of accounting irregularities that left the company in a financial and management crisis.

Then there is Phar-Mor, Inc.'s CEO, Michael Monus, who was in federal court for allegedly plundering the discount drugstore chain, duping investors, and evading taxes. And MiniScribe's CEO, Q. T. Wiles, who was indicted for shipping bricks disguised as computer disks and then trying to conceal company losses by lying about profits. Later he blamed a group of "rogue underlings."

- *The co-workers* most frequently conclude who is a poor chief. The president of Montgomery Ward quit, following the COO and several other executives below him, all due allegedly to the CEO, Bernard Brennan. Brennan's tough management style was credited for saving Montgomery Ward from liquidation, but it also caused others not to want to work with him.

- *The customers* conclude a CEO to be not-so-near-perfect when he makes decisions that affect their profitability. The warehouser and supplier of 258 retail food outlets, Supervalu, bought their own chain of competing grocers. According to the analysts, Supervalu could potentially put their own customers out of business.

- *The investors* pronounce a CEO to be inoperative: In the late 1980s, Sir Humphery Cripps, although not the CEO, controlled 67 percent of Velcro Industries N.V. (the hook-and-loop fastener) but he wanted to own the entire company. He initiated a number of actions to attack the stock price, driving it from $30 a share to $12 then back up to $20, where he magnanimously offered to buy the public out at just under $22. But investor Alan Kahn, of New York's Kahn Brothers, concluded Cripps was taking advantage of minority stockholders, sued, and Cripps called off his offer rather than go to court.

- *The competitors* make the CEO out to be not-so-near-perfect: Montgomery Securities is one of the nation's leading underwriters, acting as lead manager for thirty-one companies that went public last year. Its CEO, Thomas Weisel, is so influential that when the New York Stock Exchange wanted to open half an hour early he helped successfully defeat the plan because Weisel felt brokers were already made to get up too early on the West Coast to meet the opening of trading on the exchange. Weisel is described as "not beloved by his competitors, and he couldn't care less."

> *I can think of several cases of CEOs where you wonder, How did they get there? One man comes to mind whom everyone describes as the worst. I've not met anybody who likes the man. But the owners of the company he runs are trying to position it to sell. The CEO's job is to make the company look as productive as possible to sell. So everything he does is with that in mind. He's ruthless in cutting costs regardless of the effect on employees. If you didn't know that about him you'd really wonder how he remains the CEO.*
>
> —BILL FAIRFIELD
> CEO, Inacom Corporation

You might find that a CEO who was the nicest, wittiest, most modest, gutsy, confident person you've ever met (a number of the traits of near-perfect CEOs!) is also a crook. Does that make him a good or bad CEO? Then you have the honest, quiet, deliberate, detail-oriented, tenacious, willing-to-fight-for-his-people CEO whose company maintains a stagnant profit margin while it continues to lose its market value for the last eight quarters. Is he a good or bad CEO?

And what about Lajos Nagy, CEO of Balaton-Trade, who has made a fortune in catastrophes—such as wars—producing goods for the world's refugees? Based on where his profits come from, is he in the category of near- or not-so-near-perfect?

Obviously, aside from the proven illegal activity, it

is a very subjective subject whether a CEO is awful or an ace.

The opinion about the quality of CEOship in your company generally depends on your ability to be effective with that person. The more you become "near-perfect" the sooner you will be able to accurately evaluate CEOs. But always keep in mind, that no one meets everyone's ideal all of the time—not you or them. It reminds me of the situation in Mexico City when a group stood outside the Banco Nacional de Mexico, soliciting donations to help pay the ransom money for the chairman of the bank's holding company, Alfredo Harp Helu, who had been kidnapped. They raised $6.00 (that is, six dollars!). As awful as it sounds, apparently some people didn't want him back.

If you work for a boss whom co-workers, customers, competitors, the press, the board, and spouse regard as a rotten individual, he probably is, and my suggestion to you is, don't continue working for him. Quit. One entrepreneur was fond of bragging, "As long as I can buy people and sell them, I don't care what they think of me." This same man was described by another CEO, "He's an evil genius, and yet one of the greatest visionaries you'll ever know." The good things you *may* be in the position of learning from such an individual will not compensate for the bad things you *will* be exposed to working for him.

Don't quit if the CEO is just difficult and demanding. Everyone has had an impossible boss—including the impossible boss! You know the type:

- You can't please them, no matter what you do.
- You can't reason with them; can't satisfy them.
- You get blamed while they protect themselves first and foremost.
- You don't get credit for your work.
- You don't understand what they want.
- You get stabbed in the back by them.
- They are neglectful, sloppy, self-centered, geared toward success at any price, domineering, over-powering, authoritarian, negative, and fearful of others' success.

Even if your CEO's a combination of all the people you don't like, and you don't like him at all, he does hire good people—he hired you!

> *There are CEO types out there who take all of the credit and none of the blame versus taking no credit and all of the blame. If you understand the type and work accordingly, you will be able to work forever with them.*
> —PERRY DYE
> President,
> Dye Designs International

You have to decide what you can learn and how well you can work with your CEO type. Some are not worth the effort. Obviously avoid working for any boss who lies, cheats, steals, uses illegal sub-stances, or is involved in any illegal activity. Those are major obstacles to your climb.

People love to tell me stories of their "boss from

hell." Here's a sampling. For obvious reasons their comments are anonymous, or I'd have to label this "ex-bosses from hell":

> My boss came into my office asking for a phone number. I looked through my Rolodex but couldn't find it. Frustrated, he picked up my Rolodex and flung it against the wall. Cards fluttered through the air like snowflakes. There was a two-inch dent in my wall where the plastic case hit. Then he walked out. Another time he arrived at the office and some delivery man had left some boxes in his parking space. The CEO stepped on the gas to push them out of his space. They didn't move. One entire side of his Mercedes was gouged. It cost him a couple of thousand dollars to repair it. But he'd do it again. He doesn't learn.
>
> —a secretary to a CEO
>   who was divorced four times
>   and has been in jail overnight twice

> I once worked for a man who routinely sent out incriminating internal office memos to the press to embarrass his business foes. He doesn't do that anymore. He was fired when they traced obscene phone calls to his extension.
>
> —a former vice president to a CEO
>   who is now in therapy

For the simplest decision he has four meetings and asks everybody's opinion. He won't stick his neck out at all. He leads with an attitude of "Where do you want to go, I'll lead you there." You can't reach him because he is always in a meeting. And as things get worse, he has more meetings.

—a supplier to a CEO

After I spurned the affections of our COB, I heard he'd passed the word I was a lesbian. For Christmas that year he sent me two flannel nightgowns with a note that read, "one for you and one for your lover."
—a female saleswoman, about a COB who is so incredibly successful financially he feels he can get away with anything, and usually does

Some CEOs have dismally low personal ethics. They talk about shareholder wealth and they mean *their* shares. They scheme to pull money out personally every way they can. Some are afraid and don't know what to do. As a recruiter I have to fulfill job requirements of my clients and find the best person possible. Bad CEOs will not hire good people who they perceive could replace them.

—a headhunter to CEOs

I worked for an entrepreneur who built a fantastic corporate headquarters building. Floor-to-ceiling glass walls overlooking a panoramic view of the Rocky Mountains. No expense was spared to construct a monument to his success.

He'd stepped on lots of people's backs on his way up though. One was a man who was fired but ended up forming a competing company. The man quietly obtained a piece of land in front of my boss's headquarters. Then he built a taller, bigger, more beautiful building right across the highway, totally blocking my boss's mountain view. My boss never got over that retaliation. Every time he looked out his office window he had to see his rival.

—a corporate controller

My boss subscribes to a newsletter that recommends the CEO invade your subordinates' privacy. It advises using videotape and camera if necessary. Use body posture, height, frozen smiles, tone of voice to cut people to pieces. Be irrational, throw tantrums, be scary. Be ruthless. Cheat to advance, bail out when things get tough.

—a vice president to a CEO

Ernie Howell, retired president of Packaging Systems International, Inge Trump, president of Trump Property Management, and I were having lunch. A man walked by our table. "See that man who just walked by?" asked Trump. "He was fired from [a major computer company] I was with for embezzling funds from the company. Nothing was done to him. The company wanted to keep it quiet."

"I know of several cases like that. The companies

don't want the publicity. It happens all the time," added Howell.

We could go on and on with little horror stories about outrageous CEOs. In truth there are more good CEOs than bad CEOs, but it's more fun to talk about the bad ones.

WHY NOT-SO-NEAR-PERFECT CEOS GET TO THE TOP

CEOs are humans like you and me. Humans get spiteful or jealous and seek revenge or retaliation. Humans connive and scheme to keep their power and protect their position, once obtained. Their love of power and wealth causes them to overreach. Often their distasteful behavior is an isolated event caused only by the fury of the moment. Sometimes it's prevalent. Some could argue if it doesn't get in the way of profitability, ignore it.

Every day the news carries stories of CEOs and their staff who mislead customers, steal technology, overcharge fees, deliberately harm the environment, sell fake parts, falsify documents, finance illegal doings, accept Rolex watches, real estate, children's college tuition, or Mercedes-Benzes in kickbacks for bribes, destroy internal papers relating to investigations, and so forth. Big companies get caught and fined millions. And the public wonders how they thought they could get away with it.

You are probably wondering why there are any not-so-near-perfect CEOs at the top at all.

A series of unusual circumstances. In a company's history, at a certain time, a bad boss started out as the "right person for the job." Sometimes the not-so-near-perfect was the only person who would do the work necessary, or simply "everyone else left but him." In some cases his talent was brilliant and the company needed his specific expertise to fill a niche during a specific time period. And remember, as previously discussed, different styles work in different eras. Timing.

> *Sometimes otherwise good CEOs lose their personal motivation. Values and integrity stall. Their vitality is taken out. The willingness to take risks and their willingness to do things differently is gone. But they don't let go. They get comfortable. It sounds crazy that they let it happen because of what they had to do to get to the top. But they simply lose nerve to move forward. And lots of times the CEO is highly mortgaged and he can't quit.*
> —ED SHONSEY
> CEO, Northrup King

Things go unnoticed and unchecked. The board of directors, shareholders, customers, public, and employees put up with poor behavior. CEOs can lose touch with employees, customers, and the real world. People steer clear of atrocious CEOs and further isolate them with thoughts like, "For heaven's sake, don't upset the boss this morning." So some CEOs literally don't know (or don't acknowledge) their own poor behavior and don't know they have to stop it.

> *There are lazy people who let it happen. Remember, "All it takes for evil to occur is for a few good men to do nothing."*
> —MICHAEL P. SCOTT
> International Communications Manager,
> Pioneer Hi-Bred International, Incorporated

Politics. There are exceptional wheeler-dealer types who "play the board of directors like a violin." They are so slick they can fool the entire financial community long enough for them to call in their chips. Or they are great golfers; the selection process was based on friendship. They say the right things. (They survive by focusing on meeting needs of direct superiors. They learn to execute and follow orders. They surround themselves with people who compensate for their weakness.) They schmooze the "people who count." A CEO can go off on six different tangents at once in a staff meeting, be disorganized and filled with superfluous mish mash, but put him in front of the board, and he can turn into a mighty manager.

Maintain Luck. Some lucked into the position and remained lucky enough not to get found out or fired. Some things in life cannot be explained or justified.

Ownership. Some literally *own* the company and can frequently do, say, act, relate any way they please. Neither the banks nor employees nor investors nor the public can intervene. The not-so-near-perfect may run into trouble with customers or the government, depending on their action.

When you stop to think about it, it is easy to see how not-so-near-perfects can stumble their way to the top. But for you to deal with any boss (whether near-perfect or not-so) you need to understand how to work with that person *as long as you're employed at the same company.*

Until you walk in the CEO's shoes, you'll never fully understand or appreciate the pressures, responsibilities, and frustrations that cause different (and difficult) behavior. I'm not saying, "Tolerate the poor actions and conduct that separate the not-so-near-perfect CEO and the near-perfect CEOs," but I am suggesting, "Understand them before attacking or adopting similar conduct."

In Defense of CEOs

Unless you are a chief, you can't fully appreciate all the elements involved. Following are some comments

CEOs (near-perfect and not-so-near-perfect) have given me in defense of their behavior:

> I'm responsible for 68,000 people's paychecks. Can you imagine the pressure that puts on me?

> It goes with the territory to be considered a jerk. I'd love them to like me, but at least I'd like them to respect me. But I have to make decisions daily on who gets promoted, who gets allocated scarce resources, their pay. . . . Whenever I promote, there's one winner and several losers. There's a high chance people won't like me.

> I never relax. I'm tense all the time. Running the company the last three years has taken ten years off my life.

> I'm *always* under a fire hydrant hose from my board, bankers, the press, and my spouse.

> The popular trend is employee empowerment. Customers are the boss. Upside-down management. *Teams* take over. Let the team decide. Well I did and I failed because of it. I won't do that again.

> An employee is much more likely to be wrong about whether a CEO is a bad boss or not. I have several employees who think I am a complete idiot because I don't agree with them or believe in them. They're wrong.

You learn to accept things like being the "Darth Vader" in town.

Many times a CEO has to restructure and maneuver titles and power and ultimately it's good for shareholders and employees, but initially not so good for individuals. Tough bosses carry out difficult decisions that aren't popular. But for everyone who takes shots at the CEO there are likely twenty people who will say good things about him.

LEARN TO WORK WITH NEAR-PERFECT *AND* NOT-SO-NEAR-PERFECT CHIEFS

My advice to you is to learn to work with your CEO (and his chiefs) regardless of how less-than-perfect they are. (It's a rock wall that is imposing, but doable.) It will be for your own benefit in the short run and for the long run of your career. Also you will be stronger, more effective, and more powerful as an individual if you can effectively deal with a variety of difficult people. Why?

When you summon up your personal strengths and run a course that allows you to deal with a variety of difficult people, you push out your own limits and stand out above the norm. If you succumb to his rantings, *you* become the loser, not the rotten CEO. Most people get frustrated, get mad, give in, give up, and either silently suffer while plotting revenge or quit their job prematurely because of a poor leader.

You will undoubtedly face a similar person and situation wherever you go. People don't change; the location and company name may change, but personalities don't. If you walk away without conquering the rock wall you will just face another, bigger one when you are even weaker in your ability to face such obstacles.

You will learn from dealing with a tough CEO whether you "win" or not. You will learn what not to be like if nothing else. You might find out what works and doesn't work in behavior and strategy in human nature. (You might discover the person isn't as bad as you thought. It's amazing how many times I've talked with subordinates of CEOs who complain bitterly about their actions; then years later when they take the lead, their subordinates make the same complaints about them!)

You are constantly being watched and judged by those around you. They will note and remember your ability, or lack of ability, of surviving difficult people, times, and situations. Management, now and in the future, will judge *you*, not your boss.

One of the biggest reasons for learning to deal effectively with a not-so-near-perfect is the control of timing it allows you to maintain. When you leave the situation, it will be by your decision made from a base of accomplishment, not one of a beaten-down little puppy. You leave on a high note rather than a flat one when you choose to leave after successfully dealing with the not-so-near-perfect types. You feel good about yourself. Your family and friends feel good about you, too.

YOU will be in control of your life and career, not the boss, the company, or the government. YOU alone. And that is empowering yourself!

In theory this all sounds well and good but there is a gap between the worlds of theory and the worlds of practicality, and there is a need to bridge that gap. So how do you better understand and work with the not-so-near-perfect CEO?

Be in control of your attitude. If you lose your personal command and allow a chief's poor or destructive attitudes to determine your actions, you submit to him.

Be secure in yourself. If you know and feel in your heart and mind that you are on the right course, stick to it. Don't let pressure from people, or the numbers, or whatever is the driving force in your organization cause you to weaken.

Be tenacious. Many bosses, good ones and bad ones, love to test you to see your breaking point. You will get admiration and respect from the good ones and the bad ones if you persistently hold to your course of action. Also, with tenacity, you might outlast the dreadful chief and get a god-sent replacement. Hang in there long enough, doing the right things, and *you* might be the pinch hitter.

Be willing to see the improvement potential in the situation. Take the position that you can benefit from the experience. Fall back on the basics of effective behavior outlined in chapters 3, 4, and 5. Remember that *many* times you criticize a person for what you yourself are guilty of. Before you publicly attack others, honestly scrutinize your own actions and check if people below you couldn't complain about the same thing. Then change and improve as needed.

Be sure to think before you talk. If you are feeling hurt by others or self-righteous, now is the time to really slow down; think through your words and behavior. Imagine the ramifications for you, the company, your boss, co-workers, and your family and double-check if that is what you really want to happen.

Be gutsy. Now more than ever is the time to try something you normally may not have the courage to do. What do you have to lose? If you are considering quitting anyway, you might as well try a super learning experience by taking radical action. (Note: radical action should not include violence or unlawful steps.) Gutsy behavior may be any of the following:

- speaking up when you usually don't,
- talking to a person you normally feel you can't talk to,
- making a decision without fourteen levels of permission first,

- standing up for a position where you would generally back down.

Now might be the time that you have to try to get a new boss inside the organization. (But remember, every new boss will provide a different set of frustrations for you. You won't avoid problems, you'll just get a new set of them.) Or, you may have to go around your current boss to a higher one. It will be extremely important for you to utilize the near-perfect traits while you find the vehicle to do this; you just can't crash over him. Not only will you make an enemy of him, but others are watching and judging your overall effectiveness and future potential as a leader.

Be a tad theatrical. You may have to act like you are comfortable, confident, competent, satisfied, motivated, enthused, supportive, loyal, responsive, and so forth even though you don't necessarily feel like it. Many other people around you who behave as if everything is fine, may not really feel that way deep down inside. There is value in not wearing "hurts" on sleeves. You don't always have to let everyone know exactly what you are thinking. You may say that isn't being honest or at least genuine. My response is that as much as you have the right to act any way you want, you know from your own life experiences that it pays to selectively show your true thoughts.

Be silent. Do not feel every rumination you have must be expressed. It doesn't have to be. Being silent offers you a fail-safe. If you have the self-discipline to be quiet and let things go unsaid, you might find you were wrong anyway. If you were right, you can quietly reaffirm your good intuition. I am not suggesting hiding or suppressing feelings (that would be politically incorrect of me). I am suggesting there are plenty of times in business when you need to shut up, hold off, be patient, and let things play out.

Of course, I am not suggesting you keep quiet about illegal, unlawful, or unethical business activities you are aware of. Do carefully consider, think out, and strategize how you will address those issues so that your input makes a difference.

Be detail oriented. Pay more attention to detail than ever. For example, regarding people involved, take note of another's attitude, expression, tone of voice, dress, actions, patterns, idiosyncrasies, irritations, loyalties, actions, missed actions, inconsistencies, and so forth. Make a mental note or write things down. Regarding the CEO, pay particular attention to his schedules and rhythms of work. When he's pressed and stressed, leave him alone. Why add irritation? You don't like it when someone does it to you, do you? Only if you are observant and silent can you truly see and hear what is going on at the surface as well as under the surface.

Be sure to maintain your sense of humor. This is work we are talking about, not the things that truly matter in life like health, love, and family. Seek out the irony. Look for the silliness of it all. Don't lose sight of the seriousness, of course, but don't be overwhelmed by it. Three years down the road you will wonder why you let the bad boss have so much control over you. A financial officer with MiniScribe, the company I told you about earlier whose executives were indicted for shipping bricks instead of computer disks to falsify sales, was on trial for his role in the scam. He told the court about his preparations for upcoming under-the-table activities, which involved watching a U.S. Navy film giving instructions on picking locks, something he was called upon to do at the company. And when he couldn't successfully pick a lock he sometimes allegedly jimmied it in order to cover up a $15 million inventory shortage. "I realize it sounds pretty silly right now," he admitted during the trial. Ultimately humor can be found in most every situation.

Be nice. When people all around you are not being nice, you will stand out from the crowd because of your congeniality. Pleasantness makes you appear confident. *Try acting pleasant.* Sounds like funny advice, doesn't it? But don't you know some people who could benefit from trying that? You can be extremely tough, demanding, deliberate, certain, whatever is necessary, but in a good-natured way. For instance, don't lose your emotional control when you stand your ground. It's better to calmly and temporarily endure than have a temporary outburst of fury that you'll regret later (say after you've resigned in a huff!).

Be inquisitive. If you think you know, and act on what you think you know—you might be wrong. Ask for clarification or verification. Ask. Check. Verify. Don't assume. Even when you do know, ask. Then inquire again. Remember, asking at least three times seems to be necessary to get the whole truth and a clear understanding of a person's meaning. It may take extra courage to ask tough questions that others are afraid to. That is all the more reason to do it. Ask about details. Use your good humor. Be nice when you inquire. Be tenacious when you query. Have a private meeting with your boss and ask, "What can be done better?" Conduct the discussion with mutual respect, not a pathetic "What's wrong with me?" tone of voice or a "What's wrong with you?" attack. The more confrontational, the more private the meeting should be. Ask questions rather than making statements or accusations.

Be willing to fight for your people—upward and downward. It would be nice if the company management (from the CEO on) would support and back you always. However, I'm afraid they tend to disappoint. But you shouldn't. You should set yourself apart and stand behind all the people you work for, work with, and who work for you. *You* can set the example, the tone, the course, or whatever is required. You can do the right thing for yourself, regardless of whether others are for you or not;

meanwhile you will be benefiting the entire organization. And people in positions of power *are watching*. They may be inside the company, or outside in the industry, the community, or elsewhere, but they are watching. Your effective actions will not go unnoticed. The expression "What goes around, comes around" really is true. You know it to be true. It has been proven in life. Now you just have to be patient, long-lasting, and consistently improving in these all-important traits and *you will benefit*.

Be willing to lead. Like fighting for your people, it would be nice if the leader in your company truly led. They don't always. They dictate, direct, demand, require, nag, pester, and badger—they don't always lead. Nonetheless, you should be willing to lead and able and capable to provide the leadership necessary.

Keep your personal overhead low so you can maintain financial freedom. Many people like to see you paint yourself into a corner of luxury where you can't quit. Then they have you. You can't quit. At that point you have lost a great deal of control, and although the attributes discussed can help make your situation more bearable, few of these traits can help you get out of the situation.

Do you happen to see a pattern of recommendation here? Do you see how all these vital traits I've laid out go hand in hand and overlap and interrelate? You should, because they do. As I've said before, this is all simple; not necessarily easy, but simple.

My closing remarks on dealing with the not-so-near-perfect people in your life is best expressed by Douglas Conant, a group executive vice president for Nabisco, Inc.: "Weak leaders won't survive. It's only a matter of time. By definition leaders are visible, as is their level of competency. In today's environment, if they are not competent, everyone will know in short order. I don't know anyone incompetent who has survived the scrutiny that leadership brings."

And remember the true words of Dave Powelson, COB, CEO, and president of TRI-R Systems: "It's a good thing the metal detectors at airports aren't bullshit detectors."

And the consoling remarks of Jerry Henry, senior vice president at DuPont: "If there is a jerk as a CEO, he won't last forever. People give up on him and trying to work with him. Sometimes the board had tolerance in the past for people who had enough ability to get to the top but weren't effective once there. Today the people in power will fess up and admit they made a mistake and the bad CEO will be out the door."

OBSTACLES SUMMARY

Why do not-so-near-perfect chiefs last, or even get to the top at all?

- Series of unusual circumstances.
- Things go unnoticed or unchecked.

- Things go unnoticed or unchecked.
- Office politics.
- Mountain luck.
- Ownership.

What should you do about a bad chief above you?

- Learn to work with the individual utilizing the vital traits necessary to climb any mountain. Remind yourself that you'll face that same difficult type elsewhere. It's best to learn to deal with them here.
- Live up to their test. Outlast them, outwork them, outshine them.
- Learn from their example of what *not* to be!

PART TWO

Should you desire to go for a chief position—even CEO—you'll want to know the best route to take and what to expect once there, the job you'll do, what you'll get paid, who your boss will be, and what happens when things go wrong. That's Part Two of *How to Think Like a CEO*.

CHAPTER 8

How Chiefs Become Chiefs

How you can become one also

There is a vast climbing wilderness out there. The questions young climbers ask: What's the most direct route? What route should I take? Is it better to take a new or a well-worn path?

Chiefs can come from any neighborhood, part of the country, or class. It is true that people who had early, ongoing exposure to the corporate world probably have some advantage, but if you didn't have that in your upbringing, you just have to get it now. I sometimes discuss achievement with my seminar audiences with the following example: If you were born into the family that John F. Kennedy was born into you might be quite different. Meaning, if your family had summer and winter homes (complete with servants) that were larger than most small hotels, and your father was ambassador to England, where you met the queen while in your teenage years, and you went to private academies with the sons of other wealthy, influential men, and your mother's father had been the mayor of Boston, and as a young man you partied with the famous in Hollywood—well, you'd be different than you are!

Few people have that kind of early exposure to shape their lives. Most of us come from very middle-class families where we work ourselves up the hill, have typical childhood experiences, public schooling, and a home where too many people fit into too little space.

It's true, chiefs come from families like JFK's, but chiefs also come from backgrounds similar to yours and mine.

THE CEO'S UPBRINGING

Chiefs don't come from formula parents. Some had both parents working, some neither. Some blue collar, some white. Some parents were there, some weren't. Chiefs had the same types of parents that people who don't become chiefs have. *The difference is in the offspring, not the parent.*

Charles Koch, who runs Koch Industries' billion-dollar operation, remembers, "I had great love for both my parents. They weren't demonstrative, they didn't say 'love you' every day. But I remember being kissed by Mother and Father every night. And Dad would pat me on the shoulder."

At twelve years of age I had a paper route. I also had a checkbook because of it. My

teacher saw it one day and plucked me out of class to be part of an accelerated math class. It was the start of a pattern of achievement. The problem with early success is it makes you demanding of yourself and other people.
    —JOEL A. SCHLEICHER
       COO, Nextel Communications, Inc.

I was not a good student in kindergarten, first, second, or third grades. Both my parents were doctors. In the fourth grade they really turned on the psychology, really worked on me frequently, but without pressure. They expressed conviction that I was a lot better than I realized. I got curious to see if they were right; it wasn't out of fear or pressure. I turned around and continued for the rest of my school.
    —ELMO R. ZUMWALT JR.
       Retired Admiral, Chief of Operations, U.S. Navy

I was the basic achiever's achiever as a child—president of my elementary school, president of my junior high, graduated first in a class of one thousand from college, passed CPA exam on my first try, Harvard MBA with distinction, first in my HBS class of one thousand to coauthor for the Harvard Business Review, *fast-tracked through General Foods marketing, . . . ran my first*

marathon (twenty-six miles) four months
after I ran my first mile.
                    —STEVE SILK
                    President and CEO,
                    The Estee Corporation

One of the wealthiest men in Japan, Kenshin Oshi-
ma (worth around $1.2 billion), who heads the fi-
nance company he started, Shohkoh Fund, told
Forbes magazine, "When I was twelve, I read a book
about the Rothschilds. Since then I knew I wanted to
be a billionaire."

Another CEO said, "I knew I'd make it. I just didn't
know what journey I'd take."

And yet another one told me, "I was a jobless
beach bum, drifting from one area to another until I
was nearly thirty. I wasted a lot of prime time."

Then there is the current chairman of OmniBanc
Corporation, William Johnson. *Black Enterprise*
magazine told Johnson's story: "He was born 50
years ago in Columbus, Ohio. After his parents divorced, his mother became too ill to work and the
family went on welfare. Johnson took on two newspaper routes to help make ends meet. He was so
good at selling newspaper subscriptions that he won
a trip to Disneyland. When welfare officials found
out, they told him that the value of the prize would
have to come out of the family's welfare benefits.
Johnson didn't go.

"An avid student, Johnson took up football in 10th
grade solely because he wanted an athletic scholar-
ship to college. 'I didn't like the sport,' he recalled.

But he was very good at it, good enough to be recruited by coach Woody Hayes of Ohio State University in 1962. But when Hayes demanded that Johnson major in physical education instead of political science, Johnson transferred to nearby Capital University, where he earned his bachelor's and law degrees. He later earned a master's degree in law from the University of Houston.

"Johnson joined a law firm which gave him contacts into the cable business which he invested in, later to sell out and with his profits acquire a bank, thus starting his financial career where he is now the Chairman of a $26 million bank."

If you were talking with your boss and he revealed something like the above stories, it could be very eye-opening to you. You'd have a better idea of his history and philosophy of life. You'd better understand the chief when he says, as William Johnson says, "This [being CEO] may have been what I was born to do." *You can find out these types of things about your boss.* You do it by engaging in a conversation and asking questions. You can do that. There is no law against it.

While you're sitting there telling yourself you could never do that, that you could never be so bold as to ask such questions, consider the following:

- It would be flattering if your boss asked you.
- Bosses, like you and me, enjoy recalling personal history.
- They, like you and me, seldom get the opportunity to talk about themselves.

Note from the author: My parents ran a mom-and-pop business together, so at dinner they talked about the day's work. Vacations were usually tied in with their business trips. They didn't believe in babysitters, so every day after school I went to their office. I had my own play, or actually work, area. They paid me in nickels and dimes for errands. I'd have to patiently sit alongside my parents and listen to seemingly endless business conversations with suppliers and salesmen. Mom and Dad were real entrepreneurs. That was my world. I remember my very sweet mother saying one time, "When I see someone having to work for someone else I just want to upchuck." I admit, I'm an entrepreneur because of my upbringing.

- They will *definitely* remember someone who asks with sincere interest, tact, and discretion.
- And, very important, consider what insight you will gain.

Is there a company policy against asking? Probably not. It just takes courage, timing, technique, and availability. If you don't get to be face-to-face with your chief, ask these questions of others. If you do get to occasionally see the chief in the hallway, the company cafeteria, or annual Christmas party, there are lots of reasonable questions you can ask.

- Where were you born? What line of work did your father do? Did your mother work outside the home?
- What did you think about yourself? When did you do well? How could you tell?
- How did you get attention or recognition at school and among your peers?
- Who did you want to be like?
- What were early successes? Setbacks?
- What/who motivated you?
- What/who inspired you?
- What/who discouraged you?

Some savvy is required to weave these into the conversation so as not to sound like you read in a book to ask these specific questions. But hopefully you get the idea of learning about the person behind the title. If you understand about the chief's upbringing you can see who, what, and why he is like he is.

The purpose of learning about the chief's upbringing is to gain insight about the person and maybe even find common areas of interest. By understanding what he or she has experienced, you'll see what they value. What they value is what they promote. I don't care how much antidiscrimination legislation is passed, people live and promote in their own likeness to a large degree.

THE CEO'S EDUCATION

One CEO recruiter told me, "It holds true that people who attend the top ten or twenty schools in the country will still get the nod. They're likely smarter." But another CEO recruiter told me, "At senior executive positions the college or major doesn't matter at all. It's the easy way out to selectively evaluate based on what campus they came from or the blue-chip companies they joined. I exclude individuals if they got jobs just because of the school they graduated from."

Some of the CEOs I met with had their predominant formal education in agronomy, veterinary science, art history, theater, literature, history, English, Russian, journalism, and even massage therapy. *Most* CEOs had either finance, accounting, marketing, or general business as their major. It's like a bell curve. At one extreme you have CEOs who didn't finish high school, at the other extreme you have CEOs with Ph.D.s. But the college major did not guarantee or block success (when the future CEO had the Vital Traits).

> *I was a crammer and did well at it. One quarter, my roommate and I had a contest. Who could attend the fewest classes and get the highest grades? I would like to think I'd have been successful regardless of my college or major, but I know my major [ac-*

counting] put me in a spot to get certain po-
sitions.
> —JOEL A. SCHLEICHER
> COO, Nextel Communications, Inc.

Of the CEOs I interviewed, 66 percent had de-grees. Of that percentage, 32 percent hold degrees in general business, 44 percent in finance, 9 percent in marketing and sales, and 15 percent in other majors. Nine percent had graduate degrees, and 89 percent felt none of that was important compared to *doing the job on the job* today!

The Gallup Poll asked 315 CEOs the following question: "If you had children who were about to graduate from college, would you advise them to go to graduate school or start working?" Forty percent said graduate school, 50 percent said start working, and 10 percent had no opinion.

In a headline of a story about Kahl's department store CEO William Kellogg, *Forbes* writes, "Bill Kellogg's high-school grades were so bad he decided he should go to work, not college. Poor Bill, at 50 he's a centimillionaire."

> *I was a psychology major and also attended the American Academy of Dramatic Arts. I got into the buying side of retailing twenty years ago and went on to gain experience in product development, importing, and de-signs. I joined my current parent company six years ago as an associate catalog direc-tor and today am the president of the $300*

million catalog company. . . . My background is entrepreneurial not managerial. . . . I wish I'd studied more business and economic courses earlier on, both to help me on a daily basis and for my own confidence. Today I am very grateful for my acting and psychology background. As the president, I'm always speaking before the public. It is unfortunate but true that people frequently care more about how you say something than what you say. The psychology background helps me deal with people, which is of course the biggest part of the job.

—SUSAN YAGER
President, Domestications

In today's competitive job market, a college degree is almost a must to compete for top jobs. If you don't have a degree your choices are (one) to be exceptionally skilled in the 22 Vital Traits and be a specialist (i.e., know everything you can about the subject you will be working in) even without the certification; (two) go back and get the degree (there are many options available to securing an undergraduate and graduate degree nowadays aside from taking four years off); or (three) start your own company, where you determine whether a college education makes or breaks you.

Mentors

To scale lofty heights you frequently need "power as-sists" from other climbers. Mentors are simply the *more experienced* climbers who can guide you be-yond the rudiments to those heights.

Three-fourths of the CEOs I interviewed had someone in their life they could specifically point to as a guide to teach them how to "walk, talk, and act"—someone who was their sounding board, teacher, and thought leader. I myself have had so many mentors that a list of their names would fill three address books. They are people who have shown me the ropes, brought me along, checked if my ideas made sense or not. I'd ask them, Here's my situation and here's what I'm looking at. Here's what I think; what are your thoughts? I can readily recall things they taught me.

You need to have a coach who both helps and challenges you. That's the only way you'll get a balanced perspective. Try to always learn the best from the best. (There are people in a position of power who aren't the ones you should learn from. Remember the not-so-near-perfects?) Be cautious of the ones whose mentoring status is an ego trip. That often ends up as an amateur teaching an ama-teur to be an amateur.

How do you choose a mentor? Select someone who

- knows the territory,
- knows where he's going,

- knows where you want to go to,
- knows how to traverse the terrain,
- and is willing to advise you.

Some potential mentors don't want to help others, don't want their secrets known, don't want it known they don't have secrets, are too timid to share, or don't have time.

A good teacher deserves a good student. Find out how your "Sherpa" teaches (by asking questions). Understand how you learn. Look for a mentor whose method fits yours.

You will discover that some people teach and some people learn by engaging in one or more of the following methods:

- example (showing versus telling how),
- written communications,
- analogy (telling stories, painting pictures),
- hands on (going through a situation together).

Ask and intelligently observe. Emulate things you like about your chosen guide. Avoid the things you don't like. Either way you are learning. Be careful not to seek mentors just like you. They'll only reinforce what you want to hear. You need someone who will challenge or object to your thinking.

It's true the word *mentor* is three letters from the word *tormentor*. In reality most of the people you need to learn from are pleasant about it; some are not so amiable. Ricardo Salinas Pliego is head of the largest chain of appliance and electronics retail stores in Mexico. Through one of his suppliers he arranged to spend a day with Sam Walton, the founder of Wal-Mart. It was one of the most important learning days of his life, he says: "[Walton] asked me a lot of questions I didn't know the answers to." As expected, he soon got the answers.

You and I can get quite wrapped up in our world and lose some awareness of what is going on around us. That can be a major problem even at the top. Anthony Eames, head of Coca-Cola Canada, says, "We live in an information igloo," meaning we get lots of available information while still being isolated. Initiating and maintaining mentoring relationships (where you are sometimes the mentor and sometimes the mentee) is critical for a well-rounded view of what is going on.

Every time your personal coach offers an extra nugget of insight because he is younger, older, has a higher title, manages more people or more complex operations, or has more and different industry experience—you win. He is helping you "walk, talk, and act" with greater originality, with more control, in an improvement mode, and in a way that will make you better at your job.

Sometimes coaching goes beyond informal career guidance into sponsorship. Where someone really "takes you along." That is good and bad. One CEO who wanted to remain anonymous said, "I followed my mentor through a number of jobs. He pulled me through when I needed it because of what he saw in me. Before he took early retirement he called me into his office and warned me I needed to get out of the company too. I didn't take the advice. I thought I knew better. I was wrong. Now I'm being forced out."

A mentor's role is not to make your life easier, even though the mentor in the previous example did. Their role is to help you see things you wouldn't normally have seen for yourself because you were so involved in doing your job.

Some companies sponsor mentor programs where a senior executive is literally assigned to a junior. (You see that a lot in law firms, for example.) If your company endorses such relationships, take advantage of it, but don't rely on it. Strike out on your own to develop your own relationships. A coach from outside the company is critical to have on your team.

The same CEO who unfortunately is in the process of losing his job added, "When I look back at the responsibility given me by my 'godfather' I think what a risk he took. At the time I thought it was a good decision, but in hindsight I think, What a risk."

Mentoring is needed over and over again throughout your career. It's helping people along in business, just as you do in life. But in business, or your personal life, it still boils down to *you* doing whatever needs to be done, not expecting or counting on someone doing for you. Mentors do the easy part. It isn't difficult to teach you *how* to do something; the *doing* is the near-impossible.

NETWORKING

Two college board directors sat beside each other at a national youth leadership meeting with the usual "Hello, how's it going" exchange. One director commented, "I'm heading up a search committee for a college president. I've got candidates coming out of the woodwork, but no one is right for the job." The other director said, "Let me put a name in the hat?" That name ultimately became the chosen candidate, who as the new president said, "I have no idea where I'd be if it wasn't for those two sitting together." That college president was Dr. William Morgan, a man I mentioned earlier as being publicly modest.

A chain of interconnected people (and situations) gets you a job at the top. It's not a passive sit-back-and-hope-it-happens-because-I-deserve-it chain of activity. It's keeping in touch with people you meet—both upward and downward.

You never know when you'll have the job rug pulled out from under you. One of the best investments you can make in your career is to constantly develop business friendships that can help you when you need it. And you can help them when *they* need it. (Remember—sometimes you're the mentor, sometimes the mentee.)

You need involvement in organizations other than your own to meet outside people. You have to trade information back and forth, so when in need of a new opportunity you can call on people, tell them what has transpired, and what you're looking for.

Ask if they know someone they could introduce you to. It's important to develop contacts inside and outside of your industry. One CEO whose company provided services to penny stock companies explained his dilemma of only knowing people inside his industry: "I can't tap into my network because most of the people I know are in jail."

When things are going well it's easy to get lazy or arrogant and drop off networking activity. Don't. You must work on the contact game consistently, especially when things *are* going well and you *don't* need the help of other people in the chain. If you contact people only when you need them, you look desperate and sleazy. A good businessperson—err, climber—needs lots of friends. You need to cultivate them with effort and thoughtfulness.

Steve Silk received a call from a person in his network asking, "You're running a $30 million company now, do you want to be considered for a $400 million company?"

So how do you develop these business friendships so you might get a call like that someday?

1. *Decide to increase your business contacts.* Set a goal of at least one new person a week. "What separates winners from 'also-rans'? The Rolodex," Harvey MacKay, author of *Swim with the Sharks*, told me. Fill up your Rolodex.

2. *Initiate the contact.* Keep your eyes and ears open to prospects. Learn to recognize a potential business friend: people you meet in airplanes, at the health club, friends of friends,

friends of vendors, friends of kids, even people you read about in newspapers. Make several attempts with each person before giving up.

- Introduce yourself.
- Show interest in the contact.
- Look for common interests.
- Follow up in what common interest you've discovered.
- Maybe even inform the contact of your interest in networking with him or her.
  (Developing these business friendships is not simply handing out business cards.)

You should acknowledge every telephone call or correspondence you receive, a lesson one of my mentors, Bill Daniels, taught me long ago. He said, "For example, if you write me you *will* hear back from me. It may take a while, but I will respond." Bill Daniels is what *many* who know him would call a near-perfect CEO. He returns phone calls and answers letters. Follow Daniels's lead when dealing with phone messages and correspondence; often it's someone's attempt at networking with you. Listen to how they handle you so you can learn how to better handle others. And you never know where it will lead.

3. *Anticipate and accept the feeling of discomfort.* Usually anything new is uncomfortable. Keep networking until it feels comfortable. There is no secret method to becoming comfortable; it's simply a matter of time and perseverance. The

simply a matter of time and perseverance. The right attitude toward revving up your career will keep you motivated and create excitement that will overwhelm procrastination.

4. *Get several balls up in the air.* When some drop (and some will), you still have others up. Have lots of opportunities going simultaneously.

5. *Expect acceptance.* But if you don't get it, don't feel rejected. Remember, they probably have their own list of prospective business friends they'd like to develop also. They may not have time for you on your timetable now, but are nonetheless willing to at another time. Things change for everyone.

6. *Do for others first.* Networking is a two-way street. Demonstrate the value of your being part of their network: Give a name and phone number of someone they need to know, send a magazine article of interest to them, introduce them to someone, write a letter of introduction, take them to the Sunday football game, loan them your courtside box for the tennis tournaments, frame a newspaper article on them, call a politician you know on their behalf, send company product samples, send vegetables from your garden—or avocados from your farm, as John Bianchi got a reputation for doing.

7. *Maintain contact.* Work the phone, have lunch with people, write notes, congratulate, compliment, ask advice, etc. Lay the groundwork and plan ahead.

8. *Keep a log of your activity*. Draw a "family tree" depicting how each new contact led to another. That way you objectively test whether you are meeting your goal of a new contact a week. If you don't track it, you'll lose track.

I was in New York for a month-long business trip. When I travel, I like to try good restaurants, and one of my friends had said I had to go to Le Cirque. Four different attempts for a reservation resulted in "no availability" as the response. Walking by Le Cirque one day, I discovered it was located next to the Mayfair Regent Hotel.

So I put my network to work. A client and a friend, W. Ted Wright IV, ran a sister Regent Hotel in Sydney, Australia. So I called Ted in Sydney and asked if he could help me get a reservation at Le Cirque through the New York Regent. Ted called his friend Dario Mariotti, the general manager of the Mayfair Regent, who called the owner of Le Cirque and made a reservation for me.

Prior to the luncheon reservation I stopped into Dario's office to thank him for his assistance. We chatted, shared stories about our common friend, Ted, and I headed to lunch, after adding someone new to my network.

Lunch was perfect. Perfectly prepared and perfectly served. I barely noticed that the actor Don Johnson was seated at the next table. I particularly enjoyed watching the owner and maitre d', Sirio Maccioni, perform his craft. His restaurant patrons were treated like guests in his home. I was fascinated watching his true orchestration of every element of running the show.

When I finished eating, I noticed Mr. Maccioni sitting with a cup of coffee. So on my way out I stopped by his table to thank him for a delightful dining experience and said his waiters had been particularly gracious to me as a woman dining alone.

I introduced myself and explained my attempt at a reservation and the aid of Dario Mariotti at the Regent. He asked how I knew the Regent people and I explained I was a consultant specializing in professional effectiveness and had been to the Sydney Regent a number of times providing consulting services.

Sirio was very interested and started telling me about his sons and how he'd like one of them to talk to a consultant like me to offer an outside opinion on some business decisions. "Would you come tomorrow and meet him for lunch?" he asked.

"Sure, I'd enjoy that," I said.

The next day I had another delicious lunch at Le Cirque with the owner's son. We discussed his career options. I volunteered some direction. (Acting as the mentor!) He seemed happy with the advice.

When I returned to my hotel a message was waiting from Sirio Maccioni: "Please bring a friend and be my guest tomorrow night for dinner in thanks for your help to my son."

Remember, at the start of my story *I couldn't get a reservation*. Then by utilizing a network I ended up eating three meals in the next three days at this famous establishment! (That's just one benefit of networking.)

Unless you start a company, or buy one, you'll have to generate new opportunities *continually* in your career. Instead of reading a how-to-job-hunt book, circulating résumés to search firms and venture capitalists, or responding to the *Wall Street Journal* classifieds—work a chain of interconnected people and situations to develop business friendships.

What Path Do CEOs Take?

The CEO's path to success holds many turns: upbringing, education, mentors, and networking activity for instance. It also includes motivation and jobs.

CEOs have come from all different career starts: salesmen, staff accountants, technical writers, underwriters, lawyers, ministers, waiters, scientists, veterinarians, management trainees, assistants, juniors, nurses, to name a few.

Ford Motor Company CEO Alexander Trotman started as an executive trainee with the company forty years ago.

Miller Brewing Company CEO John McDonough was recruited from Anheuser-Busch Company, where he was responsible for the highly successful Bud Light product.

Calvin Klein Inc. CEO Gabriella Forte was recruited from rival Giorgio Armani. She is in her forties and had worked with Armani fifteen years, most recently as the executive vice president.

Olaf Olafsson, who runs Sony Corporation of America, is a novelist and best-selling author in his native Iceland.

After finishing high school in 1965, Hugh Smythe decided to skip college and become a member of the ski patrol. Today he runs three very successful ski resorts.

The leader in Hollywood for Creative Artists Agency (who represents people like Tom Cruise) is Robert Kavner, the former executive vice president of AT&T (and a former chief financial officer). Until Kavner's move to Hollywood, the word was he would succeed the AT&T chairman, Robert Allen.

The president of Children's World Learning Centers, Duane Larson, truly knows the people business. He has to; he is in the "little people" business. What route did he come up? Human resources, an unusual track for a CEO. He explains, "It keeps me keenly aware of what employees want and need to do their job."

Even from this small sampling you can see there is no specific route. Recruiters typically say the "complete CEO" has 40 percent experience in finance, 40 percent in marketing, and 20 percent from other functions. The function of finance leads, followed by operations, then sales and marketing as predominant routes up. There are fashionable functions that come and go, such as international business development or product management or technical work. You could start your career in the current fad and by the time you're seasoned enough to step onto the top ledge the fashion has changed.

As I write this, the business journals tout the trend of recruiting CFOs as CEOs. The previous month they proclaimed a zigzag path through different jobs and different companies to be the source of where CEO recruits were coming from, i.e., from technical work to business development to international business development to product general manager to finance or sales. The mistake is to think there is a predictable rise through a single discipline to ensure you the top spot. Obviously it's important to watch the events at the top of your organization (and others) to look at it as it ties into your interests.

> *The public accounting firm gave me well-rounded business background, but I wanted to learn about entrepreneurs so I joined a small company as vice president and treasurer. After some time there I knew I needed to learn how to structure financial deals so I became an assistant to the CFO of a larger company. I later joined a growing manufacturing company as a vice president and treasurer, and was eventually promoted to president. From there I was looking to grow through equity ownership and took a position as COO with Nextel [at that time a venture-backed early stage company].*
> —JOEL A. SCHLEICHER, COO,
> Nextel Communications, Inc.

Attempt to make a route for yourself that

- fits your interests,
- fulfills more than one of the company's needs,
- meets the requirements of the future business world,
- is transferable to other industries.

Regardless of the functions it's more important how you *function* in the functions. In other words, how you do your job.

Remember the trait "flexibility"? Every career path must have flexibility. You need to be able to deal with a variety of people, cultures, situations, problems, decisions, and technologies. You, of course, could not be expected to be an expert in everything or every aspect, but utilizing the Vital Traits, you will be able to handle most everything and every aspect of business.

Think about what we have discussed so far: *Tenacity* keeps you climbing back onto the hill after you've slid off because of a business swerve; *being inquisitive* allows you to explore and discover new routes that better suit your ability and the times; *being in control* of your attitude enables you to pick yourself up, dust yourself off, and present yourself to the next challenge and opportunity; needless to say, *courage* enables you to reach beyond what you've done and past where you previously failed to tenaciously try again. And since you are always trying to improve, you *learn* and get better in areas needed that enable you to move up the mountain. If you can maintain your sense of humor through all of the inevitable setbacks, despite how deliberate and detail oriented you are, you will get to the top eventually.

Résumé builders can occur at all points of your career—in the beginning, the middle, and at its height. It's been over twenty years since Harry Combs took over Gates Learjet, turning it into a profitable venture. Now in his early eighties, he had the first of a trilogy of books on the American West published. Lee Iacocca was in the auto industry for forty-seven years. At sixty-nine he remains a $500,000-a-year consultant to Chrysler. He gives six speeches a year at $60,000 each. He serves on the board of MGM Grand and New World Communications—in addition to traveling to his homes in California, Colorado, Michigan, and Italy.

Choosing a career path has to be based on what you enjoy, what you can do, what is needed in the marketplace, and what you want to do when you are finished. People usually think about the next step in their career. You must also think about the next step in your life. If your career path is successful and you make a financially profitable business, with good systems in place, you can likely step aside and it will continue. If it fails, it won't need you anyway. So either way you need to think about the next step in your life, regardless of success or failure. Otherwise, you'll have a big hole in your day-to-day life. (Interesting note: Accountemps surveyed a number of big-company executives: Half said they would become entrepreneurs, if they had the capital; the other half would retire, if they had the capital.)

A CEO who was into his second month on the job said, "I've had a steady progression upward, but it hasn't been planned. I never dreamed this would happen to me. It's unexpected. Yet I feel very comfortable in this position. But, I still find it surprising companies allow people like me to get to the top."

People luck into, happen into, scheme into, perform into, get recruited into CEO positions. Many had no idea, no thought, no dream of getting into such a situation. As NFL football coach Dan Reeves always says, "Take one game at a time." CEOs just took "one job at a time." On the other hand, some knew since childhood that they were destined to be CEOs.

> *I was born to be a CEO. I knew that right at the beginning. This [CEO position] was like coming home. I now have the opportunity to do what I could do. I always thought I'd be okay as the top guy. It's not just that I wanted to be the CEO but I felt I should be. It wasn't a power thing, just an attitude, a view, a way of looking at things.*
> —BOB HANSFORD, President,
> US Sprint, Canada

Take two people who have comparable intelligence, enthusiasm, education, and appearance. One becomes CEO of a multimillion-dollar operation. One becomes regional manager of the same company. What made the difference?

- One did more.
- One handled setbacks better.
- One utilized luck more.

Do more. Reuben Mark, COB, president, and CEO, Colgate-Palmolive Company, remembers his early days as a salesman: "I came back into the home office one day and heard people talking about a big sales meeting in another state. The personnel manager told me I couldn't attend (despite the fact my counterparts were attending from other offices). 'There is no budget for travel,' he told me. So I decided to pay for the trip myself. In the meeting one of the managers introduced me as 'Reuben paid to get here *himself.*' A bigger boss from New York heard that. Shortly after that I was brought back into the home office ahead of schedule. It's important to always try to do more than the next person. It's like I've told my kids, 'It's important to always try to do a little more than they expect.' Ask yourself, all the time, 'How can I make it better than expected?' "

Anyone at any level in any type of organization can be a risk taker by *risking* doing more than expected. Do what no one else does by two or three percent. You will surprise people by doing more than the job. You will stand out and likely have more fun.

Eight years into AT&T I had a midlevel job. A vice president called and asked me to present my ideas on a subject to the regional vice president. Unbeknownst to me, my eight peers were given the same task. The showed up at the meeting and all my peers were there. Some had a pad of paper with five ideas scribbled on it. Some had glossy presentations. Mine was modest but with a lot of solid information and analysis. Three months later I was promoted to a new job. It turns out there was an individual in the audience who was looking over people and I got the nod.

—RICHARD MCCORMICK
CEO, US West

To become a chief you have to *do more*. Why?

- Every bit of exertion adds to your career life preserver (a necessity for the ambitious).

  Note: I just used the word *ambitious*, and I meant it in a positive, productive, constructive way. Curt Carter said to me one time, "Remember when we used to use the word *ambitious* and it was a positive thing?" He meant that nowadays the word carries a negative meaning, a dog-eat-dog meaning. That is *not* my meaning.
- You seldom get fired for doing too much.
- You have less time to get involved in office politics or other problems.
- You might turn out to be a better human toward others because you feel better toward yourself. (Doing more builds self-esteem.)
- You can relish your success—and can eat better, buy nicer clothes, or buy a sharper car!

- You might turn out to be a better human toward others because you feel better toward yourself. (Doing more builds self-esteem.)
- You can relish your success—and can eat better, buy nicer clothes, or buy a sharper car!
- You become your own boss telling *you* what to do—regardless of the chain of command.

But when you *don't do more:*

- Your hopes and expectations (and demands) "while arms are folded" make you useless to the company.
- Nothing progresses, profits, or is attained.
- You desert yourself and commit career suicide.
- You will be discontented, worry, and not sleep well at night.
- Any exceptional genius or talent that you have will be wasted.
- You'll likely never get paid more—because you don't deserve more!

Now before you break out in a cold sweat concerned about the extra hours at the office—that is not what I mean by doing more. It's looking at the "fifth and sixth side" of the box, figuratively speaking.

If you do at least *one* of the following you'll likely be doing more than your competition:

- Work happily.
- Be inventive.
- Be ingenious.

- Be active.
- Be enterprising.
- Concentrate.
- Be honest.
- Enliven work.
- Exalt in work.
- Be extremely tenacious.
- Be constantly improving.
- Be nice.
- Be straightforward.
- Be willing to fight for your people.
- Be humorous.
- Be detail oriented.
- Be willing to lead.
- Work without hesitation.
- Work without complaint.

My friend Henry Dubroff, business editor of the *Denver Post*, said I was a "goody two-shoes" with recommendations like these. But let me ask you: If you were the boss, wouldn't you expect or want the above qualities from your employees?

At any point in your career, you're capable of being seen or being recognized for your unique way of working. Most people fail to take advantage of the opportunity presented. Don Hewitt, executive producer of *60 Minutes*, was talking about his show's success on the air: "I don't have the formula for success, but I do have the formula for failure: Rest on your laurels."

As the bumper sticker I saw on a Rolls Royce in Palm Springs read, "If your ship hasn't come in, swim out to it."

I literally have a brass ring hanging over my chair in my office. I believe in the theory that if a brass ring swings by you, you have to grab it. I don't believe in overanalyzing.
——BRIAN HICKEY
President and CEO,
Harlequin Enterprises

Do less worrying, scheming, planning, dreaming— simply do more.

Handle setbacks. CEOs, like you and me, meet unanticipated and sudden changes in their progress. They have boom times. Go bust. Boom again. They get passed over for a promotion, have a job terminated, make a colossal mistake or get to the realization that they are not doing what they want to do with the people they want to do it with.

How do they handle setbacks?

They realize their efforts will occasionally be thwarted. It does not derail them for long. They get back on track. Unlike one young climber who actually said to me, "If I lost, I'd just have to kill myself."

Think of the alternative to not handling setbacks. Succumbing.

Your setbacks will occur where you aren't looking for them. When they come, remember the following:

- They aren't a curse (they are life).
- They are a blessing (if you choose to see a different perspective).

- Be thankful for them (because then you'll learn).

Great people confront and overcome setbacks. Overcoming the difficulty becomes a tool they put to use to conquer the next setback, thus enabling them to build a career, not wait and hope good things will happen to them.

Overcoming setbacks

- energizes you,
- strengthens you,
- increases your resolve,
- makes you self-reliant,
- improves self-confidence.

Always have a plan B, C, and D. You know you're going to be challenged. Prepare for the possibility. Prethink potential situations that could happen—and not happen. Think out what your alternatives are. Ask yourself what Mr. Big would do, or what others involved would do. Look at the perspective from all involved. Ask yourself what are the minimum and the maximum power you have in the situation.

Learn from setbacks. Let them wake you up and shake you up. Then handle it, learn from it, so you don't have to handle *that* particular setback again. You will have the same disappointments your competitors have. They might not get through them. You can.

People who have "made it" have as many, maybe

more, problems than those who don't. The differentiating factor is what one does about them.

Success will be determined by what you allow yourself to do despite a temporary letdown.

Christopher Palmeri at *Forbes* describes the CEO of General Instrument: "Sidelined by a painful gall bladder ailment in Germany several years ago, Daniel Akerson decided to take things into his own hands. He pulled the tubes out of his arm, checked himself out of the hospital, and then got on a plane for the States. 'The German doctors were not moving fast enough,' the U.S. Naval Academy graduate complained.

"Pulling out the tubes is the kind of thing Akerson seems to do constantly. Right now he's doing it as chairman of General Instrument, the Chicago-based cable television equipment supplier."

Akerson says, "I want turmoil; I want excitement." His attitude didn't go unnoticed by Bert Roberts, the chairman of his former company, MCI, who says about Akerson's aggressive style, "It's one of his great managerial skills."

Utilize luck. Chance, fate, luck—whatever you call it—there is a far greater force in success than we're willing to admit. Brian Hickey, president and CEO of Harlequin Enterprises, related this story: "I was a protestor in college against the Vietnam War. I had no interest in business people. After four years I graduated with a degree in 'esoteric arts,' then moved home. A month after I got there, my parents said it was time I got a job. Begrudgingly I took a train to the nearest city. Got off. I knew the business district was south so I started walking east. I walked past a building that was an insurance company. Out of curiosity I went in and asked the security guard, 'How does one get a job here?' He sent me to personnel to take a test. I did. Personnel graded it and said I had the highest score ever. Within the hour I had met with the vice president of personnel and he offered me a job as an underwriter. Four months into the job they doubled my salary and gave me a promotion. I decided to try the GMAT test for business school and they reported back I had a 'rare score.' From business school I joined General Foods, then S.C. Johnson & Son, Inc., where I got my Ph.D. in marketing. I spent some time running the Asian division and was recruited by Harlequin. It was all a complete fluke."

Denis Brown, CEO of Pinkertons, grew up in California, but twenty years of his career were spent in New Jersey. He was educated in the west. When the company he worked for in the east wanted to develop operations in California, Denis got the nod because as they told him, "We need someone who understands California." Luck.

When one of my clients, Goeff, was a twenty-one-year-old junior accountant he found a statistical error that caused a significant flaw in a test program that was headed up by the financial vice president. Mathematically Geoff was right, but the embarrassed vice president would not give him an audience. On the weekends Geoff gave flying lessons. One Saturday his student was the *senior* vice president over the financial vice president. The senior vice president really liked Geoff's instructing expertise. Geoff brought the conversation around to the boss at work and explained the statistical error. The senior vice president concurred and "blessed" Geoff to correct the test. Luck.

Another lucky break came when he got to hand-carry a proposal for a new product to the CEO of the company. "Others were on vacation, it was my idea, and the boss was leaving town so if it was to be done, I had to do it," explained Geoff.

Luck does play a part in most everyone's climb. But do not count on or hope for luck. Don't trust luck. Luck turns. The best luck might be no luck, so you don't count on luck being repeated.

When David Fuente, who had just finished turning around Sherwin-Williams' paint stores, was being sought by a headhunter for CEO of Office Depot, he really wasn't interested. But being congenial, he said, "Look, I'm going to play golf that day. If it rains I'll drive over and have a peek." It rained. Was that luck? Who knows. It was just a set of circumstances surrounding a situation. The perspective you take about it determines whether it is luck or not.

Luck is extremely difficult to give credit or blame to, to hope for and wish against. Luck isn't an act, it is an attitude. An attitude that comes from effective utilization of traits that help you become even more near-perfect than you already are!

PERSONAL PR

If you do good work, you have to let people know what you've done. Of course, you have to be subtle also. A strong ego means you're confident and know your strength. A large ego is always looking for recognition, constantly in need of a pat on the back. Strong egos can effectively utilize publicity. Large egos give it a bad reputation and subsequently mis-use publicity. (You can be publicly modest but still get out the message about your talents.)

There are two main reasons for managing your own ongoing personal public relations campaign.

1. *Visibility*—inside and outside of your day-in-day-out work environment. It keeps you on people's minds.
2. *Credibility*. They'll say, "She must be good; she's always being written about."

Outside of hiring someone to do PR for you, you can take specific steps yourself.

- Write or contribute to a corporate newsletter.
- Join (and be active in) trade or professional associations. (Select some whose members are the type you need to be around; get elected to an office.)
- Take part in town meetings and community activities.

- Write letters to the editors of selected publications.
- Write editorials, for the "Manager's Journal" column in the *Wall Street Journal* or for your city newspaper.
- Send out press releases about your department, as appropriate.
- Send announcements of your promotions to the media. (Then send copies to recruiters. *Consultant News*, Templton, New Hampshire, publishes a directory of executive search firms.)
- Take part in significant social activities.
- Teach at a college.
- Earn an award or honor.
- Join boards of directors and advisory boards.
- Write a business book.
- Give speeches.

The list is endless. The key is to be creative and tenacious. Sporadic efforts might bring you some recognition, but consistent effort sets you up as "someone to know." It keeps you prepared.

You should always be prepared to contribute when called upon.

- Have something valuable for others to know.
- Organize your thoughts and points so you're understandable.
- Illustrate points with stories, anecdotes, and metaphors.
- Be able to shut up and not blurt out something you wish you hadn't said.

- Develop a voice people are able to listen to.
- Have a current, interesting, worthwhile bio on yourself.
- Have a photograph of yourself that you're pleased with.
- And then utilize all of this on a regular basis.

You don't have to go to the extreme of Donald Trump, but there is a lot of area to work in between what a person like Trump does and what you are currently doing. You don't want to overtly blast your own horn, but you have to let people know what you're doing.

Suppose your personal public relations efforts pay off and you find yourself in front of a camera? . . .

How Should You Handle a Television Interview?

With five hundred potential television channels plus all the corporate in-house videotaping and video-conferencing potential, you'll be on screen sometime in your life. Probably sooner than you hoped and more than you like.

The big difference between real life and television is that anything you do incorrectly on tape is exaggerated and recorded for posterity.

When you find out that you are going to be appearing in the little black box, arrange for a good-

pany promotion, video résumé, or, if nothing else, something to show at the family reunion.

There are some things you should keep in mind about being in front of the camera.

Expect to be uncomfortable. Expect the unnaturalness. There are men in business suits wearing pancake makeup, there are red lights on cameras going off and on, there is a fake office or living room set up in the middle of a warehouse-type studio, there are teleprompters, there's an earphone hidden in your ear, it's hot under the piercing lights, numerous people are acting very harried, scurrying around, and then you hear the seconds counted down; three, two, one and the red "on air" sign lights up.

Watch the show (or view tapes of the format) beforehand. Carefully observe the style, habits, idiosyncrasies of the interviewer/reporter you'll be talking with.

Plan the points you want to make. Initiate points or questions. Have courage to bridge between the interviewer's questions and your points. Don't wait for permission. If you do, to the camera you'll appear nervous and hesitant.

Notify friends, family, or co-workers about your TV appearance in advance. Note the time, date, and subject. Whether you do a good job or not, and whether they tune in or not, at least they were informed that you were on. (That's public relations.)

Notify friends, family, or co-workers about your TV appearance in advance. Note the time, date, and subject. Whether you do a good job or not, and whether they tune in or not, at least they were informed that you were on. (That's public relations.)

Plan to inject some humor into your answers. Go in with the attitude of using humor.

Prepare your points as sound bites. Make points succinctly, with analogies, metaphors, or stories to illustrate them. Remember, sometimes a two-hour filming session gets reduced to two minutes of air time. If you're being interviewed several times on the same subject, give fresh answers each time. Tony Bennett has sung "I Left My Heart (in San Francisco)" thousands of times. You may have to answer the same question a few more times than you'd like, but each time you must make the effort to have a fresh-sounding answer. Practice by taping a mock interview.

Gesture around your upper chest and shoulder area. That's all the camera is likely to pick up. Point into the camera maybe once. Pretend as if your entire body is being photographed at all times, because you never know when the cameraman will do a long shot. Keep nervous toe-tapping, ring-twisting, and knee-bouncing to a minimum if not totally nonexistent.

If there is a table, rest your hand on top of the table. Try to do this asymmetrically so you don't look like you're holding hands with yourself. In a sofa or chair, make sure your upper body is asymmetrical—meaning one arm on the armrest and one on your lap versus both on the armrests or both on the lap.

Check your posture. If you walk onto a set or off, make sure you stand up and sit down with good posture.

Take time. Don't rush in. Don't rush to shake hands or be too quick with a response. Touch the host if possible (hand, forearms, shoulders are acceptable areas). It's subtle but powerful control (in addition to giving him/her an effective handshake). Lean away from the back of the chair. Don't sit back and look like they are firing questions at you.

Don't watch the camerapeople or others milling around. If you do, to viewers you'll look like a robot head.

Don't wear a patterned shirt/dress/suit. A dark, solid suit with a white, preferably not a stark white, shirt.

Follow up with a note to the interviewer. Perhaps share the positive comments of friends and associates.

When you're watching the videotape of yourself later, bear in mind, you will look differently than you think you do. And no matter how good you look, it probably won't look good to you.

How to Be Photographed

You may not enjoy having your photograph taken, but the higher you go up in a organization the more of a public figure you become. Whether for the society papers or the annual report, you'll likely need to allow photographs of yourself.

A formal studio shot will be controlled by the photographer, the expert. However, you can go in prepared with samples of professional shots clipped from magazines or annual reports that you like. Showing the photographer what you want is much easier than just describing it.

But sometimes you are at an annual sales meeting, convention, or community event where there is a roaming photographer and you are likely to be a victim. Keep certain things in mind to control the results and end up with the best possible candid photos.

- When the photographer asks you to pose, turn your body at a slight angle; don't face directly into the camera. (At a slight angle you'll look thinner.)
- Take a second to correct anything about your appearance that needs attention. Remove your name tag, button your jacket and straighten your tie, etc.
- Avoid appearing dull to the camera. Smile.
- Don't be photographed holding a beverage. A drink glass limits the future use of the photo, requires cropping, and projects an image you

could regret later. (More often than not, it's death to a politician.) Develop a quick reflex to put the drink in hand behind your back.

These are details that go along with the big job of running the show. Anytime you think they are unnecessary for you, you're wrong. Many people have made that mistake; don't you do it.

Becoming a chief is a complete package of activities. Some you will enjoy and some you are obligated to do whether you like it or not.

Parts of becoming a CEO were given to you, parts you have to give yourself. You can do little about your upbringing, early environment, education, or previous jobs. You *can* do a lot about continuing education, the mentoring relationships nurture, the networking activities you involve yourself in, the fact you choose to do more than the next or not do more, your ability to handle and grow from setbacks rather than be overwhelmed by them, and of course there is the part about luck.

Some of the activities you may not enjoy on your journey of moving up the organization is the fact that you have to let people know you are good as well as being good. That takes personal public relations initiated and supported by your efforts to let people know how valuable you are. You may not like to blast your own horn, most near-perfects don't, but you do have to deliberately, purposefully, effectively, modestly, and honestly make an impact on people. All of these components are part of your path to becoming a mountaineer.

How Chiefs Become Chiefs Summary

Chiefs come from all walks of life—including the wrong side of the mountain. Change paths as necessary but keep climbing.

Get a mentor who
- knows the territory and routes,
- knows where he (or she) is going,
- knows where you want to go,
- knows how to traverse the terrain,
- is willing to advise you.

Network (i.e., crisscross your connections constantly).
- Anticipate and accept feelings of discomfort.
- Initiate contact.
- Expect acceptance of your efforts.
- Do for others before you ask of others.
- Maintain contact.
- Keep a log of your activity, contacts, and progress.

Do more than what others do by at least three percent.

Handle setbacks. Do not let them derail you.

Utilize the luck factor in life. But don't trust luck; luck turns. Depend on skill.

CHAPTER 9

Ascending the Peak

Moving from the number-two to the number-one position

Until you actually do a job you don't fully know what it will be like. *How to Think Like a CEO* will give you insight before you get the position, to keep you from getting lost or dealing with dangers you hadn't bargained for. When you are down the mountain the visibility at the top gets reduced because the summit can be wrapped in gray, wet, thick clouds. But you can disperse that fog so when you move from different ledges to the top perch you are prepared.

> *I had been on the job for only a few days when I had to make a very big decision. All of a sudden I looked back at a tough CEO I know and saw his performance from a totally different perspective. . . .The big difference is the realization, I have to make the decisions. For twenty-five years, I've been*

analyzing issues and problems, then present-
ing to the boss for a decision. Now all of a
sudden there wasn't anybody else to go to. I
was the last guy! I was stuck with it. I swal-
lowed hard and made the call. . . . Occa-
sionally the thought comes across my mind,
I miss working for some of the good bosses
I've had; I wish I could just make a recom-
mendation. Yet I can't stand the thought of
not being the one to make the decision. I'd
die if I couldn't make the decision.
—SAM SANDERSON
President and COO,
Rogers Network Services

At the number-two position (or whatever position
you are in) you are the person somewhat behind the
scene, likely engaged at every level and maybe even
running the show (in some situations) without the
glory that number one gets. The key decision you need
to make is if you want to be a good support person or
become the leader.

Your acceptance of the 22 Vital Traits and ability
to incorporate them into your work style is the first
step. Your thorough comprehension of what kind of
environment you're in—entrepreneurial or not—determines the approach you can take. That, combined
with your continued efforts at networking and mentoring, *while doing exemplary work*, will get you the
nod.

When you succeed in making the move to number

one from number two you can expect to discover the following situations:

1. You'll ask yourself, "What do I do now?" The first time anyone goes in as a quarterback it is natural to wonder, at least a little, if one can do it.

   Your skill-set of Vital Traits needs to rev up; you'll want to work a little harder to make sure you avoid failure. You'll basically have to go all out to prove to yourself and others that you can do the chief's job.

2. You will no longer have the same people looking over your shoulder. There will be different people to tell you what to do. Some of the ones who used to direct you are now directed by you. *You* are now the decision maker for those people. Where before you could rely on someone else, it's up to you.

3. The day after the promotion announcement has been made, constituents will come into your office or call you on the telephone and expect solutions to problems. Instantly you're in the spotlight for solving issues. You'll have to be prepared to resolve rocky issues *right away*.

4. You'll be in the enviable position of being able to say no to certain groups you've never been able to say that to before. You'll also be able to say yes. Pronouncing either word gives you power. The critical requirement is saying one or the other, though! An inability to make de-

cisions strips your power. And now, as number
one, your action (or inaction) is more visible
to more people. You can't back down now.

5. You'll have a number of new outside-of-the-
direct-job demands on your time. They will be
more than you expected and planned for or
want to have. With power comes obligations.
Corporate socializing, representing the organization at civic events, public speaking for your
department, and similar activities increase proportionately with steps up the mountain.
(You'll probably wish you had spent more
time preparing for the corporate affairs and
political side of being the top person.)

6. You will discover new enemies among your
former peers and friends, i.e., the other people
who wanted the job that *you* got. They might
feel disappointed, jealous, and maybe experience loss of face. You *will* likely need them as
you take the lead. One of your first tasks will
be to win those people over onto your climbing
team right away. If you don't you'll lose their
contributions or they might attempt to sabotage yours. Now more than ever it's your time
to take the initiative, make determinations, and
handle the potential setbacks caused by co-
workers.

7. You'll find that you are all of a sudden surrounded with more yes-men (and -women)
than at any other time in your life. Some want
to please and help; some want to ingratiate
themselves. As uncomfortable as it is, you

have to sort through the yes-people and seek out the no and maybe people. They will be the ones most honest with you. The last thing you can allow is people who say one thing to your face and a different thing behind your back.

8. You will have many people insist on meeting with you. These are the same people that prior to your becoming number one had no time for or interest in you, even though you had tried to meet with them. Again you have to sort out the ones who simply want to become popular with you versus the ones who want to join and support your climbing efforts.

9. You will no longer have much of a buffer between you and the mountaineers. Now you are accountable for most things. You have direct contact with more of the Mr. Bigs in the business. You have more authority too, fortunately. Still you want to be careful (which doesn't mean you fear taking risks). Because of the higher visibility and fewer people to fall back on, you'll have to slow down and think things through more. Mistakes cost more at towering levels.

10. You'll realize the job is not that difficult if you work diligently. You are doing many of the same things you did when you were lower down the mountain. It's just that some zeros have been added to the money you're responsible for and hopefully the money you make. You might even find your office is bigger and there is a lock on the door!

There is the possibility you will move to number one from farther down the ladder than number two. The more distance between your current position and the chief slot the greater the number of changes and surprises you'll likely encounter. Monte Roulier was an intern in my office during the summer of his final year at DePauw. After graduation he joined a new company, Service Adventure, Inc., that was doing business in Russia and central Asia. He hit the deck as a fresh-faced, energetic, bright young man who so impressed the founder of the company that within seven months the founder made Roulier the president of the company. That required a *fast* learning situation for the new mountaineer.

Regardless of the job level you leave to take over the top position, there will be changes. No matter how much you prepare, anticipate, and plan, surprises will occur at rapid speed. If you've worked on the Vital Traits all along, you'll be far better prepared than the next person. Actually, if you're working on those traits all along that is probably the reason you got the nod for the top job!

CRITICISM

Regardless of how effective you are, you will get criticism. There are people who feel that giving critiques is in their job description. The higher you go up the mountain the better view others have to find fault.

That is part of the price one pays for being an emerging mountaineer. It's best to learn to take criticism and give it rather than futilely try to avoid it.

One CEO who takes criticism as a chance to improve said, "We put in a suggestion box six years ago. Some of the comments zinged me: 'You are arrogant and hard to work with sometimes'; 'You don't intend to but you make comments that border on sexual harassment'; 'You should lose weight and stop smoking.' I've changed half of those things. That box has helped me communicate from the bottom up. But as the CEO I feel like I am wearing bull's-eyes in all directions. Many days have felt like someone put me inside a clothes dryer, threw in a couple of pairs of tennis shoes, and kept it running all day long."

> *It's healthy to be criticized. It gives you a pause for introspection, and an opportunity for improvement. I encourage a certain amount, but it does depend on who I'm hearing it from.*
> —BILL BLOUNT
> President, Power Motive Corporation

Chiefs get criticism from everyone, all the time, deserved and undeserved. Top people get it more than others because they are an easier target. If a CEO tried to respond to all the criticism levied from all the constituents, it'd be a full-time effort.

When dealing with criticism, consider the source. People frequently attack you for their own weaknesses. Those who hunt for blemishes, the severest critics, often have failed themselves. (Plagiarists are always suspicious of being copied, for example.)

Criticism can make you mad, even if you might deserve it. If you follow these steps, you'll minimize a negative reaction.

- Don't lash back.
- Talk about the conflict or criticism when it happens if possible.
- Ask questions.
- Allocate a limited, specific amount of time to evaluate the comment.
- Evaluate yourself honestly.
- If wrongly accused, calmly deny or vehemently deny once.
- Acknowledge your actions.
- Accept the reality that a certain percent of the population will not like you.

Don't lash back. Defensiveness makes one look guilty. Try to lean over backward to avoid overreacting.

> *I used to write page after page to defend myself against an unwarranted attack. Now I let it roll off my back. Age has a lot to do with what is important and what is not.*
> —MARIE MCDONALD, President,
> Access Disability Advisors/
> McDonald Elevator

Talk about the conflict or criticism when it happens if possible. Putting it off makes it grow out of proportion.

If the comment was made in person, right then and there ask, "What do you mean by that?" (Be sure to ask with a relaxed facial expression and tone of voice. Do not go for the jugular.) Then be quiet and let the person answer. If not clear, ask again, "I'm still not sure if I understand. What do you mean?" Again, ask a third time. As I said before, it often takes three queries to get to the heart of the issue. Stopping at one or two is insufficient. Most people give criticism in writing because they feel safe doing so. They know they won't be confronted as readily.

Ask questions. And continue to ask until you fully understand and agree on how to handle similar situations in the future. Listen. Seek real substantial facts.

Allocate a limited, specific amount of time to evaluate the comment. Consider the source, the relationship, and the situation. If there is some truth to the comment, decide how to make a change. If the comment was not deserved, dismiss it.

Evaluate yourself honestly. Was the comment valid? Consider the complaint people make about you. It is often their own weaknesses or problems that they transfer onto you. Take the complaint seriously, not personally. Look at it and check for accuracy.

Later tell the person, "I'm always open to constructive criticism. Thanks for taking the time to better explain things"—and mean it.

If wrongly accused, calmly deny or vehemently deny once. Ignore the accusation. Ignore the person. Some people aren't worth worrying about. Go on with your life. Forget it. Laugh it off. Defuse with humor. Expect it. Control your thoughts to remind yourself of the good comments versus the bad ones. Don't remember the negative only.

Acknowledge your actions. If you did something differently than expected, immediately ask openly and honestly, "What can be done now?" Ask for an accurate assessment, not an emotional, opinionated one.

> *I used to stew about it; now I'm not so thin-skinned. I take a broader perspective. If I'm blindsided for something when I am just flat-out wrong, I'll fess up and fix it.*
> —LINN LEEBURG
> Executive Vice President and
> COO, WestGas

Accept the reality that a certain percent of the population will not like you. And they are never going to like you. Jealousy is the root of a lot of it. Expect it. Be aware of that fact and condition yourself for it. Remind yourself that life goes on.

If comments are presented as constructive criticism but are really personal attacks, follow the first four steps listed above anyway. Always talk issues, not people.

> *I don't take criticism as well as I should. But as I wean myself from day-to-day operations, I can look back and be more objective. They are probably right. I made decisions people didn't agree with or what I said irritated people.*
> —VIC MILLA
> CEO, New Method Textile Services

"I turn on the farmer routine—stutter, stammer, draw pictures on the floor with my toes, look embarrassed—all the time while my position is being bashed. *Then* when I have my five minutes to present my case, I'm forthright, to the point, and tell them what they want to hear, rather quickly," explains one CEO.

When I asked about others doing the same to him, he responded, "One advantage I have is the ability to pick out these fakers really quickly. You know the saying, 'Don't get into a pissing match with a skunk.'"

> *How do you handle criticism? Face up to it. Correct the situation or improve communication if that's the problem. You can't eliminate mistakes if you are doing things but you can face up to them and hopefully benefit from them. Then keep moving.*
> —WILLIAM WALLACE
> CEO, Phoenix Home Life

If you truly want to set an example of keeping the lines of communication open, you have to take criticism—particularly if you've asked for feedback. Remember, criticism will sting a little; you might be embarrassed, even insulted, but you must not overreact. Don't take any action that looks like retaliation then or later. Listen. Say thanks. Think about it. Register if there is accuracy and change as necessary. Casually thank the person later again.

A question I get asked a lot is "How much criticism can I give my boss?" Let me answer it regardless of your chief's title, even if he is the CEO.

- Don't get carried away with criticizing the boss or anyone, particularly if they specifically ask you for feedback. That is, don't go on and on. Make your points, then stop.
- Don't criticize in public. The conversation should be between only the people directly involved. Ideally you and the other person only.
- Remember, even those who openly welcome criticism don't always mean it.
- Consider your own motivation. If it's to retaliate, to look smart, or curry favor—forget it. It won't work.
- Be particularly good at your job so you speak from an effective perspective and you have his respect.
- Keep your comments to a short list of three. No more.

- Don't speak of the criticism to others unless you say it with the same tone and use the same words you say directly to the boss.
- Follow up with something positive.

At Sun Microsystems, the CEO, Scott McNealy, has an open e-mail policy, like an "open-door" policy. People are welcome to voice criticism upward. McNealy says he receives two or three suggestions a day, some of which get passed to appropriate departments and some of which stay with him. Other companies have similar policies with the option for anonymous messages.

Two truisms of criticism:

1. As you build confidence, criticism won't bother you so much.
2. Criticism falls harder on your ears if you're rife with self-doubt already.

GIVING CRITICISM TO OTHERS

You cannot hide dissatisfaction with some aspects of co-workers' work. You do have to constructively engage in candid conversation if you're going to get anywhere. Your fellow hikers and climbers prefer and feel more secure knowing exactly where you stand on issues. You remove ambiguity.

I presented some bum [wrong] information. Instantly I realized I was wrong. My boss did too. Privately, one-on-one, he reamed me out. But he did it in such a way that when I left I said to myself, I'll die before I let this guy down again.
            —WILLIAM PERRY PENDLEY
            President and Chief Legal Officer,
            Mountain States Legal Foundation

Many bosses complain that subordinates take critique as a personal attack. They say, "I can't say anything without the employee taking it personally and thinking I don't like them. Nothing is wrong with them, it's the way they did a specific job that I didn't like." (This comment is made most often by male bosses about female co-workers.)

There are some things you should think about when you need to *criticize* co-workers.

- Remember how it feels to get it before you give it.
- Plan a private time to clearly and simply explain your criticism and what you want in the future.
- Maintain an even tone of voice and facial expression. (Don't apologize, coddle, or get nervous.)
- If questioned, repeat your critique. Don't take it as a challenge. Stick to the issue and don't personalize.
- Keep the conversation confidential.

- Set a good example; don't practice a "Do as I say, not as I do" philosophy.
- At another time, compliment the person you have criticized on something they have done well. Simply, clearly state, "I appreciated your work when you . . ."
- Always be firm, fair, and consistent.
- Separate performance from personality.

Whether you're providing a requested or unrequested critique to the boss, a co-worker, friend, or spouse, be aware of certain points.

First, keep in mind that everyone will act differently regardless how well-thought-out your approach is. It's hard to judge. Their self-confidence and personality are the key to how they will react. Regardless, don't avoid bringing up the difficult. At least you'll know their reaction and attitude rather than getting an ulcer for the next three years trying to figure out what to do.

Second, take the time to research the person's background. How good is he at his job? Is he new and still testing the waters? Has he been with the company forever and doesn't care about it? Does he "own" his job, where he truly cares with all his passion to do the best possible? More information on why the person is a certain way helps you understand him and therefore address him more effectively.

Third, with the problem clearly identified (and what you want to achieve clear), initiate the conversation with the person. You might pose the problem to the individual at fault in a third-person form. For example, say, "Joe, if you had someone you work with who should be told about a distracting habit, how would you go about doing that?" Listen to his answer and ask, "That's a good idea, anything else you'd do?" Listen to his answer, and a third time ask, "Good, anything else come to mind?" Then do what he suggests. (Note: Don't expect consistency. Some people will fly off the handle when they are criticized no matter how they are approached. And some CEOs have been known to fire people for the same things they congratulate them for and encourage them to do. But regardless of the uncertainty and risk it is always better to take care of problem issues than simply hope they will go away.)

If you have regular meetings or a company newsletter or e-mail that encourages "issues of concern," use the forum to bring up your issue. Write it in a "potential problem" format that does not even hint at attack but simply discusses the topic.

You might discover that you have a fair-minded supervisor who has been enforcing what his boss has dictated and he's relieved to hear a differing opinion. He may now have more ammunition to confront his own supervisor to make changes. Or you may find you have a pure jerk to work with and you have a choice to put up with it or move on.

My final advice regarding taking and giving constructive criticism:

To take: Ask, ask, ask for it.

To give: Give very, very, very, very little. But do give when needed, and do it right.

We've looked at the changes (or surprises) you can expect moving to the number-one position from somewhere down the path. With any move up there is a cost. A significant price to pay is being the target for incessant criticism. But as in all things in life there is a reward for moving up. In the case of CEOs, one reward is their latitude to be eccentric!

LET'S PEEK BEHIND THE SCENES AT THE TOP

Since every chief is unique (just as all humans are), it's a mistake to make major conclusions from limited exposure. One purpose of this book is to provide you an up-close, personal report on chiefs and how they think.

Having so much direct contact and exposure, plus learning about CEOs from reliable sources, I've seen behind the scenes of the top people.

The human side is interesting. It's eye-opening how the CEOs of IBM or Exxon or Pepsi or United Airlines (and on and on through the list) are just like you and me. True, they might live in bigger houses, have more money, know more important people, wield more power, go on more exclusive vacations, and own fancier toys (e.g., yachts, jets, ranches, cars, art), but as humans we are all alike.

I do admit there are some dissimilarities. A CEO of a prestigious company is likely to have standing reservations and his own table at the better restaurants where the maitre d' knows his favorite drink. (When one particular CEO I know finishes with his meal, his favorite waiter automatically brings a "doggie bag" of shrimp from the salad bar for the CEO to take home to his cat.) Some CEOs rent islands for their summer getaway or visit the islands on their sixty-foot motor cruisers. They have his-and-her Harleys beside the Ferraris and Rolls Royce parked in their garages or in the extra space in their jet hangars. They've gone to Betty Ford's clinic; their spouses have been to European "fat farms." Their children have trust funds that set them up financially for the rest of their lives. They buy original art, not prints. Instead of just going to Vail at Christmas they also hop over to Antarctica to view the penguins. When they consider moving to a new city, they interview the mayor of that city, not just the Century 21 representative. Money received from fat paychecks allows a lot of these dissimilarities.

Regardless of the money, all of mankind is very similar. These same CEOs worry about their kids on drugs, have a favorite pet, visit in-laws, divorce, experience heartache, like their team to win (especially when they own the team!), get sick, sometimes get tongue-tied, forget to carry pocket money to pay the baby-sitter, get awed by celebrities, grow beards on vacation, get voice-mail messages messed up, question themselves, like to read their own press clips, overuse the television remote control, drive beyond the speed limit, mourn a parent's death, don't like aging, get scared sometimes, have midlife crises, go bald, go deaf, forget anniversaries, perspire when nervous, save paper clips, overeat, fear dentists, lose virility, like praise, take the free shampoos and soaps from hotels, get in fist fights, pick their noses, aren't always politically correct, get angry, cry. . . .

My guess is you can relate to about 80 percent of the above list.

Just as some humans have idiosyncratic eccentricities, there are CEOs that do. The following are some of the ones that stood out to me. (For obvious reasons these are intended to be totally anonymous.)

CEO "Jane" always travels with a particular pillow. It's the same one she has slept on since high school, and she has total insomnia if she doesn't use that particular pillow. She had a canvas briefcase sewn to carry it incognito on airplanes.

CEO "Joe" has a stuffed rabbit and bear tucked into the corner of his private sleeping compartment on the corporate jet.

CEO "Bill" makes each Sunday a "no-talk day." From sunup to sundown, he speaks to no one.

CEO "Al" has been in therapy for twenty years. He always travels on business *with* his therapist and his personal trainer.

CEO "Bob" takes a grand nap every Sunday. He explains, "I have a glass of wine, put on a sweat suit, switch on the ceiling fan, turn on some music, slip onto my down mattress, elevate the foot of my bed, and sleep for an hour while my friends are out playing golf or tennis."

CEO "Dave" has sixty-seven working televisions in his house along with two swimming pools and a fireman's pole.

CEO "Carl" sleeps on a single mattress on the floor. His entire house is furnished with one sofa and one chair at the dining table. Nothing else. Not even a curtain on the shower.

CEO "Ralph" has a strict understanding with his stockbroker: "The instant he opens his mouth to give me a recommendation, he's fired. I make the decision of what I'll buy and sell; he just executes the sale."

CEO "William" has homes in San Diego, Phoenix, Las Vegas, Kaanapalli, and Palm Springs with identical kitchens—same pots, silverware, dishes, and food inventory in each. Bathrooms are identically stocked as well. When he finds some new appliance he likes he automatically buys five of them and has them shipped to the different locations.

CEO "Dale" lives in a mansion reminiscent of the old *Dynasty* television show with twin descending staircases into the foyer. He does his own wallpapering, fixes his own car, and hitchhikes into town for replacement parts.

CEO "Cliff" lives in an apartment above the factory so secretly almost none of his employees know he's there.

CEO "Phil" *sketches* his daily activities on his calendar. One calendar day had a pictorial rendition of him meeting the mayor, giving a speech at a chamber of commerce meeting, and firing a manager, complete with guillotine.

CEO "Bill" goes to country-and-western bars and dances across the floor—even participating onstage with the musicians' gag routines. His blue-collar employees unknowingly stand beside him not recognizing him because there would be "no way" their company CEO would be in a place like this!

CEOs can be eccentric and just plain wild. A group of CEOs gathered at a Colorado ski resort. The evening started out as a 1950s flashback with hot dogs and Rice Crispy treats on the menu, and the Everly Brothers onstage. The evening progressed to six male CEOs dancing onstage wearing only women's pantyhose and fur coats. Meanwhile, a number of the CEOs in the audience were dancing along with the music *on top* of the dinner tables in their long underwear!

There is a human side of the CEO—even your CEO!

ASCENDING THE PEAK SUMMARY

What can you expect when you finally reach the top?

- A little apprehension and questioning, "What do I do now?"
- There will be fewer people to tell you what to do.
- You'll have the power to say no more than you had in the past.
- You'll have more and different demands on your time than you expected.
- You will discover new enemies among former friends.
- You'll find yourself surrounded by yes-men (and -women).
- You will be expected to solve problems and make decisions sooner.
- You'll realize there is another mountain to climb.

CHAPTER 10

CEOs in Action

What exactly do they do at the top?

I asked Larry Johnson, COB and CEO of the Bank of Hawaii, what exactly he does as CEO. He paused, smiled, and humorously said, "I'd have to think about it." (If someone asked you for an explanation about what you do, you'd probably have the same answer! It's tough to dissect exactly what one does in a job—particularly the CEO.) The job title "Chief Executive Officer" encompasses a vast range of activities. The CEO job is considerably more difficult than it appears, not that it requires supreme intelligence or extraordinary competence but because it takes so much of everything one could list as requirements for any and all job positions!

So Larry pulled out his calendar from the day before and told me about his schedule.

6:20 A.M.   Out of the house.
7:45   Finished at the gym.
8:00   In the office.
             Read local papers and the *Wall Street*

	Journal. Breakfast with staff without a set agenda. ["We just talk about philosophy and direction. It's amazing how fast word spreads regarding what we talk about, plus the fact that I hold the meetings," explained Johnson.]
9:00	Credit committee meeting.
10:00	Testimonial dinner planning meeting for an employee who has been with the bank for forty-two years.
10:30	Met the son of a Wells Fargo executive and friend who heads up the finance committee for a woman running for governor.
11:00	Met with the brother-in-law of a friend who is new in town and wants to get the lay of the land.
11:30	Met with a state representative about the local symphony funding.
12:00 P.M.	Canceled lunch with a marketing consultant. Had lunch in the employees' cafeteria, unannounced.
1:30	Met with a physician seeking support to prevent a waste incinerator installation near a residential neighborhood. Gave advice on the public relations side of the fight.
3:00	Human resources meeting regarding an audit with the Office of Federal Contracts and Compliance.
4:30	Went through the morning mail. Returned telephone calls.

6:00   Left the office.

7:00   Dinner with customers.

"But what about the work of running a bank?" I asked. "Not much time was spent on specific operations."

"They pay me to lead. I hire good people to do the details. If I let it, that could be my job. But I don't because my job is to be the leader of the bank," Johnson answered.

In the simplest of terms it could be said the CEO's job is basically to put the right people in the right job at the right time, and to lead those people from where they are to where they ought to be—setting a direction to the business. Of course, the job implies a capacity for business.

> *My job is dealing with people and dragging out the best and stomping out the worst. It's not magic. Take one problem at a time. Some actions you take now and another one tomorrow.*
>
> —JACK LUNDBERG
> President,
> Denver Sala/Svedala Industries

The quest for a one-sentence or one-phrase statement to describe the CEO position is not new by any means. People will readily give an answer to the question about the CEO's job based on the outcome he or she produces, such as "enhance shareholders' wealth." Traditional descriptions of the

CEO's job tend to be expectations rather than a description of what they actually do for the desired outcome.

When I ask the question, What do you do? a lot of CEOs came up with a metaphor to describe their job.

The job is similar to being an orchestra leader, making sure all the musicians play in harmony. If you have people who can't play well, you won't have very good music.

It's like golf; the test is in the distance and direction that a CEO can take the venture.

The CEO job is like auto racing. You have to know how to round a corner. Every turn is important. And once you come out of one corner, you have to think about the next one and the next one and the next one.

It's like I'm the ramrod, it's my job to keep the cattle headed West, and not stampeding out of control.

Some say business is war without the shooting. And becoming a CEO is comparable to being a military officer. You have to wait your time and grade to get promoted—and you have to dodge the barrage of bullets on your way up and once you get there.

Some CEOs feel like the rider and the company is the horse. When the "muscles" work together we can make the jumps.

The CEO job is simply a combination of caretaker and performer. When something needs attending, he sees it is attended to. When something needs fixing, he sees it is fixed. And all the time he moves from one thing to another, he must be able to keep juggling and keep the audience dazzled.

By far the most frequently used analogy to describe the CEO's work is that the job is akin to sailing: "You never know for sure what the wind will be like at any one time or one place. But a good sailor knows how to use the wind, whether predictable or unpredictable, to take him where he wants to go. And when the winds turn violent, he knows how to either use the storm to his advantage or ride out the storm with the least amount of damage for the right course at the right time. Different circumstances continuously arise and they have to keep the ship afloat and heading on a course to the desired port."

Moving away from the images to the actual, on a daily basis a CEO's job entails the following:

- *people*—works with people (managing, corporate socializing, office politicking)
- *decisions*—sets up and makes decisions
- *meetings*—conducts and attends meetings (time utilization)
- *selling*—creates and maintains a prime environment for selling
- *operations and profits*—oversees operations and ensures profits

Tasks might evolve around unionization, competition, the global marketplace, weak (or strong) dollars, competitors for the job, meeting payroll, avoiding bankruptcy, consumer changes, or maintaining power during an acquisition—all part of the CEO job.

With so much involved in their work, you can imagine most CEOs think about the job all of the time. What comes easy to them, they do well. What is difficult requires them to work harder. (Just as you and I have to do—and anyone else. As the cruiser-weight world boxing champion Kenny Keene from Emmet, Idaho, said before one of his fights, "I'm not that good a boxer, I just get in the ring and do the job that needs to be done." That's what makes a world champion!)

This chapter is about the different elements of the CEO job. Unfortunately, until you actually do their job, as with any job, you won't fully comprehend the magnitude of it. But what I can offer you is a picture of what your CEO does all day, as given to me by the ones who are already at the top, doing the job.

THE CEO JOB—PEOPLE

"A CEO leads people."
"Eight hours a day?" I asked.
"No. A lot of time they are trying to figure out which way to lead."
   —DAVE POWELSON
    Chairman, CEO and President,
    TRI-R Systems

CEOs tell me, almost unanimously, that the people side of running a company is the most demanding, time-consuming, and difficult. It's no wonder that not only does the CEO have to try to get qualified people in jobs that enable him to comfortably delegate (a major task in itself) but he has to deal with the complications of myriad styles, personalities, and situations.

- in-office workers versus telecommuters
- top-down style of management versus consensus management
- working parents versus childless workers
- smokers versus nonsmokers
- flextime versus nine to five
- WASP workforce versus culturally diverse workforce
- politically correct versus the totally incorrect
- workaholics versus punch-the-clock workers
- dress codes versus ethnic or casual dress
- young versus old
- substance abusers versus nonabusers
- company loyalists versus job-hoppers

A chief's job in managing his people, in essence, is helping employees maintain self-esteem—unlocking fears and inhibitions; keeping stress off their backs; helping them be productive, be challenged, and experience a little dignity of contributing something; helping them come to work and go home with smiles on their faces; and, most importantly, teaching them to develop to the point that they can (and want to) take the chief job on themselves.

> *A good CEO is an ally and a colleague versus a superior. He clears the deck, gets rid of garbage, noise, and distraction, so subordinates can actualize their goals.*
> —DAVID VOGEL
> President,
> David E. Vogel & Associates, Inc.

The CEO (and his chiefs) create a climate of growth, an environment where each individual carries his own weight. A near-perfect sympathizes on down days, disciplines on others, nags when necessary, sets a good example, runs outside interference, filters out the BS, and stays involved with people's work. To stay involved with his seventy thousand employees, Chuck Knight, CEO of Emerson, surveys them every two years with a lengthy questionnaire that contains questions such as, "If you were to start over, would you go to work for this plant again?" and "Is the plant manager competent and doing a good job?" The surveys are paid attention to. If more than two-thirds of the responses to one question are negative, the division manager must develop a plan to correct the situation. Knight isn't concerned just with the almost entirely nonunion personnel but with his executive staff also. He has a private room where 650 of his top managers' photographs and bios are posted on the wall. Beside each are stickers indicating level of experience and status for promotion.

The CEO constantly upgrades the management team by finding and trying to keep qualified employees. Top chiefs are absolute nuts about finding the best people. As well as finding good people to upgrade the management team, they are also in the position of having to remove those people who are no longer an effective part of the team. Sometimes they fire people. As one CEO who wished to remain anonymous told me, "Employees can be a real pain in the ass. Some people look right at you, smile, nod in agreement, and have no intent of following through. As their boss I have to hold them accountable. I help them set goals, set strategy, and let them achieve if they will. Sometimes they don't get the job done and I fire them."

People make it all happen—most of the good things and most of the bad things. Mother nature causes some business disasters, but humans are usually to blame for the majority.

A small percent of the people create the majority of the problems. So a big part of a CEO's job is to spot "empty suits" and get rid of them before they ruin the "good suits." What is an empty suit? A person

- who has catchy solutions to complicated problems,
- who is a "flash in the pan" needing to be supported by the troops,
- in over his professional competence,
- who uses excuse and blame,
- who is a liar for hire,
- not qualified for his responsibility,
- who has a many-faceted face,

- who is 5 percent value and 95 percent wind,
- who gets calluses from patting himself on the back,
- with whom it takes an hour to get through the facade,
- who puts so much energy into projecting, he has to be hiding something.

Simply put, an empty suit looks the part but does not have substance, qualities, or skills to effectively do his job. His presence jeopardizes the integrity of the entire operation.

A CEO doesn't fool himself into thinking that maybe they aren't that bad. They are. You cannot count on empty suits for satisfactorily completing work, for timeliness, or for coming through in a critical situation. They must be removed, and an effective boss does not hesitate to remove them. Just as a good chief should not hesitate to eliminate an empty suit, he should not mistake someone he simply dislikes as an empty suit either. At the top, CEOs have to deal with so many people they inevitably find some they dislike but who are nonetheless good workers. The result is called office politics.

People and Office Politics

Whenever two people work together there are office politics. At least one of the two, but more likely both of them, will try maneuvering tactics to get what they want in the situation. The one who is least ef-

fective often cries, "It's so political here!" *Office politics* is not an inherently bad thing; it is just a business label for interpersonal relationships that occur
in the workplace. If left to run completely unchecked
without boundary and out of control, office politics
can become bad and very destructive.

A big part of the chief's job is managing office politics—one employee's little power plays, slight decep-
tions, and aggressive schemes designed to purposefully
hurt a co-worker. The CEO's tolerance or intolerance
will be emulated by the people close to him.

> *It constantly comes to the CEO desk: con-
> flicts among and between divisions and de-
> partments. Little fiefdoms and power bases
> tend to evolve. Normal human beings are
> naturally inclined to expand their sphere of
> influence, control, and authority. People are
> scared that attention from the CEO and re-
> sources and money for their pet project won't
> be there! CEOs need to set the stage of colle-
> giality among the various components.*
> —DAVID VOGEL
>   President,
>   David E. Vogel & Associates, Inc.

A CEO, and everyone else in the company, must
realize the potential for the destructive and devastat-
ing environment office politics can cause, and how
easily it can occur. You also have to realize that the
natural competition among humans to strive for limited resources will cause a personally aggressive of-

fice environment, which isn't necessarily office politics.

1. Don't get overly caught up in the negative aspects
   of interpersonal relations at the office. Few people wake up in the morning and consciously plan
   how they can take advantage of another person.
   Most everyone wakes up and plans how they can
   protect themselves from the enemy, elements, etc.
   If the results hurt someone else, well, so be it. If
   the person getting hurt cries foul office politics,
   that individual is naive. Competition for power,
   position, and results *is* business. That does not
   mean a person should avoid defending themselves; it means a person should be realistic about
   the environment he is in and make the best of it
   and do what he can to exert some control. Most
   have more power than they utilize.

2. Don't take unnecessary offense toward others'
   attitudes or actions. A lot of interpersonal behaviors are done out of innocence and ignorance. Openly, and immediately, correct and
   rectify any misunderstanding or problems.
   Only the interpersonal acts done out of arrogance should be aggressively confronted. In
   other words, don't ignore "traps" set for you,
   but don't instantly assume traps were set.

3. Do not assume you are more cunning than the
   next. You aren't. There are masters out there in
   all walks of life. You don't need to attempt to
   be as cunning, but you do not need to be a victim either. Take action *openly* and *quickly* to

diffuse the effect of potential power plays. Hoping it will go away won't work. Attacking the aggressor in a fashion similar to their attack on you won't work. Sitting back and taking it won't work. Complaining to others won't work. What works is deliberate, decisive, swift action.

4. Do try to make as few enemies as possible during your climb to the top, without being a wimp. You *will* run into those people again and next time they might be your boss.

5. Do learn from the tough competitors you deal with inside of the organization. The ones who give you the most grief are the ones you will learn the most from. Your "enemies" find your faults first. Note what they seek out as a weakness and work on what they found.

Office politics are inevitable. If you choose the "That's awful" perspective, well, you are right. If you choose the productive perspective "That's part of business life, now what can I do about it?" you will also be right and are positioning yourself to be less vulnerable to it.

A headhunter, who recruits for some of the companies whose CEOs I interviewed, explained it this way: "It's impossible to end all office politics. I understand Watergate because that is what goes on in some large corporations in America every day."

The higher up you go in any organization the more politics you'll have to contend with. You will encounter it in direct proportion to your success. For example, President Clinton encounters it more as the president than he did as the governor of Arkansas. When I talked with Caroline Roehm (former wife of Henry Kravitz of RJR fame and a successful CEO herself) about the surprises she discovered when she got to the top, she said she was surprised about how much jealousy she experienced from her friends as she became better known and financially successful. And that is the root of a lot of negative office politics: jealousy!

The essence of office politics is no different from family politics. Sisters sabotage sisters. Brothers scheme against parents. Some siblings hate other siblings. Office politics is no different except money is attached to it.

People and Corporate Socializing

Another important task of the people part of the CEO's job is the corporate socializing. Rick Holley, president and CEO of Plum Creek Timber, talked to me one month after he became the CEO. He said the job requirement he'd paid the least attention to prior to his promotion was corporate socializing. "I didn't realize the amount of time consumed by public demands outside of running the business," he said. "If I had to do it over, I'd spend more time honing social skills to prepare for the CEO job." (I might add, I've seen Rick at social functions and he is very effective representing Plum Creek. He realizes it's an important part of his job, and he does his job well.)

As another successful business leader, Duane Larson, president of Children's World Learning Centers, put it, "I'm pretty good at it, but I don't like it. I spend an inordinate amount of time doing my job, so I feel intruded on when I have to spend an inordinate amount of time in company social obligations. However, if there are opportunities to do some good for the company, I'll likely go through with it."

Inge Trump, president of Trump Property Management, relayed the dream she'd had the night before an important business social gathering. "I was in the restaurant; people were talking to me and my stomach was churning. I couldn't think of a thing to say. All of a sudden the maitre d' approached our table and announced that Russia had just declared war on the United States and all the Southern states had already been annihilated. Upon hearing the news, I gave a sigh of relief, thinking that now at least we'll have to cancel the rest of this social gathering."

From all my interviewing it is clear the job that CEOs dislike most is the inordinate amount of corporate socializing that is required. Their biggest time consumer, outside of direct work responsibility, is public activities. It's easier for some than others, but good ones know the importance of putting extra effort into the business social scene. As many CEOs have said of the job, "Fifty percent of the time is spent managing the company, 50 percent of the time promoting the company."

A typical list of the social activities required by the CEO:

- entertaining out-of-town customers, suppliers, and other guests,
- "wining and dining" important customers, employees, potential employees and their spouses,
- sponsoring and attending employee gatherings like the annual Christmas party, company chili cook-off, and Fourth of July picnic,
- community fund-raising,
- participating at company retreats,
- civic clubs (Rotary, Sertoma, Optimists),
- industry and professional association conferences,
- employee retirement parties,
- advisory board gatherings,
- political causes,
- ongoing corporate and personal public relations activities.

That's just a *short* list of the events the CEO is fairly obligated to attend; it doesn't include the ones he wants because of his own interests: Porsche Club rallies, Yacht Club meetings, neighborhood lawn parties, family gatherings, dog shows, cat shows, flower shows, gun shows, and so forth as they relate to *his* interests outside of the company.

As Duane Pearsall, cofounder of Columbine Venture Funds, says, "CEOs need public visibility to maintain an image as a good corporate citizen." Since corporate socializing is inevitable, here's what CEOs do to make it more productive and less painful.

- *Go with a cheerful attitude.* Maintain a relaxed, friendly expression throughout. If you frown or take on a serious demeanor, you'll look scared. If you want to appear relaxed and confident, smile.
- *Take the opportunity to talk with people you don't see day in and day out.* Initiate conversations; do not wait for others to break the ice. Do not stick only to people you already know. Talk with people you seldom get to talk to—your boss and his boss, your competitor's boss.
- *Go prepared with things to say to start a conversation,* such as: What brings you here? How are you involved in this group? What do you like best about gatherings like this?

  You'll note these are not necessarily show-stopping questions. They are just casual conversation openers to get others involved, break the ice, and take pressure off of yourself to perform.
- *If your spouse accompanies you, treat her with respect and courtesy.* Everyone watches how you treat your significant other, and they draw conclusions about you accordingly. Make sure your verbal message is consistent with nonverbal behavior. But do not spend the time with your spouse exclusively. If she's drop-dead gorgeous do not parade her around like an arm trophy. (The same goes for male spouses of female CEOs.)
- *Be inordinately conservative in alcoholic consumption.* Career fatalities increase in direct proportion to alcohol consumption. If you think you're the exception to the rule, you're incorrect.

But if you hate your job and want to get fired, a corporate social gathering is an excellent opportunity to achieve that goal by following these suggestions (all of which I've seen people do!):

- After shaking someone's hand, smell your fingers.
- Tell old jokes poorly and laugh uproariously.
- Come drunk and stay that way.
- Get really close to people and talk in their face with bad breath.
- Lie; start a rumor.
- Avoid displaying any interest in people; it only encourages them.
- Call people by the wrong name—repeatedly.
- Remind co-workers of their mistakes and point out where they were wrong in front of others.
- Maintain an attitude of superiority with everyone.
- Frequently pull out a brown bag and take a sip.
- Interrupt people repeatedly and change the subject.
- Say over and over, "Your wife looks really familiar."
- Grope members of the opposite sex.
- Spill drinks on people.
- Turn up your nose at what everyone else is eating and order take-out food to be delivered in.
- Clean your fingernails or floss your teeth while talking to people.

Now back to constructive advice.

THE CEO JOB—
DECISION MAKING

A CEO's job is to make decisions. (Make them wisely, of course!) But above all, make them. If you can demonstrate an ability to solve problems early on in your career you will get the nod most every time for advancement. Remember, even those who don't decide, decide.

Jim Rupp ran his own business for twenty years before he retired. "I always felt so relieved after making a decision; that's why I always made them so quickly."

Whether it is reaching a conclusion making up your mind, passing a judgment, or pronouncing a verdict, it's still a decision. People judge a chief's character, courage, and determination by his ability to come to a conclusion and get it implemented. No one is so admired as someone who can decide what needs to be done and does it. No one is as short-lived as a chief who can't make a decision.

Surprisingly there's lots of indecision in the workforce, even at the top. One ex-CEO of a consumer products company was described as one who "knew everything about everything; you couldn't bring up anything that he hadn't thought of. The person was consumed with work but couldn't make a decision." The individual who can't make a decision, can't narrow down options, and as a result of keeping options

open too long has people stymied, will in time get
the company stuck.

> *With the pace of technology, you really need*
> *someone to set priority, direction, and make*
> *the decision.*
> —Larry Kirshbaum
> President, Warner Books

All day long a parade of people ask for decisions
from the CEO. What to do about a new competitor's
product? How to resolve a personnel policy dispute?
What can be done about a key employee paralyzed
with grief over the death of a spouse? Who should be
promoted? You can see judgments and resolutions
consume the CEO's day. Being willing and able to
simply decide is the CEO's job.

> *It's just as important what decisions you*
> *don't make as those you do make as the*
> *CEO. I've discovered that some of the issues*
> *people bring to me—first, I don't need to*
> *make the decision about it, and secondly, I*
> *don't need to make it in the time frame they*
> *want it made. The CEO can get really hung*
> *up on things they shouldn't be involved*
> *in. . . . Management books preach empower-*
> *ment. As the CEO, empowerment is real*
> *easy to do. But it's shocking to me that I've*
> *found a real lack of people who are wanting*
> *and willing to take on the responsibility. I*

hear, "Let us manage." I say okay. But half
of them talk a better game than they play.
                                —BILL FAIRFIELD
                                CEO, Inacom

People really want to be led. We make the mistake of being incredibly polite and holding back on determination. People want direction. People want decisiveness. Individuals would rather disagree with a decision than have ongoing indecisiveness. They want to give their opinion but they want the chief to decide.

Don't let the sun set on a decision. Every-
one will have input as to what you should
do, some people will be angry regardless of
what you choose, but you'll make a lot
more people angry if you drag it out. You're
going to make a choice anyway. Do it ear-
lier rather than later.
                —JACK LUNDBERG
                President,
                Denver Sala/Svedala Industries, Inc.

To Make Decisions:
1. *Ask and ask and ask questions.* The more information you have, generally the better the decision. Questions cut through people's emotions and opinions and get to the facts. Take nothing on assumption. Ask. Bring all data together and *listen* regardless of whether the ideas come from the youngest employee or the most senior.

Gathering all the facts minimizes a wrong resolution. Get people to explain. Give them reasons to object. Let people fight for their
position.

Take the initiative to get a broad range of
input.

- Ask your five most critical advisors.
- Ask someone totally unrelated—your twelve-
  year-old daughter's friend, for instance.
- Evaluate likely consequences to all parties in-
  volved.
- Then decide.

2.   *Set a timetable.* Draw conclusions. Make rec-
     ommendations. Act.

     The time to work through a complicated
     issue should have set limits. A wrong decision
     is better than no decision. You can decide to
     wait on a resolution. That's a decision. Need-
     ing a conclusion against the clock ensures one
     gets made. All sporting games have a definite
     set time; therefore, the game gets resolved.
     The same is true in the game of decision mak-
     ing. Even the right decision can be wrong if
     it's made too late.

3.   *Rest with your decisions. Live with them.* Any
     decision will be unpopular and seem unac-
     ceptable by someone. Leave it lie. The cycle of
     acceptance will come around *sometime* if you
     maintain a pattern of seeking input, consider
     all facts, follow a sense of values, and keep
     motivation intact. If you're delegating the

process, rest with whatever decision your people make. Don't jump down their throats and tear out their livers after they have made the decision you'd given them the responsibility of making.

Nothing is more frustrating to employees and destructive to leadership than indecision, fluctuation, and actions suspended. In all decision making you finally have to choose. What separates winners from the rest is whether you end up finding good in what you've chosen. The ability to live with a decision that could prove you either right or wrong takes confidence.

> *Hire good people. Make decisions fairly rapidly. Use their recommendations, then* don't look back. *It's over.*
> —DENIS BROWN
> CEO, Pinkertons

There is a myth that all chiefs are rational people, making rational decisions. Not so. You may think they study the hard facts and launch the right response every time. "I grew up thinking adult decision making was more black and white than it is," says one CEO. In fact, chiefs' decisions are often based on human emotions of greed, fear, even naivete. Even they can be a little less businessman and a little more human. "Everyone is out for themselves—including the CEO," as one executive matter-of-factly ex-

plained it to me. "He may preach 'team, empowerment, pluralism,' but if he has a chance to get a $10
million bonus the year the company takes a $50 mil-
lion loss, he'll take it."

The reality is, sometimes chiefs have their minds
made up before they go through the exercise of the
decision-making process. Whatever the request or situation might be, the answer is always no. One CEO
spelled it out: "I have a sign outside my door for
everyone who comes in. It says, 'NO.' It saves me a
lot of time. Fifty percent of the people won't ask, another large percent won't ask again, so it cuts my
work load in half."

Be modest about your own grand decision-making ability. Maybe it is one of your better qualities;
I hope so for you. But being able to make the right
decision may come from some other source, such as
superior marketing angles, a superior brilliance,
fortunate timing, or pure luck—not from you
alone.

The CEO's total existence is based around decisions: He has to anticipate them, make them, change
them, argue for or against them, correct them, delegate them, and live with them. Warren Buffet says a
career boils down to "a tiny handful of very well-
considered decisions."

The CEO Job—
Meetings

A big chunk of the CEO job is completed in meetings. His day, on an hourly basis, is filled with meetings. He meets in person and on the telephone with staff, customers, investors, board members, reporters, friends, relatives of friends, peers, politicians, potential politicians, community leaders, salespeople, vendors, job candidates, competitors, and a few others.

Effective chiefs run productive meetings. Too often people don't just run bad meetings, they run awful meetings. Yet at great expense in money and time they continue to have them.

A lot more people have the power to run meetings than ability to run good meetings. People frequently aren't organized, can't shut up, or can't diplomatically shut others up.

Here's a list of productive meetings "dos" that I developed after interviewing CEOs whose daily success depends on effective meetings.

1. *Have fewer meetings.* Get together for very important reasons only: to identify a problem, solve a problem, or dispense information to a group. Do away with a meeting if the only reason to have it is that it's Monday morning, unless it's an informal gathering to simply stay in touch with the troops. Don't let meetings become the work.

2. *Prepare, so you can focus.* Use an agenda as the tool to keep focused on the issues to be dealt with. Send out an agenda in advance if possible. Have an answer for the questions: Why are we here? What do we want to accomplish?

3. *Keep the number of people at the meeting as small as possible* while still including everyone that needs to be there. A meeting becomes more complex with more people. It also consumes more of everyone's time just because they physically are in the room.

4. *Decide who will run the meeting in advance* and how others will get feedback from the meeting. Free form may be good for brainstorming, but not for dispensing information. Structured may be too burdensome for spontaneous staff update meetings. Preparation (and following these guidelines) does not diminish spontaneity. People prefer prepared.

5. *Physically set up the meeting.* Arrange the configuration of the room, where various people should sit to enhance the meeting objective. If the meeting is in the chief's office with the boss behind his desk, it will be more intimidating. It might be more effective to go to another person's office, a board room, or a totally neutral place (a restaurant, for example) or even someone's home.

One CEO's setup for his meetings includes a way of getting out of them: "I have a standing arrangement with my secretary. Forty-five minutes into every meeting she comes in and hands me a piece of paper. Sometimes it's blank. But I look at it, excuse myself, and leave."

6. *Consider the time of day* when people are in attendance, emotionally and intellectually. If you're going to "come down" on people, do it at the end of the day when they can go home and think about it. If you're going to praise them, do it first thing in the morning so they are in a good mood all day.

7. *Deal with difficult issues first.* Present key ideas and keep coming back to them. Stay on track. Be flexible as new directions come up but don't let someone's pet peeves dominate. Survey, establish criteria, and set task teams to get things done. If necessary, set a time limit to spend on each and stick to the limit. Tap a glass of water to give warning that two minutes are left. Most decisions get made under the gun. People get so wrapped up in what they are talking about sometimes they don't want to stop. You must stop them sometimes.

8. *Use humor.* A serious discussion can be equally effective if an attitude of good cheer is maintained. Humor relaxes people and eases candid communication. Although one CEO wasn't laughing when he told me, "I've stopped having meetings. I just write a memo that says, 'Do this my way.'"

9. *Make the meeting quick*; don't let it drag. One CEO likes to come into the meeting at the very last minute with a frenetic pace "to get the people pumped and keep up a good pace to get it over with."

10. *Rehearse.* Some meetings hold more significance than others because of the issues or the attendees. For example, if the meeting involves people from the outside that are forming an impression of your company, it's probably very important. Rehearse your ideas, your pitch, and the answers to possible questions and objections when you need to do all you can to control the outcome.

11. *Ending meetings.* To keep the meeting on track set ground rules for ending it. Don't let yourself or others digress. "Let's get back to the issue" can be said as many times as necessary. Control the meeting hangers-on by controlling the "meeting closing ritual." Instead of clipping your fingernails, tapping your toes, or repeatedly glancing at your watch,
    • make a decision,
    • hand out assignments and deadlines,
    • stand up,
    • or provide a concluding line:
        "The idea is good; let me think about it."
        "Can you think of anything else I can do to help you? I have to do————now."
        "Are there any other problems I should be aware of? We need to wrap this up."
        "I need to get back to my desk."

One CEO told me, "I simply don't discuss further. I direct them even if sometimes it is a nothing thing, but just to get them on their way. Otherwise, you get the same effect as sitting in a hot tub drinking white wine."

Another has a Westminster clock in his office set twenty minutes fast. "It keeps me on time, but more importantly it helps me end meetings faster. People keep glancing at the clock. They know it's fast but they aren't sure *how* fast. When the chimes kick in I say, 'Time's up,' and everything gets sped up!"

Follow up meetings with a recap in writing. Even if it is two sentences on your calendar, note what was decided and what needs to be done by whom. In many cases, for legal reasons alone, documentation is necessary. People who weren't there know what went on and people who were there get reminded.

Part of the chief's job in meetings should be to build attendees' self-esteem. The chief's work becomes easier with people feeling good about themselves and their work. People feel good when they are prepared and not caught off guard. Preparing so people know your objective and therefore meet your objective makes people feel comfortable in meeting you. You won't get cooperation if you put co-workers down in front of others. If you can't listen as you should, then draw people out. If the decision has already been made, then it's better not to have a meeting at all. The damage you do will be multiplied by the number of people there.

If you, the reader, wish to be more effective in dealing with your boss you should utilize the techniques used by top CEOs. Be empathetic; the chief could be sitting through eight or ten hours of meetings a day! It's very difficult to pay attention that long. It may be up to you to make it easy on him so he readily agrees to meetings with *you* again in the future.

Of course there is the option one CEO uses but one I certainly don't advocate: "I make the meetings such a miserable experience so people work hard at getting things done on their own to avoid having to have a meeting with me."

Crisis meeting. Regardless of how well-thought-out, well-planned, disciplined, and organized a CEO might be—crises still occur. Something goes wrong.

Near-perfect managers don't have crises happen very often in which "you are running around like a fireman most of the day." As Larry Johnson, CEO of the Bank of Hawaii, says, "I surround myself with individuals in the company who can help us solve the problem at hand. Fortunately they don't happen very often."

A client was in my office preparing for his upcoming move into the president and CEO position of a large cable company. We were discussing the usual going-on-board process. The phone rang and it was his wife. "The man you are replacing and his secretary were just shot and killed by a crazed customer. They need you at the company right away!" Our meeting changed from the usual going-on-board focus to a crisis focus—to deal with the media, the community, the victims' families, the parent company, the shareholders, the co-workers, competitors, and even my client's spouse.

We strategized his written and verbal communication to all involved, tried to anticipate the unexpected, went through several scenarios, prepared answers to expected questions, then he caught the next flight. He even scheduled in potential nap times so he would be rested to handle what lay ahead.

The CEO's job is to handle crises. (Your ability to handle similar situations will get you noticed as promotion potential.) The following are important in handling a crisis:

- Identify the source if possible.
- Set a plan of action.
- Allocate resources, time, and people.
- Be flexible for the unexpected.
- Expect criticism.
- But above all, act and act fast.

The CEO's job is to prepare his organization before a crisis occurs. He might periodically cause "planned upheaval" to keep people from being complacent and overconfident. Or he might create crisis scenarios and play them out entirely with people who'd be involved. Bob Elliot, president of Elliott Associates, calls it case analysis before they become real. By going through problems before they happen, he controls the outcome better and likely avoids the problem altogether.

The big difference between the crisis that happens to you versus the one that you make happen is that if you initiate the situation on your timetable, people have the time to think through and plan, and to allocate resources necessary to solve the problem. For example, a CEO of a beverage company called his top ten managers for a three-day summit meeting and proclaimed, "Most executives might be happy with 10 percent annual growth in earnings, but I'm not. From now on it's 15 percent." And he handed each person a model train on a track headed toward ten tiny, frightened figures. Then he instructed, "Now tell me how we're going to do it." Then they spent the next three days brainstorming. Instead of waiting for bad times to hit, the CEO claimed an artificial doomsday *now* to get people to take action.

You can never plan for every potential critical problem but you can rehearse what-if scenarios. Crises from today's headlines give you plenty to work with: product tampering, murdered employees and customers, plant malfunctions, illegal behavior from executives, and so on.

Time utilization. "I get into the office at 8:30 A.M. and the phone starts ringing at 8:35 A.M. Key managers from around the country call to talk about what's going on in sales, personnel, general business conditions. Often I'm only in the office two days a week. I'm out calling on customers, visiting other offices, attending outside board meetings the rest of the time," said Gay Mayer, president and CEO of MEM Company Incorporated.

A big part of the CEO's job is utilizing his and his staff's time. It's not so much a matter of time management as it is time conservation. You can recover lost profits, reputation, friendships, and knowledge, but you can't recover lost time anywhere up or down the ladder. As Hyram Smith, who heads Franklin Quest

Company, which manufactures day planners, says, "The key to managing time is controlling events."

The higher up you go the less your time will be your own, the more important it is to do what you can to control events. A CEO's time seems to belong to everyone else. His plans are preempted by matters of importance to most anyone else. It's part of the CEO's job to get it to all work together.

A CEO's time has to be spent with senior people, important customers, day-to-day operations, and community activities. He makes and receives phone calls, writes and reviews written communication, follows up on delegated work (or does things that should have been delegated), and responds to panics. For some it's not unusual to send out three hundred different pieces of correspondence a week. One CEO has five wastebaskets sitting under his desk, all of which are full at the end of a day.

Most CEOs' consciences bother them a little all of the time. They balance time and the continual stress of doing all that's required to do the job. Like you, they seldom have enough time to do all the things they need to get done. As William F. Buckley Jr. says, "The demands I have are always greater than the time I have to do them. . . . I'm always up against infinity."

An effective CEO conserves time by *prioritizing*, controlling distractions as best as possible, and focusing on one project. Then they *start, continue,* and *finish* that project. Above all one can't procrastinate. Highly productive people don't spend time on anything they'll:

- apologize for,
- regret,
- repent later.

Franklin L. Child, principal of Project Control, Inc., has learned that "fortunately your ability to do seems to expand with your responsibility."

One CEO I interviewed for the book agreed to "thirty minutes." He was generous with his ideas, but when thirty minutes were up he said, "Time's up." During the conversation I asked, "You run three different companies in three different locations overseas and in the United States. How do you have time for a week of golf every month?" He answered, "Good planning. Good time management. Delegating. Respecting other people's time. Not fussing with paperwork, keeping a clean desk." He didn't say "good people," but I suspect that's part of it.

A CEO works with the same amount of time that employees do. Any chief or employee who doesn't know how to spend his time will likely be terminated or at least left behind. People are controlled in how they spend the company money; there should be similar controls on how they spend the company's time.

If you feel you can't afford to lose *a single moment* you'll likely be one who gets the nod for promotion.

THE CEO JOB—SELLING

The CEO's job is to sell *all the time*. He has to sell change, sell his ideas, sell his vision and strategic plan, sell his image. The CEO has to sell to his board, his employees, his customers, the public, the bankers, and the media. The top person in the company has to be the top salesman. Everything starts with the sale.

You may think people try to sell the CEO but mostly it is the CEO trying to sell people on his ideas, direction, decisions, goals, vision, support, or anything else he wants or needs. Everyone in life "sells." A big part of the chief's job is to sell as well. It is his responsibility to make known to the whole group how he thinks, his perspective on what the future holds, and how he wants to rise up to meet it—that takes constant and effective selling.

> *Although I don't have sales responsibility most of my time is spent in sales and marketing. I'm in direct contact with the customer; my ear is to the ground, listening to what's going on. We have to convince people our product and service is better than our competition's. To do that I listen to their concerns and needs.*
> —BILL BLOUNT
> President, Power Motive Corporation

The higher you go, the more you have to sell yourself and your ideas upward and downward. If you have a negative attitude about selling, you'll not advance very far very fast. Selling is not arm-twisting, swindling, or glad-handing.

Selling is marketing yourself, your ideas, your work, your organization constantly. You don't do it just when you hold a "salesperson" title. The new CEO of Norwest Corp., Richard Kovacevich, says, "Hey, this is all about selling, about going out and convincing." Selling might mean giving a Mustang to the founder of Honda, Soichiro Honda, as Lee Iacocca did when negotiating for three hundred thousand front-drive power trains for his minivan. It might mean talking to the CEO's wife when her husband is considering purchasing a company plane, as Bob Cooper, executive vice president of Gulfstream, knows: "Wives are behind the CEO's decisions on a lot of things."

Selling is simply giving them what they want in a way it will work for you and them. There isn't one way to do it. In fact, your first way of presenting something probably won't be the way it finally gets accepted, but you keep at it. No matter how well you have done before or how well you're doing now, keep selling yourself, your ideas, your work, your organization, and anything else that is necessary.

Don't think you can do soft, fuzzy selling. You need hard-core, purposeful, directed, goal-achieving selling, which by the way doesn't mean arm-twisting à la encyclopedia sales. From my discussions with CEOs I learned how they sell both subtly and not so subtly. Following is a compilation of what the best do.

To sell to people:

1. Find out what people think they want by asking questions.
   • What do you want to achieve?
   • What do you hope to gain?
   • What are you unhappy with?
   • What do you want to avoid?
2. Find out what they will pay for what they want by asking questions.
   • How have you budgeted for this?
   • What do you hope to pay?
   • Who has authority to approve this?
3. Offer what they want as long as you can provide it.
4. Ask them to buy.
   • Will you give me your okay?
5. Methodically repeat the above process as often as necessary.

A chief sells outside and inside his organization. Internally people may "pay" with support, time, energy, resources rather than money per se. And buying may mean "buy into," but the concept is the same whether selling internally or externally.

Now you may ask, "What if they want something I don't have to offer?" That's where your tenacity, creativity, and resourcefulness come in. You may need to ask better and different questions. You may have to adjust your timing, your attitude, your approach. Or the alternative is to give up and walk away. Many do. But those people don't become the chief.

"When I give a 'no' answer, it's not necessarily 'no,'" one chief explained to me. "I'm not always right with that answer. But if the person who wants a 'yes' gives up and doesn't come back at me, I assume that I was right. I usually say 'no' in a negotiable tone of voice, which leaves the door open for them to come back if they have the courage and tenacity."

A chief's selling and negotiating are pretty interchangeable terms. He has to achieve a workable balance between what *he* wants and *they* want. He does that by questioning, listening, *hearing*, and questioning more.

A client told me this story about a company president who was talking to a potential investor during lunch. The investor had thrown out several dollar figures— $100K, $250K, and $500K. But the president hadn't received any commitment through the meal. The waiter came to offer dessert. They decided to split a piece of cheesecake. The president reached to split the piece between them. He needed to get a commitment. So he took the knife and, indicating the portion he would give the investor, placed the knife on a sliver-width and asked, "Will you go the $100K? . . ." Then, moving the knife to the middle of the piece: "Or $200K? . . ." Finally, moving the knife to just a sliver size for himself he asked, "Or the $500K?" The investor watched his piece of cheesecake get bigger with the $500K and with that jumped in and said, "$500K."

Sometimes people think selling and negotiation is a game of bait and switch where you come at people in an oblique way. They think negotiation is talking about issue one, two, three, when really four is what you are interested in. It isn't. Selling is simply getting things done.

—DAVID M. HOLLAND
Retired Senior Vice President,
DSC Communications

THE CEO JOB—OVERSEEING OPERATIONS

The CEO job written about most frequently in the pages of *Forbes* and *Fortune* is the ability to run the operations of a business and earn profits for the organization. As Joel Schleicher, COO of Nextel, told me, "Every business has well-known ways of making money. There aren't any big secrets. The differential between those CEOs who profit and those who don't is *how well* they do the known things."

The CEO operations job is rather like a NFL game. All of the professional teams have the same numbers of players on the field, all have the same field dimensions, rules, and regulations, and all teams have the same amount of time to execute the game. They also have comparably talented players with each team getting a shot at the better ones every season via the draft system. Yet only two teams out of twenty-six candidates get to compete in the Super Bowl! The difference between the winners and the also-rans is the leadership of the coach—the team CEO!

> *I don't think just about how to grow the business and to create new opportunities. I think about how to manage my owners to ensure that they remain supportive of our business whether or not this month's results are positive. I review many reports and analyze information to understand if we are executing excellently. I think about creating a company that does good things for people and gives its employees a fair opportunity to prosper. I think about how to make it fun and rewarding for everyone involved with our company—employees, customers, suppliers, the media. And despite the bumps and bruises of daily business life, I constantly wish to create something unique while remaining focused, on a daily basis, on "the numbers."*
>
> —STEVE SILK
> President and CEO,
> The Estee Corporation

The CEO's job is to make sure the resources are in place for the core business. Products and services are the heart and soul that enable the company to stay in business. The CEO puts all the core competencies together: design, engineering, supplies, products, labor, plants, marketing, sales, and distribution through his people. His generalist skills kick in here to be able to manage functions he's not a specialist in.

> *I was practical, had common sense, involved with people. I always knew enough about everything versus a lot about any one thing . . . and the ability to motivate the team to make decisions.*
> —RICK HOLLEY
> President and CEO,
> Plum Creek Timber Company

CEOs work to create a coalition among the different specialists or teams of people. But the key job is still to run the whole operation. One CEO who had tried and failed to pass responsibility down the line told me, "I thought I was mentally ill. I wanted to go to a therapist to learn to be a team player."

Team input and team execution are important. But team decisions can also cripple a company. If a CEO is not managing the process, it goes nowhere.

A major flaw of the concept of teamwork: Everyone assumes someone else will do the work—because it's the *team* work. It doesn't always get done, and what does get done takes too long. Sometimes teams are formed so more people can share the credit (or blame) with the one who does the work. The chief's job is to make sure what needs to be done *is* being done by whoever should be doing it.

Part of overseeing operations is introducing change to accommodate employee problems and subsequent progress. There are three basic reasons good CEOs constantly come forth with new directives:

1. The old way isn't working.
2. It's expected of them.
3. They need to plan for the future.

As one CEO put it, "My job is to decide what we will be when we grow up." That's why every six months you read about a new management trend. One year chiefs are trying to "right-side-up" the organization and next year "upside-down" it. Then they take the company from a centralized system to a decentralized, and within a few years it's back to centralized. And each cycle carries new labels or catchy titles for the change.

Barbara Thomas, president of Pillsbury Canada Ltd., told me, "As the boss my job is to get people to tell me what's going on. But I always have my own projects going in addition to supervising others. Therefore I don't get isolated in an ivory tower and tell others they are accountable when I am not accountable for some specific project." Carrying out the company mission is also a CEO job.

But while the CEO oversees operations on a big scale, he has to make sure employees see where they play a part on an individual scale. The CEO might need to literally sit down with them and say, "Let me see if I can be more clear about where we're going."

The near-perfect CEO wants people to be able to carry the message around (figuratively if not literally) on a wallet-sized card stating the following:

- the business objective,
- how they personally gain or lose if the objective isn't met,
- how they personally contribute.

Some employees will complain about the CEO's operations regardless of efforts to involve everyone. The CEO job is to take and hear those complaints from his various specialists.

The "Pyramid of Crud," as Hal Krause, CEO of Crestcom International, puts it, is part of the CEO's job. "Everything that can't get taken care of is shoved up to the next level where it all accumulates in the CEO's lap. It's very important the CEO keeps a good attitude so he doesn't think the whole world is crud."

THE CEO JOB—PROFITS

An obvious requirement for the CEO job is earnings and profits. That's what enables the CEO to keep his job and the company to stay in business, grow the business, pay salaries, make investments, acquire other companies, pay taxes, and keep the enterprise going.

A CEO develops, implements, and follows up on plans for boosting profits and adding value to the bottom line. He deals with declining sales, rising costs, obtaining financing, warding off bankruptcy, cutting overhead, automation, and so on. Outside complications pop up from government regulations, health insurance costs, family leave, or litigation.

Every quarter is analyzed for the numbers side of the business. Are earnings rising faster or slower than sales? Is the worldwide unit sales volume up or down? Are gains being diluted overseas because of unit sales declines in North America? Are profitability gains lifting and gross margins going to raise profit margins for this year over last? How much will even one point profit margin increase price per share? How to explain that inventory adjustments are the cause for the sharp slippage in volume? What do we do next about our 24.3 percent share of the market compared to our biggest competitor who is at 36 percent? What costs can be whittled away? Do the gross margins allow for more advertising and promotion to increase the value of our company? How much of the capital spending budget goes into investments to reduce costs? How much revenue savings will occur through cost reductions? CEO bonuses often depend on delivering a good return on their capital spending; how does that affect some decisions? What could be some new high margin products to come up with? Should a parallel product company be acquired? How to decrease debt ratio? Should we borrow, do a stock swap to acquire? Should we sell an operation to raise cash?

Well, you get the picture. The operations/profit side of a CEO's job is rather complicated. That's why he needs good people around him. That's why he has to be a good leader to *keep* good people.

Earning profits and deciding what to do with them

is another factor that separates the successful CEO from those not so successful.

The CEO can utilize profits in different ways:

- "wear them" on the company building, facilities, equipment, decorations, brochures, etc.,
- share them by supporting public causes,
- hoard them to build net worth,
- spend them shamelessly on extravagances up and down the line (usually so more *up*—for a fleet of corporate jets, executive retreats, etc.),
- invest them in other businesses, product expansion, the stock market,
- gamble them on untested investments,
- use them to pay the company bills, keep the operation afloat, and for employee development.

Too much profit can make companies soft; it has been known to corrupt, and to ruin empires. When profits are low, the CEO can motivate with the hope of future prosperity. Adversity makes strong teams. When profits are high, the CEO's work is to prepare for adversity. A chief is never tested more than at times of excessive good fortune. Employees are more difficult to manage and less cooperative at work during good times. The CEO's job is easier if he has to endure continued hard times rather than continued prosperous times. The CEO, the employees, the products, and the organization seldom get better during good times.

Every company and every chief experiences cycles of success and setback. Some experiences are less visible, less public, less costly, but they are there. The CEO's job is to manage through those cycles, the ups and downs in the dollar, marketplace, or the country. It is no different for anyone. They all have a comparable size field, regulations, and talented players. The rules are the same. The difference is *how* they play.

WHO BOSSES THE BOSS?

CEOs have less freedom, are more controlled, are more closely measured, watched, and looked over than anyone else in the company. They are truly under a microscope.
—BILL FRANK
President, Careerlab

There is some satisfaction in knowing even the boss gets bossed. Right?

Virtually no one else in the company has to deal with all the factors that the CEO does. He is responsible to groups inside and outside of the company. He must fulfill their needs, meet their demands, understand their perspective, serve their interests, and still meet long-term and short-term business objectives.

If you think you have a lot of people to please, consider the CEO, he has *lots* of constituents to please:

- customers,
- employees,
- board of directors,
- shareholders,
- corporate CEO,
- bankers or Wall Street,
- government,
- media,
- family,
- public.

Satisfying constituents is the key to longevity for a CEO and his company. It's also vital for the CEO's reputation inside and outside the organization. Every relationship is unique. But each stockholder needs to feel the CEO is

- comfortable in himself,
- confident in his decisions,
- secure in what he's doing,
- keeping advised of issues from constituents,
- availing himself of advice from his constituents.

Customers. The number-one constituent to answer to is the customer. The customer (or client) is the reason the business exists. It's so basic and important yet so easily forgotten and replaced with "the business of business."

> *Spend the travel time to get to know the business and your people. Don't spend a lot of time in the office. Don't spend a lot of*

time at home. Travel and talk with customers. *That's the CEO's job.*

—DENIS BROWN
CEO, Pinkertons

Michael Bloomberg, whose estimated net worth is $500 million in the financial news business, doesn't have a secretary, partly because "it impedes access to clients and customers."

One of the corporate sayings of Mars Candy is "The customer is our boss."

But the CEO is usually the furthest from direct customer contact.

Good CEOs make a concerted effort to spend time with the customer face-to-face. Some regularly supply (and subsequently read) feedback surveys to check how the company is doing, whether it's one-on-one, on the phone, or on paper. If the CEO loses touch with customers' happiness the company will *not* survive.

The CEO must satisfy the customer constituent.

Employees. One of the most important constituents to the CEO is his own employees. They generally think of trying to please the boss, but in fact the boss has to please his employees as well. Employees feel the top guy has more control than he does. In truth, subordinates have tremendous power over the boss: they can do or not do what he wants. They can make or break his objectives and goals and ultimately the company.

I don't worry about the competition. I worry about someone on my payroll.

—Leonard Abramson
CEO and President,
U.S. Healthcare

If the CEO's people don't like him or don't trust him they can undermine in subtle and not-so-subtle ways: lack enthusiasm for projects, mistreat customers, and let the entire process down. Steve Cornforth, a partner at Price Waterhouse, told me, "Employees say to themselves, 'I can tell if the CEO cares about me. I can tell in his voice and see it in his eyes.' Then they decide, 'I won't go the extra yard for him. I won't work enthusiastically.' While they secretly hope he will be replaced soon."

The CEO must effectively lead, guide, and motivate the employee constituent.

Board of Directors. The BOD sits in judgment of management and specifically the CEO. If performance is inadequate they are supposed to do something about it. The board has committees on audits, regulatory groups, compensation, profit sharing, strategy, marketing—things shareholders don't want executive officers doing unilaterally. Committees review and stay in touch with issues. Theoretically they represent the interest of the owners. The CEO is legally answerable to the board and morally answerable to everybody else.

Traditionally boards of directors haven't been very strong. That's changing. They are getting embarrassed. They look silly when CEOs they support head huge losses, mismanage finances, stock prices plummet, and confidence is lost.

Although board members represent constituents, specifically the shareholders, they frequently serve at the pleasure of the COB who is often the CEO.

Board members get paid director fees. The COB can *raise* director fees. Directors want to keep their seat of power. They get attention lavished on them. They get to go on fun travel junkets—golfing at top resorts, jetting off to Wyoming dude ranches, meeting celebrities, etc.

To be a BOD member you have to have some specific expertise, be a celebrity (head of state, politician, astronaut, actor), be a CEO, president, senior executive officer, or be a pal of the chairman of the board (COB) or CEO. The current chief's predecessor usually is on the board, a fellow company senior executive, sometimes a family member, if the company has professional management such as Campbell's Soup's, and sometimes big shareholders. Rumor had it that the CEO of Seagrams, Edgar Bronfman Jr., wanted a seat on Time Warner's board. He also wanted to increase his stake of stock ownership to 20 percent without triggering an antitakeover provision. In exchange for his seat he stopped what appeared to some to be an attempt at a hostile takeover.

Shareholders. Shareholders are individual investors (you and me) and institutional investors (pension funds, mutual funds, insurance companies). The latter are called super-shareholders and currently own over 50 percent of corporate America. In entrepreneurial ventures stakeholders may be venture capital firms, friends, family, and/or banks.

The idea of shareholders is to give people (investors) a reason to give the company money (investment/purchase stocks) while the company gives them some reward (dividends) that is worth their risk in giving their money to the company.

A shareholder's key interest is price per share. For example, a share of Nike cost $3.30 in 1984. By 1992 it was worth $90.30 per share. In 1993 it dropped to $43 because of customer trends: athletic shoes were out and leather "grunge" workboots were in. That same trend caused Timberland's shares to go from $9 to $85 in 1993.

The investor and Wall Street "boss" is huge and complex. An example of the power of this constituent was when Wall Street didn't like the approach the founders of Ben & Jerry's were using to recruit a new president. Remember the essay competition on "Why I want to be the president of Ben & Jerry's"? The ice-cream company's stock, which had started at $5 a share and had gone to $300, was devalued to $150 until a more orthodox approach to recruiting a president was found. The retainer search firm, Russel Reynolds, was hired to find the new president. Stock values shot back up.

The spring is the general time for annual shareholder meetings. With powerful funds and personalities the event can turn quite raucous with individuals taking the microphone, questioning, challenging, attacking the CEO and the board. It's the chief executive's "annual interaction" with the people who own his company. CEOs rehearse their slides and polish their scripts, buy new suits, and hire consultants to evaluate their performance. Some meetings are broadcast by closed-circuit television to other parts of the country.

In past times the meeting was significant to keep shareholders abreast of corporate decisions. Today, with detailed information accessible to shareholders via technology, annual meetings hold few surprises for shareholders.

Shareholders are hoping for a high return on their investment. They are more interested in the CEO's financial acumen than his leadership style. They can be assuaged only so long by the charismatic CEO if he doesn't produce.

Bankers. Another significant boss is the financing company. For a private company that might mean bankers and venture capitalists. Frequently the bank president will sit on the board becoming a double constituent. CEOs tell me bankers are the most difficult group to please. They are often physically close in proximity, close to the community, and close to customer rumblings. And bankers have the deserved reputation for being conservative, which is often counter to the risk-taking founder or head of a private company.

"My bankers are coming tomorrow. They are sending over two young MBAs. I need to entertain them. And want to learn under what conditions they'll continue to be nice. I know one thing, their arrangement of a boot in my neck won't be satisfactory," says an entrepreneur who despite his strong words still gets dictated to by his banker.

Venture capitalists are private for-profit lenders,

usually to risky new businesses where the venture capitalist in turn receives a piece of the company ownership. Less than 10 percent of new companies get funding from venture capitalists.

A CEO needs to be able to talk influence and get confidence from the "banker" constituent.

Corporate CEO. I believe you've come to understand everyone has a boss. Even the top mountaineer in your organization has a master. In the case of the CEO, he has many masters. Just as you have a boss, they have a boss. If the company you work with is a part of a larger company, your CEO has a corporate boss. For example the CEO of Lever Brothers has a twenty-person board that reports to a three-man special committee at Unilever. Loews Corporation has two co-chiefs. With every addition of a layer above there often comes additional shareholders, employees, customers, government regulations, and so forth.

Lots of times the CEO is better known than the person who recruited him and bosses him. Such is the case of Bob Magness, who found John Malone to run Tele-Communications, Inc., the largest cable operator in the country. Malone is the person Vice President Gore calls the Darth Vader of the cable industry. With Malone at the helm, he takes the flak for the changes in the cable industry while also getting notoriety. Meanwhile Magness, Malone's boss and founder of Tele-Communications, holds shares of stock recently valued at $1.2 billion and far fewer people know his name.

The corporate boss is a major constituent the CEO must please.

Government. The government constituent takes on many forms. Some companies try to avoid extra attention from the regulatory agencies, like the FDA for example.

Many CEOs feel, with frustration, that business is governed not to make money but to provide a social institution for government legislation. The government is a constituent not to be ignored. It has resources, time, legislation, and the threat of holding new legislation and regulatory compliances over corporations. A CEO has to steer clear of potential problems, respond to agencies' inquiries, keep them informed to varying degrees. They are one constituent who doesn't care if the CEO is a good leader or makes money; their concern is that he stays within their guidelines.

Gas, electrical, airline, cable, telephone, insurance, and transportation companies have regulatory agencies to deal with. Any time a rate change, service addition, or deletion is requested it needs to be approved by that constituent. Questions can be leveled at any time by the regulator. Employees, customers, and almost anyone else can file a complaint with the regulatory agency and the company has to answer those complaints.

A CEO has to comply with government constituents and their regulations.

Media. You think of the top boss as having power. They hire and fire. They sign paychecks. They tell employees what to do where and when. That's power inside an organization to a limited group. The media has *real* power, destructive and constructive power. They can make or break an individual executive or a company with a few words in print or a few seconds on the air.

Only a foolish, arrogant CEO dismisses the media as a constituent. Good CEOs do not necessarily act on the media's behalf but they do consider the effect as seen through the eyes of the media before they act. Their public affairs, public relations, crisis management, and legal advisor teams plan how, what, and when new information is presented for the press exposure.

Many times CEOs have bitterly complained about dealing with the media. The complaints range from invasion of privacy, to Geraldo-type sensationalized attacks, to simply being misquoted. As in dealing with all constituents, the CEO has to look upon the media as just one more customer.

Public. Some companies get more public attention than others. Public attention translates into becoming a constituent for the CEO.

Hospitals, for example, are widely regarded as rife with public scrutiny even though they might be a private, profit-making operation similar to the local furniture manufacturer. Legally the hospital has the same responsibility to the public as the manufacturer, but from the public perspective the responsibility is quite different.

The CEO needs to be constantly in touch with the public as a constituent because the public makes up the employees and customers.

The CEO is not ruler of his domain. He has *many* different interests to satisfy daily. As one CEO pleaded, "I wish they'd understand I'm doing the best I know how. I'm trying to serve them well, to serve their interest. I'll inadvertently irritate them. I'll make mistakes. It would be nice if they accepted it isn't always on purpose that I make them."

Despite this long list of constituents, the toughest person on most CEOs is the CEO himself. Most will say, above all, they work to please themselves. Few will be satisfied if the world is happy about their work unless they are happy too.

> *CEOs work for themselves, they judge self, set standards, change standards, elevate standards. It's very difficult to be satisfied because you're always redefining success. You therefore must enjoy the process because you spend so little time at any pinnacle.*
>
> *The CEO's toughest critic is himself. Every success puts the person in the position of what will he do as an encore. If he fails, it's awful. A lot of people glory in it—those who'd never risk themselves.*
>
> —DAVE POWELSON
> COB, CEO, and President,
> TRI-R Systems

POWER

The CEO's job includes dealing with all kinds of constituents, decisions, meetings, and operations. With all those responsibilities sometimes he has tremendous power, sometimes he's relatively powerless.

Part of the CEO's job is the *utilization* of power. Some of his power comes from the title but most comes from his style. The CEO who told me "power comes from always carrying five thousand dollars in cash around; it gets me to the head of the line," is not speaking of power but pull.

There are different kinds and levels of power that the CEO has at his disposal via the job.

Title power. This comes from the CEO office and position. The CEO is the "mayor of his city and the governor of his state."

Dollar power. The CEO allocates or authorizes money for projects and people because he holds the purse strings. That's "putting money where his mouth is" power.

Punch power. When the CEO bosses, polices, or parents employees he's using punch power. He carries the muscle to make life painful.

Expert power. Special knowledge, a skill, or an ability that no one else has constitutes expert power. The person who invents a cure for cancer will have tremendous clout and prestige anywhere worldwide. A mentor who takes someone under his wing has expert power. Accountants have expert power when accounting expertise is needed. Data processing people have it when data processing expertise is needed. An AAA tow truck driver has expert power when you need to be towed.

Hex power. This is the indisputable, intangible ability to spread charm and charisma even without identifiable justification. Some CEOs have run a company to the ground while still being thought of as outstanding, charismatic "community business leaders."

A chief's dominance and effectiveness increase with each additional type of power. The CEO automatically has title power. If he founded the company because of his special knowledge he gains expert power. As the company grows and becomes a "financial player," dollar power is added. Because of having title, expert, and dollar power, punch power comes into play; he can hire and fire. Only if the CEO develops people skills will he have hex power as well.

> *CEOs have power, the ability to make things happen on a routine basis with very little distraction.*
>
> —PAUL HOUSTON
> President, Results, Inc.

Any power loses its effectiveness if too frequently or indiscreetly used. Any power is soon questioned and challenged when used without equity.

The chief who constantly works on developing personal power rather than relying on position power is doing his job. Really effective power comes not from title or money but character. The CEO has power if he has the following:

- patience,
- calmness,
- forbearance,
- ability,
- energy,
- sympathy,
- spirit,
- ethics.

Everyone has power *sometimes*. You do not need to be a CEO to have it. Shelley Monfor, director of investor relations at Plum Creek, tells me about power: "My first job was with a public utilities company. I was a high-school student whose job was to turn people's power off when they didn't pay the bill." In the eyes of a customer, she held more power than any CEO on a day-in-day-out basis.

I can't emphasize enough regarding power that unless people give it to you, you don't have it. People react to their perception of you—not your perception of yourself. For example, the CEO of Company A has influence with his employees, customers, and shareholders. Right. But when Company A's CEO goes into Company F he holds very little power. Or when Company A's CEO goes to the grocery store, he has little power with the produce man.

The CEO job has many ramifications, from people to profits to operations to crisis management. Each aspect of the job requires varying skills and abilities based on the situation at hand. *Very* little is stagnant, repetitive, typical, or easy. A person headed to the top will never be able to fully prepare for *all* of the demands required of the CEO. A start is awareness of the full realm of responsibilities to be able to go into it with open eyes.

CEOs IN ACTION SUMMARY

The CEO's job entails the following:

People: Works with, manages, socializes, and politicks with all kinds of people all of the time.

Decisions: Makes tough and easy decisions all of the time.

Meetings: Conducts and/or attends an unrelenting number of meetings.

Selling: Needs to be the number-one salesperson for the organization.

Operations and Profits: The buck stops here in terms of operations and profits.

The payoff for the CEO job is power. You get
- an impressive title,
- control of other people's money,
- "muscle" to get things done,

- reputation of being an expert in something,
- the aura or charisma of a "leader."

CHAPTER 11

Moving On

What chiefs look for in who they promote, hire, and fire

When you're climbing Mount Everest, who you choose as a partner can make the difference between success and failure.

The people side of running a business is the most demanding, time consuming, and difficult part of a CEO's job. Hiring and promoting the right people for the company is the most important thing a chief does. The ability to spot potential in others surpasses the value of being exceedingly capable himself. If a chief does only one thing well, it should be finding and supporting good employees. *Nothing* happens without the right people in the right place at the right time. Almost all CEOs (the near-perfect and the not-so-near-perfect) agree on this one thing: The people make the difference.

When a person is promoted it is the result of an arbitrary decision on management's part supported by some evidence of justification. If you were a person passed over it may not seem fair and just, but it is nonetheless "the decision." If you were the person

who receives the promotion you likely feel management really knows what they are doing!

In reality, whether you were the "loser" or the
"winner" it is based on judgment and opinion—
opinions you can shape. Judgment is formed by observation (or reporting) of how well you're doing
your job today and how well you'll do it tomorrow
and if you can do the next job.

Keep in mind that tangibles and intangibles come
into play.

> *Sometimes it's just a pair of fresh eyes*
> *wanted by management. If you patiently*
> *wait your turn, it may mark you as the next*
> *in line. Maybe that newly promoted person*
> *is so good they blow your socks off and you*
> *agree they deserve the promotion. Some can*
> *be a flash for two or three years then they*
> *start to wane. If you stay in for the long*
> *run, you might get the next shot.*
> —LINN LEEBURG
> Executive Vice President and COO,
> WestGas

This chapter will examine what CEOs look for in
people they hire and promote and what to do when
someone is promoted over you.

> *I was in college ROTC. The first year no*
> *one has any rank; that comes in the second*
> *year when you have the opportunity to be-*
> *come a sergeant, corporal, or a nobody. The*

*commanding officer explained, "To deter-
mine next year's rank, I need you to write a
list of five people from among your peers
who you would like to work for, like to
work with, like to work for you." The guys
that moved ahead were on everybody's list.
If you were on nobody's list, you were in
trouble.*
                    —DAVE POWELSON
          Chairman, CEO, and President,
          TRI-R Systems

People who get hired and promoted have the following to show for themselves:

1. Results in their specialty.
2. Chemistry, attitude, and fitness.
3. They do more than the next person.

Results in their specialty. The person who gets
hired has demonstrated the ability to get results. The
person who gets promoted does likewise.

Do the job. Get things done. What chiefs care
about is *what gets done.* Bear in mind: Doing the job
may be boring and uncomfortable sometimes. But as
long as you accept payment from a company, do the
work that management wants done. (As one city
planner of an East Coast city told me, "Early on in
my career I pledged my support to each boss. I told
them in a manner of speaking, 'I'll support you despite how stupid I think you are.'")

A proven-results person is someone who succeeds

at a task the best. Peers, bosses, and subordinates have the same supporting resources available to them, but the results person is able to get things done.

People get successful outcomes in different ways. Some put in twenty-hour days. Some did nothing more than follow through reliably. ("I've paid executives six-figure incomes yet I still had to bird-dog them to follow through," says John Bianchi.) Some lucked into good situations.

Establish a pattern of productiveness by taking a pattern of action. That way bosses know they can count on you to do the following:

1. Identify a problem or opportunity.
2. Think it through to the point of coming up with two or three solutions/options.
3. Offer recommendations/suggestions.

Some made sure their results got noticed. Don't be afraid to sell yourself internally as much as you'd do externally, verbally, and in writing. "I finished the 270-page strategic plan." Fact. No brag. Results. Eighty-five percent of hikers think, "Let work speak for itself." That works in part but it's not sufficient. Find out how others in the company effectively communicate their results. Try that. Ask bosses *how* they want to be kept informed. Try that.

When higher-ups recognize that you achieve results at one level, they surmise potential to do the same in the next job. But be patient; it may take a while. Bosses are looking and working on their timetable, not yours.

The times are changing in that individual results are insufficient in some large organizations. Team results are what's emphasized. But almost every team has a leader. And the leader gets credit for both good and bad results. So if you want to be the one promoted, you have to work to stand out among team members and then as the leader, among teams.

Whether individual or team results, they must be where the company is focused. If it is an engineering company the results have to be engineering related; if a marketing company they have to be marketing related, and so on. The higher up you go, the more important it is to achieve results along the fundamental drive and beliefs of the company. People who get promoted are associated with successful business efforts and their part in meeting business goals (generally speaking increasing sales and earnings). Spend time finding out what is and isn't important.

There are trends, cycles, and fads in who gets promoted inside a company's organization. One time it is the technical wizard, the next time the financial whiz kid, the next time Mr. Personality, and the next someone fresh from the outside who is hired to be put on the fast track; the next is the old-timer with maturity and depth of experience from being entrenched in the corporate culture. And then the cycle works back to the beginning or someplace in the middle and the cycle continues.

Usually an individual thinks they deserve being bumped up more than their bosses and co-workers. That's because the person naturally wants more prestige and money and hasn't thoroughly and honestly considered what the company needs. It's typical to think, "They *need* me, I deserve it." While that may be true, it is the person in the position of power to decide who gets hired who has to see it that way also. You get promoted by meeting the company's needs, not your needs.

> *It's like in football, if I don't need another quarterback, no matter how good he is I don't need another one for my team. I may need a runner, or punter, or receiver and that's who I'm going to hire . . . someone who fits my team's needs . . . and it doesn't matter if I like them or not. If I believe they can do the job, that's who I'll hire.*
> —DENNIS WU
> Partner, Deloitte Touche L.L.P.

To be promoted, your name has to pop up as the answer after each question the boss asks regarding who should be advanced.

- Who does a good job?
- Who does more than their job?
- Who consistently produces results?
- Who fits well in our company?
- Who has the attitudes we want?
- Who has the courage to take on more responsibility?
- Who has the character we espouse?
- Who wants to be promoted?

One thing is certain: Not everyone will agree on who deserves the advance rank. Not the peers, bosses, or subordinates. But all of those people aren't privy to the screening an individual goes through, and they rarely are objective anyway. I'm not saying the decision maker is always objective or even right, but at least they have more information to make a more qualified decision.

> *Regardless of their careful consideration of candidates, CEOs do make mistakes, they do get fooled. You never really know what you're getting.*
> —Bob Hansford
> CEO, US Sprint, Canada

People who emphasize their personal agenda over accomplishment will be found out. Try not to be so driven by increased job status as to ignore your current real situation.

Simply put, the people promoted because of results make the right things happen at the right time. They provide a predictable path of doing things no one else did, or maybe wanted to do, and they got the desired results.

> *Who gets promoted? Someone with the knowledge and skills to do the task. He does his tasks in the context of the bigger picture because he understands the broad context. He has a perspective on the job and*

how it fits into corporate needs and his own
needs. Add luck to that.
     —LINN LEEBURG,
          Executive Vice President and COO,
          WestGas

It's a given that you must have intellectual horse-power, which does not mean simply a high IQ. Intellectual horsepower is a combination of basic intelligence, drive, willpower, passion, and common sense. And those attributes are all that's required *to get results.*

Jim Rupp, retired from his oil and gas exploration company, told me he always remembers a time in Europe during World War II when he thinks about a results-oriented person. "My commanding officer, a medic, and I came across a U.S. paratrooper who had successfully secured a clearing for the ground troops. He was alive but sprawled unconscious on the ground. The CO commented, 'He deserves a purple heart.' The medic said, 'But he hasn't shed any blood.' Whereupon the CO took out his knife, slit the paratrooper's surface skin, and said, 'Now he has.' That's getting results."

Chemistry, attitude, and a good fit. Good chemistry comes to someone who listens and learns, responds, relates, gets respect (from superiors, peers, subordinates, clients), keeps ego in control, gives and shares credit, and is objective. It's virtually impossible to have good chemistry without a sense of humor. It's common sense, good judgment, and being people-wise to know not to rely on smarts alone.

Everyone notices your effectiveness (or lack thereof). One CEO told me, "My secretary comes to me and lets me know who she thinks is doing a good job and who people like to work with. I admit she influences who I promote. I try to make sure the person deserves it and is right for the job."

> *Many believe hard work and intelligence will get you to the top—it's just a start. In my experiences, more quantum individuals do not achieve their expectations because of their poor people-quotients than they do because of substandard intelligence.*
>
> *As managers we make or break our careers on our ability to affect others' thoughts and actions. Some are smart as hell and work long and hard, but unless they can relate to and motivate others they won't maximize their effectiveness, the results they get, and their worth to their company.*
>
> —JOHN P. WILSON
> President, USC

Chemistry is a word that is often used to address the intangible feeling of fitting with the values and attitudes of a CEO and his team. Being on the same wavelength helps in liking people you work with.

> *Charisma is a big factor and can't be underestimated. Enthusiasm, charm, salesman-*

ship all put together can really move people. Then of course you have to do something productive in addition. I recommend in an interview my clients give candidates an hour to determine if there is chemistry. Spend the second hour to prove the chemistry wrong or right.
　　—MARCIA P. PRYDE
　　　Vice President and Managing Director,
　　　A. T. Kearney

On the other hand many CEOs told me the person who can do the job best is who gets promoted. Near-perfect chiefs get along with them whether they like them or not. They don't have to be friends but they try to be. Good CEOs put aside personality differences or preferences to see if the person is best for the job. (Unfortunately, chemistry can sway the decision whether the job specifications are clearly met or not.)

A big mistake a CEO makes is to hire people he feels comfortable with. That isn't what he needs. Look for people who can do the job best, even if you don't get along. My CFO never supported me on anything. He was honest and kept the books right. And he pointed out all of my mistakes. He really made me think. You're not going to have growth if everybody is thinking the same.
　　　—ERNIE HOWELL
　　　　Retired President,
　　　　Packaging Systems International

Attitudes, like values, aren't easy to change if they don't mesh. Anyone who's ever attempted it will say it's easier to hire a good attitude than change a bad one.

> *I want an individual who is excited about living life. An optimist who wakes up and figures they're going to get it on today. Someone who addresses challenges in a positive way and doesn't bitch too much, that's what I look for in people I hire.*
> —JOHN KREBBS
> President, The Parker Company

Whatever attitude helped you get hired is the disposition you likely need to get promoted, as long as you can maintain it. Too many lose their "good" disposition. It has to be continuous through the honeymoon period and on into the long haul.

> *I make it a rule to stay away from negative energy. I find it difficult to tolerate negative employees and immediately try to stop it if I can.*
> —SUSAN YAGER
> President, Domestications

> *What do I like the least? Dealing with negative non-team players or nonperformers.*
> —WILLIAM WALLACE
> CEO, Phoenix Home Life

Good attitude doesn't mean sweetie, nicey-nice. You can have a good attitude and still want change and improvement.

"People who are costing us business because they are in the wrong job or because they don't care about the business and their work, lose their job," says one chief. "If someone is just in the wrong job I'll do all I can to help them get into a different job. But if a person has a negative approach or an attitude where they really aren't trying, it's not that difficult to let them go."

A simple, straightforward (universal) good attitude as defined by the bosses interviewed is: *If you work for someone, they are the boss.* Most welcome input to bring up opposite opinions, but once a decision is made they expect their lead to be followed. They may be wrong; you may be right—but they are still the boss. If you become the boss, you'll likely make decisions that subordinates disagree with. Then you can say, "I'm the boss; do it my way." But until then, they are the boss. You have a job now. Manage it. It will be enlarged soon if you keep that outlook.

> *People are sometimes so busy planning their careers they don't get today's job done. They've got to do the job that they are getting paid for today. If they do their job, their career will take care of itself.*
> —LINN LEEBURG
> Executive Vice President and COO, WestGas

An important aspect of fitting in is the ability to handle people above you so the person doesn't feel intimidated by you. If they feel threatened in any way they won't help move you up. Avoiding a situation where your bosses feel threatened by you means simple action on your part.

- Don't say the first thing that comes to mind.
- *Think* through what you need to say and how it could be taken.
- Fully consider the effect it might have on all people involved.
- Choose to say what you want in a diplomatic way so as not to offend.

It means, for example, that when told a secret, you keep it. You make sure they can trust you.

> *New employees must conduct business with the same principles we do. Some people don't value the same things we do and despite the good backgrounds don't work out.*
> —BARBARA THOMAS
> President, Pillsbury Canada Ltd.

One CEO overheard an engineering manager refer to a company-sponsored training program as "pseudo psychology, touch-feely, bullshit." That didn't get him fired; it only alerted the CEO to watch the engineer more carefully. A few other comments caused the CEO to conclude, "I just don't think I can trust him anymore. He's two-faced. He feigns cooperation to my face but is uncooperative behind my back."

The interesting thing is almost everyone's chemistry, attitude, and good fit is good going into a job. Then many lose it. They stop finding solutions to problems they used to solve. The situation was always the same. They used to ignore or correct things about the company; now they create problems with the same things. They say, "It's a dumb policy," even though it's been there for seven years. "The boss plays golf every Wednesday afternoon. If he has the day off, why shouldn't I?" Now all of a sudden it bugs the employee because of his change of attitude.

Bob Hansford, president of US Sprint, Canada, tells of an attitude problem that cost an employee her job: "I had a very bright, capable, talented salesperson, but she could not accept working in Canada; she was constantly running the country down. I had to fire her."

Competence and intelligence are valued, of course. They are necessary to succeed *but not sufficient.* You must also have chemistry and attitude, and be able to fit in to get hired and promoted. Once on the job, to become a top climber, you have to do more.

Do more than the next person. David Packard, half of Hewlett-Packard, talks about building his company: "If something needed to be done, we just had to get in there and do it." He's worth many millions, so you could say that doing more paid off for him.

Remember chapter 8 on how CEOs become CEOs? One of their "secrets" was *doing more.*

The person who does his job, does more than required, and gets positive results gets promoted. That
same individual gets more contact, attention, and
help from higher-ups in turn; also more promotions.
It's a cycle of events that goes on and on as long as
the climber keeps generating the activity.

> *What holds most people back? Not going*
> *the second mile.*
> —LOLA SCOBEY
>   President, Audio-Therapy Innovations

The "new volunteerism" in business requires you
to leap at any opportunity to stand in front of management. Avail yourself of every chance to interact
with as broad a base of people in the company as
possible. Initiating more and broader exposure
broadens your chance for promotion. So when a
group of managers are sitting around the table trying
to decide who to promote one of them will say, "I
have an idea, how about Harvey, who gave that
good presentation in Puerto Rico. Okay?"

Do more of what the boss wants and what the
company needs. How do you know what that is?
Ask. The surefire best way to find out what your
boss looks for in people to promote is to *ask* before
the opportunity arrives. You need to correctly identify what the chief wants. If you won't ask and ask
and continue to ask over time, you won't learn how
to get promoted. Every boss is different, and they
might be very different from your thinking. So ask
for clarification.

Sometimes when climbing you have to carry a heavy pack. To move ahead you can't get away with slacking off. The thing that happens after mediocrity is unemployment.

Ed Shonsey, CEO of Northrup King, asked his daughter, Katy, a young career woman, what she would do if she wanted to move ahead. She answered, "Do what they tell me to do." So she and Ed discussed it. As he related to me, "When they say, 'Here's what you need to do,' do the basic, on time, in a reliable way. But also do more." Shonsey went on to relate this story: "Be sensitive to how they make decisions. One boss I worked for wanted numbers. One wanted a picture of how it was going to work. One time I'd walk in and address the numbers. Next day I'd come in with a picture. I got sophisticated and was able to give them both what they wanted at the same time."

There are three kinds of people in most organizations.

1. *Inactive ones*—who won't be let "into the game" at any level.
2. *Reactive ones*—who we all need to be some of the time.
3. *Proactive ones*—the ones who move up.

> *You need to declare yourself. Be proactive and put yourself on the line. You can't lie low and see if some project is successful, then pop up from behind a shield and claim a part. You have to clearly say to your orga-*

nization, Here's what I think we should be doing and here's why it will make a difference. Then you have to make it happen. A leader will proactively stand up and be counted.
    —DOUGLAS CONANT
        Group Executive Vice President,
        Nabisco, Inc.

Being expected to do more is good and bad. The good part is management figures you can handle it and want you to prove yourself to get noticed for promotion. The bad part is they could be trying to overburden you so you'll quit, or are just trying to take advantage of you. It's better if you do the job completely as expected and then do more on your own. The financial rewards will hopefully follow. But the experience adds to your net worth regardless.

Captain Odegaard of the USS *Clark* helps his people do and therefore learn more. "There are no officers in the pilot house when anchors aweigh. . . . I give the authority to the enlisted men. It builds their confidence, gives them experience for their evaluations because a commanding officer can say, 'Oh, they've done that,' so they get promoted faster."

Doing more doesn't mean outrageous acts of extra effort but simply doing a little better, putting a little more effort in by doing the following:

- *Talk to your boss.* Find out his/her pet projects and get involved in those. Few bosses will fire someone who is working on a favorite project.

Simultaneously, if possible, get off any project the boss doesn't like.

- *Initiate cost reductions in your department.* Don't pressure the boss for an expanded budget—that's a sure way to get laid off. Instead ask for a leaner, tighter budget.
- *Lower your own overhead.* Tell your boss you know that times are tough and you are willing to accept and promote an across-the-board pay cut.
- *Volunteer for additional duties.* Find a vacuum and fill it. Show your crossover ability. You'll become too valuable to terminate. Improve your relations with other departments; this is no time for empire building.
- *Maintain a positive, cooperative attitude.* It takes pressure off the boss and you won't appear like a malcontent. Likewise, maintain a sense of humor—and keep away from negative people and conversations.
- *Have guts to make decisions.* If you appear scared and timid, you decrease others' confidence in you. Have guts also to ask more questions, don't allow ambiguity. Miscommunication gives people an excuse to terminate you.
- *Show implicit trust in your boss.* When a tough situation comes up, show you trust that your boss will figure a way out of the situation and that you can help be part of the solution. Work on increasing others' trust in you; make sure people aren't nervous around you. Be honest.

Being dishonest is the surest way of getting fired at any time.

- *Come early and stay late.* Get out of the carpool if necessary so you aren't tied to leaving at 5:01 P.M.
- *Have a mental Plan B*, e.g., "If I do lose my job I'll take steps 1, 2, and 3. . . ." The mental preparation will relax you and therefore improve your performance. Care but don't care too much about keeping this job. Remember: Desperate-looking people are not wanted.
- *If you are involved in an interoffice romance—stop it.* If you are entertaining the idea of starting one—don't do it. At least one individual in the couple will inevitably lose their job.

A business is like every good sports team: They try to get rid of the worst players. The aim is to keep the best, even if that means changing positions. If you are a player worth keeping these steps can protect your job. "If you want success you have to work for it twenty-four hours a day. You have to work for it, eat for it, sleep for it," says Uta Pippig, winner of the Boston, New York, and Berlin marathons.

Here are some steps to help you keep revved up, as well as your career.

1. *Take a career physical.* Appraise yourself. Find out what people think about you. See how closely it matches your own evaluation.
2. *Decide what you need to change.* Sit down and think about it. Set goals—not just your career goals but your health, family, and life goals too.

Set big goals. It's better to fall short than not
aim high enough and sell yourself short.

3. *Turn goals into an action plan.* Write down what
   you plan to do, how, with whom, by when.

   - Initiate five telephone calls with new prospec-
     tive business contacts per week.

   - Exercise forty-five minutes four times a week,
     with your spouse, starting this week.

   - Set out to evolve a reputation from decision
     taker to decision maker by taking a risk and
     making a recommendation once a week for the
     next fifteen weeks.

4. *Get several balls up in the air.* When some drop
   (which some will), you still have others up.
   Have lots of goals. Be multidimensional. Aim
   for continuous activity.

5. *Anticipate and accept the feeling of discomfort.*
   As I've said before, anything new is uncomfortable. Keep working with the balls up in the air
   until it feels comfortable. There is no secret
   method to becoming comfortable; it's simply a
   matter of time and perseverance. The right attitude toward revving up your career will keep you
   motivated and create excitement that will overwhelm procrastination.

6. *Keep the balls up.* Keep up the action. Get into
   a discipline; make it your second nature. Get to
   the point where you feel discomfort if you don't
   have several goals working at one time.

An exciting career comes from personal initiative.
It's like the old saying, "Have one hand for the ship

and one for yourself." You must work on doing your job, but work on career *umph* also. It doesn't just happen to anyone. You make it happen with thinking, planning, action, and persistence.

Doing more is not necessarily laboring extra hours overtime long after everyone else is gone. That can upstage co-workers and bosses who will subsequently resent you. Or the other extreme it makes you look inefficient and unorganized. Also unnecessary excessive hours cause errors, burnout, low morale, and even divorce. Doing more is not translated to a burdensome work schedule but just asking a little more of your brain and your body.

> *People I notice accept responsibility, sometimes even without the authority. They pay the price; then all of a sudden they become a very important person. They know things no one else knows. They're indispensable because they just did a little more.*
> —NEIL GEORGI
>   CEO, Neil Georgi & Associates, Inc.

Ask for more work. Take on additional responsibilities on your own. Let the right people know you are doing that. State what you're going to do and meet the expectations you set (which should be beyond what they set). Set goals for yourself (or your team), then let management know those plans. Keeping people abreast of your activities is not buttering up the boss, it's helping the powers that be plan.

How do CEOs react to this information?

*In the end, we look the competition over and
promote those who stick their heads above the
crowd. Most times it is those who get results
and meet or exceed our expectations. It's always those that improve whatever situation
they are dealt because of their involvement. We
then say, "Show us what you've got at your
new level." You could get promoted again!*
                                    —JOHN P. WILSON
                                    President, USC

Your actions are most CEOs' best indication of
your thoughts. You have to act like you want them
to perceive you. (It's interesting that someone who
does more comes to enjoy it.) It does not go unnoticed and it is never lost effort. Yes, there are people
who will take advantage of you and pile more on if
they see you can handle it. (We'll talk about those
situations when we discuss added responsibility
without added title or money.) But in the end, you
work for yourself, your own satisfaction, your level
of expectation regardless of whether or not it is immediately recognized.

*The exceptionally good people who dazzle
me and the exceptionally bad are the ones
who are brought to my attention.*
        —VINCENT OKAMOTO
        COB and CEO, Pacific Heritage Bank

And while you're at it, if you think the boss is
doing a good job, *tell him.* It's okay to tell the boss

he did a good job, just as you want recognition from him. One CEO wrote me a note on the back of his business card after he heard me speak. "Why are people afraid to praise the boss?" Heck, many are afraid to even talk to the boss.

Sometime in the company cafeteria, introduce yourself to the CEO. It takes guts, but the CEO will

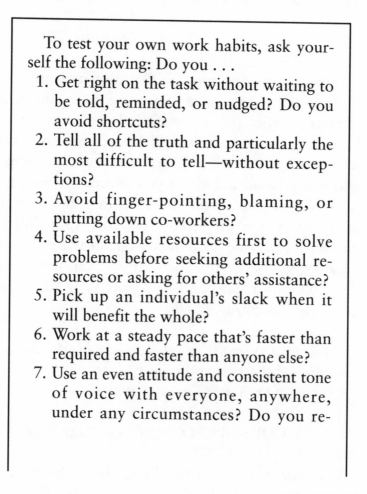

To test your own work habits, ask your-self the following: Do you . . .

1. Get right on the task without waiting to be told, reminded, or nudged? Do you avoid shortcuts?
2. Tell all of the truth and particularly the most difficult to tell—without excep-tions?
3. Avoid finger-pointing, blaming, or putting down co-workers?
4. Use available resources first to solve problems before seeking additional re-sources or asking for others' assistance?
5. Pick up an individual's slack when it will benefit the whole?
6. Work at a steady pace that's faster than required and faster than anyone else?
7. Use an even attitude and consistent tone of voice with everyone, anywhere, under any circumstances? Do you re-

frain from "putting on" for special people?

8. Treat small and big tasks with equal importance and results? Do you complete the work even if others beg off?
9. Think through actions before taking them and consider the consequences rather than blindly, thoughtlessly doing as told?
10. Avoid complaining even when others are moaning around you?

Give yourself a grade for each question: A, B, C, D, or F.

Aim to have at least seven As and Bs to be considered for promotion.

If it sounds like a tough test with extraordinarily high expectations, consider it's what *you'd* expect if *you* were the boss. Now, in these changing economic times, is the time to stand out from your co-climbers with effective work habits. When pay raises and promotions happen, you will be the one who earns and receives them because not only are you doing good work, but also a good job.

likely appreciate it. True, there are some exceptions, but most will appreciate it. Then the next time you see the CEO, he'll probably say hello. The next time he sees you, he might ask you a question: "How are things going?" You've just been *invited* by the CEO to give your opinion! You can answer. "Pretty well. I have an idea; do you mind if I talk to you about it sometime?"

One CEO explained to me, "I promote people I can trust."

"How do you know you can trust them?" I asked.

"They aren't afraid to talk to me, and when they do, they don't hesitate to tell me bad news."

One of the most important things you can do is *level with the CEO*. You must give him an honest opinion of what's being done or not being done.

Have the courage to tell the boss what you think. But be sure to think before you open your mouth. Bring up good news and praise as well as bad news.

Seldom will a human resource evaluation profile rate you on being too much of a risk taker. Instead it will say "self-starter, requires little supervision, has goals of the corporation in mind. Recommend promotion."

Over and over again CEOs told me, "I'd rather employees not say 'Yes' but rather 'Here's the problem!' I hate having to say, 'That's news to me.'"

To bring up bad news better, tell the boss

- these are the problems you're going to run into,
- here's what you'll hear,
- here's a rebuttal.

"I've never been afraid to bring up bad news. I even have a little prayer I say," one CEO told me:

"God, secure me from security, now and forever. Amen."

Extra visible results come from steps that keep you ahead of the competition. Find out what the best in the class does and use that as a benchmark to work from. Do more.

Who gets fired? The person who does not do his job and can't get results. People who don't respond to problems or don't follow up after repeatedly being told. Individuals with bad attitudes. One formerly employed person admitted to me, "I went into the job unprepared, with no tools. And things didn't change. I didn't want to fail, but I didn't want to work very hard either."

If you don't do the job like the boss wants (or better) you don't deserve the job. She can find someone else who will. You can't take full pay for doing part of the work.

All my life I've heard from important people, work hard, persevere, and use your common sense. The reality of business is that it is not all that difficult. Simply put, if you fail, you gave up, didn't persevere, and didn't use your common sense.
—MICHAEL FIELDS
CEO, OpenVision

I've replaced four of my senior managers this last year. Some of them were fourteen-year employees, some friends of mine outside of business. It was extremely tough for me. If a

CEO ever feels uncaring, he's getting too cal-
lous. As the person making the decision I
think about whether I'm doing irreparable
harm to the other eighteen hundred employ-
ees. But I've discovered most all of the other
employees wonder why the boss hadn't taken
action sooner. In fact some of them came up
to me and said, "I wondered when you were
going to do that." People below see poor
performance in their bosses and they don't
like it. Their careers and income suffer from
the wrong people in management.

—BILL FAIRFIELD
CEO, Inacom Corporation

GLASS CEILING/CEMENT WALLS

There is a special obstacle female climbers have regarding promotions: High-powered females (particularly if they're single) can be a threat to the female
corporate spouse. "Corporate spouse" means the
woman married to a male executive or CEO who
raises children and does not work outside the home.

The two types of women have chosen different life
paths. The corporate spouse feels confident in a lot
of areas—but not necessarily regarding her husband's
business. When the spouse feels she cannot compete
with the female employee, the female employee can
become a threat—especially if she is also single.

It's the female employee's responsibility to minimize the potential threat. If she doesn't manage the
situation, it could hinder her effectiveness. Not every
corporate spouse will feel intimidated, but why take
chances? A negative encounter usually first occurs at
a corporate social function. There are some precautions a female manager should take to avoid jealousy
and establish a rapport with a corporate spouse.

- *Consider the possibility of a threat in advance.*
  Put yourself in the spouse's shoes; take yourself
  out of the hunt-and-kill mode of business and
  put yourself in the home-and-hearth mode.
- *When together, initiate conversations with the
  corporate spouse more frequently than with her
  husband.* Do it first; don't wait for her. Have a
  one-on-one discussion with her about common
  interests. You can always ask advice, ask a favor,
  or compliment her. If her husband interrupts,
  don't switch to him. Complete the conversation
  with her.
- *Don't be overly physically demonstrative with
  co-workers or customers—touching and hug-
  ging—unless you do it equally with both sexes.*
  Be more reserved. A good rule is not to do anything you wouldn't want to be photographed
  doing.
- *At all times, be aware of your body language.*
  Don't be coy or flirtatious toward any men—not
  just the husbands.
- *Be conservative in dress.* Don't let your clothes
  be more interesting than you are.

- *Limit dirty jokes or profane language.* But don't be bothered by those who use profanity. You don't want to appear judgmental. But don't use any sexual connotations yourself.
- *Don't allow yourself to get physically isolated with a male.* Whether in a car, hallway, or outdoor patio; any such situation can and will be misconstrued and read the wrong way.
- *Don't be defensive about the corporate spouse's being defensive.*
- *Above all, approach the situation with an attitude of good cheer and expect acceptance.* Try for rapport, but don't try too hard. There are some insecure people you will never be able to deal with effectively.

How the female manager behaves around any man is how the corporate spouse expects she behaves around her husband. It's just good business sense for female workers to take precautions. The spouse has been around the boss (and likely will be around him) a lot longer than the employee. After all, you never know what the corporate spouse will say to her husband about the female employee afterward. When the event is over, the spouse will have his ear and the female executive may be the topic of their conversation. That conversation can make or break her career.

To get promoted regardless of whether you are a man or woman, clearly understand your job responsibilities, then do them. Then do more. A boss should be able to delegate, go do what he needs to do, come back, and have the job done *right*, and done *on time*, the first time. It's really just a matter of problem solving. If you can solve problems, you'll be an asset in business. Yes, it is head down, chin up, nose to the grindstone, shoulder to the wheel time. Take no shortcuts. You know what to do. Do it. Don't count on someone else. As the old cowboy saying goes, "Make good or make tracks."

You may claim you earned a perfect score on the test earlier in the chapter. You ask, do, act, get results, over and over. But promotion has eluded you. Worse. You're passed over by someone else. What then?

WHAT TO DO WHEN SOMEONE IS PROMOTED OVER YOU

The person least likely to get promoted is the person constantly looking for it. Douglas Conant, a group executive vice president of NABISCO, said to me, "It's like dating when you were a teenager. If you weren't interested in girls, dating came a lot easier." Very seldom will you get too much recognition and reward for your efforts, too soon; 97 percent of the time, it will be just the opposite—at least in your eyes! Most everyone (at every level) feels overworked and underappreciated—including the CEO!

Despite all my comments about scaling the summit, the fact is you have to:

- live and work for the current situation,
- do good work,
- and don't be so worried where it is taking you.

Of course, you also have to ask yourself if you're comfortable waiting, and then you must also ask if you can afford to go somewhere else.

You aren't the first to have this happen. One vice president who thought he'd get the nod for president relayed to me, "If the boss sends me a note, I send one back to answer all his questions sooner than it took him to write it originally. Always by the end of that business day. I'm humble and thoughtful when necessary, but I can take on a tone of righteous indignation to carry the company's banner. So I was extraordinarily rocked and decimated when they brought a new president in over me."

> *If the door is completely shut, go at it again. If it is continually shut with no possibility of movement, vote with your feet. I can think of people who have left for one reason or another and are a lot happier. They weren't using their capabilities here. It's true that in some situations, regardless of what you do, you aren't going to win. Most of us undervalue ourselves and don't know what a good commodity we are, and we don't test it.*
>
> —RICHARD MCCORMICK
> CEO, US West

Make your decision to stay or leave with complete information on what they liked or didn't like. It does not mean they are right; it just means that that's their perspective. But you need to understand it to do something about it. So ask what you need to be working on so you don't miss out on the promotion next time. When passed over, take heart; everyone who is hot cools. Everything has an end. Just keep doing your job. If you don't get the nod this year, you might the next or the next.

Karna Kruckenberg-Schofer tells of interviewing prior to becoming CEO of Poudre Valley Hospital. Remember, things don't happen on *your* schedule.

I met with various staff, small groups, and key individuals from 7:00 A.M. to 9:00 P.M. for three days. The interview process in total was over a three-week period. There were some social things mixed in and I had many opportunities to think on my feet. One was at a community meeting where I was told I had to give a brief presentation on health-care reform, then answer their questions—without any notice! But I know when you give a speech, people won't remember a lot, only about three or four points. So I quickly organized my thoughts and presented. People said I did a good job. Some of the interviews were formal with a panel of people who literally went from one to another asking one question, then the next person and so on around the room. Some were very informal. Then they concluded Friday afternoon with odd questions:

"You've done a wonderful job. We have no more questions. What are you going to do now?" I knew I didn't have the job, and then I found out on Saturday the search committee offered the job to a man from Cedar Rapids.

A board member called me Sunday morning a week later to see if I would be there for the next two hours. "Wait for my call," he said. Nine hours later they called. That happened three times over the next four days. Instead of letting me and the other candidate know preferentially or at least simultaneously, I found out by reading in the paper that the man they'd offered the job to had turned it down. On Thursday, they asked me to meet the search committee and offered me the job. I accepted. Many people immediately wrote and called saying I should have been first choice. That would have been nice but it didn't happen that way.

Be a bit patient, a bit trusting. You don't always know what's best for you in the company. They are going to miss occasionally also. But every CEO told me that at least once (if not more times) in their careers, they didn't get the jobs they wanted. It happens to everybody. Don't too quickly conclude that you'll just go out and get a new job. Be patient. Find out why you were passed over. Change. Then if you get passed over again consider leaving.

Ideally the boss promotes the *right* person, then deals with others who didn't get it. Top chiefs let you know why and what you can work on to be considered next time.

I'm honest. I tell them who's being consid-
ered and why. I tell them why the individual
got promoted and why they didn't and what
they can work on to be considered in the fu-
ture. I'll say, "I'd like to promote you as
vice president of sales. I promoted John be-
cause of ———. *If you want to work on*
———*next time, I'll seriously consider you.*
—DENIS BROWN
CEO, Pinkertons

"Leaving mad is the worst thing you can do. The second worst is going in with a proclamation, 'I should have gotten the job.' It will be a major strike against you. It could be a short-term aberration, so just swallow your pride," advised Reuben Mark, COB, president, and CEO of the Colgate-Palmolive Company. Unless it's a real brick wall you're up against, hang in there. You can't look at things in chunks of time measured in days, weeks, or months. You've got to break time into bigger chunks. As Mark says, "Say to yourself, 'I'm not going to let this bother me.' You might even go into the boss and say, 'You've been my boss for two years and I've learned a lot. I know John got the promotion. He's a good man. I'm pleased for him. I want your straightfor-ward critique on areas I need to work on so I can get the shot at the job the next time.'" Do not try to change their mind. It will not happen. It's a done deal.

You have some choices.

1. Crawl into a shell and whine that you've been dealt a dirty deal.
2. Write a six-page letter demanding an explanation.
3. Analytically write a checklist of reasons why you didn't get the job from the perspective of all people involved.
4. Seek constructive criticism from your chief and co-workers. Ask the following questions: What should I consider doing differently? What am I doing now that is hurting my chances? Any suggestions at all?
5. Handle it mentally and physically.
6. Attempt to rectify weaknesses.

Numbers three through six are preferred!

When you seek promotion, make sure the star you reach for isn't a satellite. Be sure it's what you want (and deserve). The old expression "Be careful what you wish for; you might get it" is true. Many happily, successfully, productively employed people became unhappy, unsuccessful, and unproductive people at higher levels in the organization. If that happens, get out. If you don't like your job, and it's not likely to get any better, you'll suffer the rest of your life and be miserable.

But never ever, ever, ever, ever give up on yourself.

What Do You Do When You Aren't Promoted but Are Given More Responsibility

Go into the chief's office and discuss the situation in a relaxed frame of mind—not with irritation. It could be a test to see if you can handle additional responsibility. Or it could be a test to see if you're vulnerable and usable, in which your chief chooses to take advantage of your good nature.

Or you might find out there is a different and better opportunity waiting.

You cannot read the chief's mind. Eliminate guesswork and ask. If you stay and work through it, choose to stick it out cheerfully. It might turn out well. Take the long view; it's the only thing that works.

Ed Shonsey, CEO of Northrup King, told me his experience of getting more responsibility put on his shoulders: "Early in my career I joined a company where no one had ever been brought in from the outside at a management level. My first task was to ask three people to leave the company. Turns out they didn't understand the culture. After each one was let go my boss asked me to take on their job. I grudgingly said, 'Okay,' although I secretly loved the opportunity." And that's what added responsibility can mean in your job—an opportunity. It depends on your perspective on the entire situation.

With more responsibility you have the opportunity

to become more valuable and invaluable. You may not get a title or pay raise but you may be able to get some budget for continuing education, flextime, financial planning assistance, health-club memberships, a bigger office, child-care expense reimbursement, extra vacation or comp time for travel, use of the corporate car fleet or jet.

In a way you can be honored about being given more responsibility without a fancier title. (How's that for choosing a different perspective?) You might say to your boss, "You've done a great job planning someone's career by . . ." (spelling out the duties they've demanded of you. Then lay out where that successful effort typically leads to job promotion). You can imply whether that is "inside or outside" of the company. In other words, manage your boss into your plan. But simultaneously do some career planning. Don't threaten to walk but prepare to walk.

If you can see the potential for advancement, play the situation through. It might just happen. If you've been doing a good job—and more as they've requested—you have to approach your boss. Don't say, "You told me if I do this, you'll do that. . . ." You may have thought you heard them and they didn't, or they forgot anyway. It may have been something you just want to believe. Either way, if you say "You said . . ." they will become defensive. Better to say, "My recollection was . . . and I sure wish we could put this together. . . ." Present it with a nonoffensive tone of voice, facial expression, and words.

Almost everyone at every level (CEO on down) voices this complaint at some time. It is a reality of business life that more and more is constantly asked of you. Consider the fact that you constantly ask more and more of your spouse, children, boss, co-workers, the government, and on and on. It's easy to feel put upon when you are on the giving end but when you're on the receiving end it's not that bad!

If the situation honestly gets to an inhumane point, you have the choice to quit. Before you leave in frustration and anger, make sure you've discussed the problem with the boss. He may get a new, improved perspective on the problem. But at least you've attempted to solve it rather than just complaining about it and leaving prematurely.

I remember the marketing manager with a recent promotion to vice president. Unbeknownst to his employer, the marketing man had been looking elsewhere because he felt the promotion was too slow in coming. The new VP had to tell his CEO he was taking a different job with another company. The boss was furious; he'd made the recommendation, pushed the promotion, got it through, and was now losing his person. "You're just a marketing soldier of fortune. If someone offers more money or challenge, you're gone," screamed the boss.

Final note regarding promotions: Should you get and accept a job promotion, remember that this is the time you must really be aware of management watching you. You will be in the spotlight and under scrutiny much more than ever or than anyone else is. You are a "pioneer" likely to get "arrows." Do not relax, rest, or be relieved at all. Do just the opposite. Turn up the effort on everything written about in this

chapter on how to get promoted because you'll need
that to stay at the top of the hill.

MOVING ON SUMMARY

Who gets hired and promoted?
  1. People who achieve results in their specialty
  2. People who have good chemistry and attitude
     and are able to fit in
  3. People who do more than the next person

Who gets fired?
  1. People who don't produce results
  2. People with poor chemistry and attitude
  3. People who don't do any more than the mini-
     mum required

CHAPTER 12

How Much Do CEOs Get Paid

Is the price they pay worth the amount they get?

In general, CEOs make a lot of money.

CEO compensation will always be an interesting issue of discussion. A survey conducted by *Worth* magazine and Roper/Starch Worldwide showed that 40 percent of Americans think about how much money they make during a day versus 14 percent who think about the weather in a day and 13 percent who think about sex. Only 8 percent didn't think about money in any context during the course of a day. Earning potential is and should be an interest to you as you climb the ladder. It's *one* gauge of success.

How much money is enough? Well, legend has it that John D. Rockefeller answered, "Just a little more than what you have."

According to *Fortune*, the CEOs of two hundred of America's largest corporations made on average $4.1 million each annually. The total compensation included salary, bonuses, and the current value of awarded stock grants. (For example, stock options the CEO chose to exercise, not including the long-term payouts, were on average twenty-three times their base salaries. Michael Eisner at Disney had $202 million in long-term payout.) The average cash compensation was $1.5 million in real terms. Notice, that was the average. The highest paid, at this writing, was Sanford I. Weill from Travelers, Inc., at $45,700,000. (That same year Weill reportedly cut some workers' benefits such as pensions and health coverage.) The lowest was Warren E. Buffett from Berkshire Hathaway at $305,000. (Buffett does own $7.8 million of company stock.)

> **Note:** As a frame of reference, one million dollars a year equals approximately $3,860 per work day, about $480 per hour if each working day were an eight-hour day.

President Clinton's after-tax income was $190,000.

It can be typical that a CEO gets paid twenty-five times the lowest-paid employee in the corporation. Some receive one hundred times as much.

"I used to get very angry when people made more money. I'd go home and kick a chair. Today I don't get angry," one CEO who earned $22.2 million in 1994 told me. He added, "I'm not worth the money they pay me. And you know, it actually was a lot more fun when I had less."

There are other compensations for CEOs as well:

- club memberships
- access to a fleet of cars and planes (not just for business but for personal use)
- exclusive residences
- landscaping, architectural, and interior design services for their residences
- home security systems
- use of company-owned resorts (in places like Aspen, Palm Springs, Acapulco Bay)
- private bathroom at the office
- private exercise room (and showers)
- private dining room (and personal chef)
- life-size portraits of them and their families
- low-interest or no-interest loans
- support services for personal side businesses
- salary during extended leaves of absence (with personal support staff)
- reimbursement for travel and entertainment costs
- financial counseling
- retirement counseling
- reimbursement for taxes attributed to use of aircraft, auto, etc.
- car and driver
- golden parachutes

(As an example of the latter, when John Akers left IBM as CEO, he walked away with a $2.5 million severance check, $1.3 million annual pension, stock options, and a $125,000 bonus. William Agee walked away from Morrison Knudsen with $1.5 million. Steve Ross of Time Warner had a death benefit that paid his personal estate his salary and bonus for three years after his death.)

Big CEO paychecks make some people (particularly shareholders) unhappy. Since 1983, CEOs' cash compensation increased 44 percent on average. Managers' and administrators' salaries dropped 2 percent over that same period, and factory workers' annual salaries were down 10 percent. Pay packages are a politically explosive issue. Theoretically there's no such thing as too much pay if pay relates to performance. If the company earns money and shareholders earn money, then the CEO should earn money. Justifiable pay is proportionately tied to long-term stock performance or specifically targeted goals such as sales or earnings. Pay goes not just to the man for what *he* does but what he can get *others* to do. Pay has to be competitive or companies can't recruit top people. Problems occur when massive compensation packages are given in spite of lower earnings and huge layoffs. Pay isn't always relative to performance.

The government is initiating legislation to limit corporate compensation deductibility and to add new disclosure rules in proxy statements. Both are attempts to quell the public and media outcry about high bonuses paid CEOs for poor performance.

You definitely read the public complaints about CEO compensation and you'll also read the argument that a CEO's money is nothing compared to a professional athlete's, including salary and endorsement totals in one year: Michael Jordan, $36 million; Jack Nicklaus, $14.8 million; Evander Holyfield, $12.0 million; Joe Montana, $10.3 million; Steffi Graf, $8 million; Mario Andretti, $5.5 million.

Bill Reagan, CEO of Reagan Companies, said to me, "The difficulty of accomplishment in running a business isn't more important than raising a family or getting through life. The professional basketball player is the biggest joke when it comes to compensation. They have the big salaries and all they do is take a ball and put in into a hoop."

Theoretically you could say when the company makes money, the CEO should make money. For example, when the CEO leadership can provide payoffs as Eisner at Disney did there will be companies that will continue to pay it (e.g, ten thousand Disney shares purchased in 1984 and held until the end of 1993 saw market value rise from $588,750 to $3.4 million). A *Forbes*/Gallup Poll of CEOs found 97 percent of CEOs said their compensation was tied to performance and 57 percent admitted they work harder than they would if the compensation were a fixed amount. (If you didn't have any hope of earning more you wouldn't work harder either.)

The same should go when the company is losing money. But it doesn't happen that way. As *Newsweek* writes about Peter Guber, who formerly ran Sony Pictures Entertainment, "He cost hundreds of millions to hire. He spent hundreds of millions more building what his bosses hoped would become a dazzling media empire. He bought the fleetest corporate jets, decorated his offices in the most lavish style (i.e., $100 million to remodel the old MGM lot, paying $100,000 for one office credenza), hired the most famous writers, actors, and directors. And now, at the end of it all, he will cost his employers many millions more to pay him off for a job less than well done . . . capping off what is widely considered to be one of the most expensive chapters in the history of the entertainment industry." Guber walked away with a $40 million golden handshake and an agreement his former employer would invest $200 million in his new company.

For heads of publicly traded corporations, compensation is more dependable; as long as they have a job, they have a paycheck. Entrepreneurial CEOs aren't always so certain of a paycheck.

It is common for the entrepreneurial CEO/company founder to take a modest salary—say the amount that would be given a first-level manager—to keep money reinvested in the company. Of course, they are still making money if they own the company. A CEO who owns a privately held company can ultimately pay himself anything he wants and it won't show up in an annual report or make the newspaper.

Entrepreneurs (of public companies) who took huge risks (that might have failed but didn't) often reap the biggest reward: Craig McCaw started McCaw Cellular in 1982 and today owns $697 million worth of the now-public stock. The founder of Conseco, Stephen Hilbert, owns $47 million worth of his stock.

"$22,500 a day for 365 days. That was my favorite year," I was told by a retired CEO, an entrepreneur who even in retirement brings in nearly a million dollars a year from consulting and investments.

CEOs can increase their compensation in different ways: get the board to change their package, produce a good year for the company and get paid for the performance, or change companies. CEOs who get hired to be a CEO in another company often experience big jumps in compensation. When George Fisher left Motorola to run Kodak he was paid a $5 million signing bonus. Louis Gerstner received a $4.9 million signing bonus to leave RJR for IBM.

CEO compensation is important to CEOs for lots of reasons. It's true money buys forms of power. As one CEO confessed to me, "Money doesn't buy friends, but something closely resembling them."

What money really buys is time. With money you can pay to get things accomplished. You can hire a chef, gardener, someone to do errands, and a maid at home. At the office you can hire more and better-qualified people for sales, marketing, operations, administration, public relations, and so on. By having more good people working for the CEO, he had more time to spend doing what he chooses. Bottom line: Money gives you flexibility and independence.

The following are forms of compensation to a CEO:

- desire to prove oneself and fight a good fight,
- power to run something, accomplish something,

- enjoyment of creating something new that's never been done,
- exercise ability,
- ego fulfillment,
- achievement,
- prestige,
- revenge.

As Herb Pinder, president of Goal Group Companies, said to me, "I don't do this for money. You can only eat one steak at a time. True, the quality of the steak can improve, plus you can hire someone to prepare it for you with more money."

Bill Daniels is a cable legend in the industry and in the business community from coast to coast. If you remember, he was the CEO from my book *Lions Don't Need to Roar* who had the "you never know" philosophy. That means he always returns telephone calls, acknowledges letters, and responds to people he meets day in and day out because "you never know where it will take you and what door it will open," as he told me. Well, Daniels looks at his employees' contribution to his success as justification for "merit" pay out of his own pocket.

In 1994 Daniels sold his Los Angeles sports cable channel, getting $130 million in stock from the sale. Part of the contract included $10 million to be divvied up among all the employees, from the president to the night janitor. Then Daniels gave another $2 million of his money, to total $12 million that was dispersed. Each employee's bonus varied, but they all received a minimum check for $9,500.

This wasn't the first time Bill Daniels paid employees way above and beyond the normal salary. Some years prior he distributed $6 million to 108 employees—some receiving checks of $100,000—after the sale of another cable television system. His company is also full of numerous stories of his generosity in other ways, like the time he sent an analyst and his wife on an all-expense-paid trip to Hawaii following her cancer surgery. "That's just the way Bill is," say people around him.

Bill Daniels is an exceptional person, much less exceptional among fellow CEOs. His generosity extends beyond his company. He gave $11 million through a grant to the University of Denver's College of Business Administration (which was subsequently renamed The Daniels College of Business.) Interestingly, Bill Daniels never attended college.

Not all CEOs are rich. The majority experience only modest wealth. But some truly rich CEOs have done grandiose things with their money: build hospital wings, open art museums, donate their palatial homes to the community, endow scientific research, erect college gymnasiums and libraries, donate to charity or churches, and some even fund a search for extraterrestrials. Others struggle to pay the bills, like you and me. A big difference is they just have more zeros in their bills!

How Much Do CEOs Get Paid?

Typical: Twenty-five times the lowest-paid employee in the corporation.

Extreme: One hundred times the lowest-paid employee in the corporation.

CHAPTER 13

Taking the Lead

The wrap on getting a greater thrill from your climb

I talked with some of the best CEOs in the country, and you and I both benefited from them. As wonderful as they are, they are living their time and ascending their own mountaintops. *Now it's your time.*

You will scale your own lofty heights by the questions you'll ask, the rethinking of information you receive, and the experimenting and adapting that you'll do. A good climber starts by learning from the best then proceeds up his or her own path. As great as the seasoned mountaineers are, they are set in ritual and tradition that worked for them and their time. *Now it's your time.*

Unfortunately only 10 percent of the current group of hikers out there will actually strap on the backpack as outlined in this book. Those 10 percent will make up the pool of people who will actually take their turn at the top. *So make sure you are part of that 10 percent.* (Ninety percent of the people won't do what it takes.) If you do, right away you're ahead of that 90 percent, those who don't have a chance.

There are very few real guarantees in life, but this is one of them. The material presented here is a workable thing. It's a guaranteed guarantee, but it's up to you.

No big outlay of money is required. You don't have to spend two to four more years in college. You only need to decide to explore your personal limits, take responsibility for your actions, and think for yourself.

The climb is for you, not for others. Follow your heart; don't be scared and lazy, clinging to fears of possible failure. It's okay to occasionally flounder because it's your life anyway. It doesn't matter what other people think about you; it matters what you think about yourself.

What matters is that you are being yourself—your best self. (It'll be a hard act to follow!) And wouldn't it be a shame if someone else was having more fun simply because they were climbing a little harder than you? You know in your heart if you are really trying hard.

I've been a management consultant running my own business for over twenty years. I've lasted and flourished while others comparably (or more) competent failed. Why? Because I strap on the ropes every day in an effort to be a better climber.

I, like you, read *Forbes, Fortune, Business Week,* and the *Wall Street Journal* to see what the competitive climbers are up to. Then I do more by approaching selected ones to go beyond the articles in getting to learn something from them. (I have to go up my Gutsy Scale every time I pick up that telephone.) Because I take the initiative and go out on a risky ledge I have a network a lot of people envy. I don't wait for them to find me. They might not!

I've found in my years of mountain climbing that more critical than the summit is the internal knowledge you gain: the sense of how far you can push yourself; how to deal with your own internal fears; how to be intuitive and humble and aware of every detail; and how to live fully. And, most important, I've learned my goal is not just to climb up the mountains, but to give back to them.

Climbing is inherently dangerous. If you slip up in your preparation and execution of actions, it can be fatal. Be knowledgeable about the risks involved and be willing to personally assume all responsibility associated with those risks.

It's your turn to reach lofty heights. Climb hard and you will reap the rewards.

Now is the time to check your gear. How are you doing on the tools needed to successfully reach the summit?

Use the 22 Vital Traits Evaluation Form below to rate yourself and have other climbers rank you as well. From the joint information you can draw your own conclusions about developmental needs. The form should be reproduced and used every three months for a one-year period to check your progress. (It is also a good review for your resolution list every New Year.)

Trait	Your Self-Evaluation	Others' Perception of You			What Top CEOs Strive For
	☐	☐	☐	☐	☐

First, review the traits and rate yourself.

Next, talk to fellow climbers who you will ask to rank you. Get their views verbally so they can't read others' marks. Often their spontaneous spoken response is the most genuine.

How do you find out what other climbers think? Ask. (There are three boxes for three different people so you get an average from them rather than give one person's opinion too much weight.)

How do you ask? You say, "Would you rate me on a scale of one to ten on the following traits?" (Yes, I know, this takes guts! But you have a lot to gain and little to lose.)

I caution you that some people will rate you lower than expected, some higher. Their opinions are just personal judgments—that is, perceptions that can be changed by you over time. Your own honest self-evaluation is the most important.

And what do top CEOs strive for? Obviously, a perfect 10!

I know the test is tough; it takes a lot to become a chief. Remember, only 10 percent will do it. But it's those 10 percent who become near-perfect mountaineers.

22 VITAL TRAITS REVIEW FORM

Trait	Your Self-Evaluation	Others' Perception of You			What Top Chiefs Strive For
1. Secure in self	☐	☐	☐	☐	☐
2. In control of attitudes	☐	☐	☐	☐	☐
3. Tenacious	☐	☐	☐	☐	☐
4. Continuously improving	☐	☐	☐	☐	☐
5. Honest and ethical	☐	☐	☐	☐	☐
6. Thinking before talking	☐	☐	☐	☐	☐
7. Original	☐	☐	☐	☐	☐
8. Publicly modest	☐	☐	☐	☐	☐
9. Aware of style	☐	☐	☐	☐	☐
10. Gutsy/a little wild	☐	☐	☐	☐	☐
11. Humorous	☐	☐	☐	☐	☐
12. A tad theatrical	☐	☐	☐	☐	☐
13. Detail oriented	☐	☐	☐	☐	☐
14. Good at your job and willing to lead	☐	☐	☐	☐	☐

Trait	Your Self-Evaluation	Others' Perception of You			What Top Chiefs Strive For
15. Fighter for your people	☐	☐	☐	☐	☐
16. Willing to admit mistakes	☐	☐	☐	☐	☐
17. Straightfor-ward	☐	☐	☐	☐	☐
18. Nice	☐	☐	☐	☐	☐
19. Inquisitive	☐	☐	☐	☐	☐
20. Competitive	☐	☐	☐	☐	☐
21. Flexible	☐	☐	☐	☐	☐
22. A good storyteller	☐	☐	☐	☐	☐

If you get a ranking from a co-climber that is particularly surprising, ask about it. Do not put them on the defensive or appear like you are upset. With a calm, curious tone of voice and sincerely inquisitive attitude say, "Your reaction is important to me and I want to understand your thinking; can you tell me why you responded this way?" Listen to their answer. Then ask again, "Can you give me an example?" Listen. Ask a third time, "That's very helpful to me; does anything else about it come to mind?"

Many times you have to ask three times to get people to provide clear thinking. They won't mind if your attitude and manner are sincere.

To help you review the vital traits before you complete the self-evaluation form, here is a recap.

22 VITAL TRAITS REVIEW

1. Secure in self:
   - No one makes you feel inferior without your consent.
   - Don't be overly concerned with what people say about you. If you constantly seek approval it gives them power over you while weakening yourself.
   - Trust your way; do it your way—regardless of what people or the "numbers" say.
   - Don't become arrogant in your self-confidence. (There are bullies at all levels of an organization; unfortunately some are quite successful and thought of as a confident boss. But these are not to be admired for they are cowards with poorly developed egos that retard accomplishment and success.)
2. In control of attitudes:
   - If you lose control, you lose. Period.
   - Any time you have contact with anyone you broadcast your disposition through facial expression, tone of voice, posture, handshakes, handwriting, voice-mail message, decision making, managing, leading, and the rest.
   - Emotional strengths, not intellectual strengths, are what is most required to get to the top.
   Note: Handle crises with calm and diplomacy. Very few do.

3. Tenacious:
   - Tenacity is a commitment to the result regardless of what has to be endured along the way. (Accept the fact that the climb may frequently be burdensome and lonely. Every ounce of physical and mental effort, attention, thought, fight, and moral fiber that you have may be called upon. But once at the top, hopefully you'll conclude it was worth it.)
   - If you slack off, waver, vacillate, and fizzle you deserve to fall short of your destination.
   - If you are determined, everything else is easy. You'll be sitting up at the top looking out at the view saying, "It's so simple, I can't understand why more people don't get it."
4. Continuously improving:
   - Your education is just starting when you get out of school. Professional life is just like life itself. It's one big learning experience. Those experiences are your lessons. No path is wrong, if you acquire knowledge or insight from it.
   - Don't go to sleep without recalling something new you've learned each day.
5. Honest and ethical:
   - Your integrity and values matter more to your co-climbers than business savvy.
   - Rock slides turn into avalanches when you tolerate deceit, insincerity, lies, or dishonorable or illegal behavior in yourself or others. Don't do it. You will cheat yourself out of a clean climb.

- Good people make it to the top.
- Don't assume people are honest with you. There are many people who can look you in the eye and lie. You need not go around suspicious and skeptical of everyone's business dealings but unless you ask questions (i.e., inspect, don't expect) you may get hurt. Do spend more of your time concerned about not cheating a co-climber yourself, than time fearful that they are cheating you.

6. Think before talking:
   - Talk a lot less and listen a lot more. Avoid wearing the T-shirt that proclaims, "Help! I'm talking and I can't shut up."
   - You must discipline yourself to slow down, take time to think, and prioritize. Few matters are as urgent as others want you to believe.
   - Think before taking action as well. You can't let others control you by letting *urgent* crowd out *important*. There is a time to push and a time to take it easy. When a decision has to be made, make it quickly. (But if at all possible, wait until the next morning.)

7. Original:
   - The more opportunities you create for your company, the more you create for yourself. You'll never run out of growth challenges. Your task will be selecting and executing the right ones.
   - There are many more paths to the peak for you now than there were in your parents' time.

8. Publicly modest:
   - Avoid pretentious, ostentatious, braggart behavior full of bluster and ego *but* on the other hand let people know what your contributions are.
   - Too many times people think achievement is solely due to oneself. You must also have a cooperative marketplace, team effort, professional managers, good coaches, luck, and timing. Focus on the mountain not your individual place on it. A successful climber understands the "big picture" and perspective and shares the credit.
9. Aware of style:
   - Sustaining success is much more difficult than achieving it; understanding and utilizing all styles enables you to do that.
   - Style is based around choice. People choose to be a certain way; choose to react in a specific manner. Choice involved tradeoffs. (That is, a tradeoff of too early triumph is that you might discover it isn't all that great, there might be a bit of a letdown, and you may wonder why you were in such a hurry to get there.)
10. Gutsy/a little wild:
   - Take risks with money, strategies, plans, operations, and people. It will help you develop courage (i.e., don't be afraid to quit a bad job situation). Appreciate the fact that jobs have life spans. They have beginnings and endings. It's up to you to monitor the timeliness and actively decide when to move on.
   - In your everyday life, and in business, there are boundaries, restrictions, precedents, regula-

tions, and expected behavior. Every once in a
while go outside of them.

11. Humorous:
- Don't just have but use a sense of humor.
  That's the only way you'll enjoy the rockiness
  of it all. Make it fun every step of the way.
- Work can be a lot of fun. (Something you may
  not fully appreciate until you're retired.)

12. A tad theatrical:
- From the outside, business looks logical, organized, structured, realistic, and practical. In reality, business is impersonal, chaotic, often unfair,
  and rewards don't always go to those who earn
  them.
- From the outside, chiefs look confident, certain, self-assured, and "on target." In reality,
  many chiefs are uncertain, anxious, worried,
  concerned, and maybe even fearful *but* they
  don't show it!
- Every leader in the world acts more self-
  assured than they really are. (Be grateful for
  what you don't know about behind the scenes
  in business. If you did know it might discourage you from trying.)

13. Detail oriented:
- Every detail you dismiss will rise up and bite
  you in some manner at some time. Leave nothing to happenstance.

14. Good at your job and willing to lead:
- If you can't clearly point out where you have
  added obvious value to the organization by
  your efforts, you have a big problem looming.

Producing results helps others to believe in you as much as you should be believing in yourself.

- Make fewer plans and take more action.
- Your relationships with people are as important as your performance. Leading, teaching, and supporting, in the end, makes all the difference.
- Allow others to get past you; support them. Respect their efforts. Save them from a dangerous fall. That's how you become the leader.

15. Fight for your people:
   - Always hire people smarter than you so they are worth fighting for.
   - If you only have yes-men around you, one of you isn't right and isn't needed (i.e., *you* for letting that situation occur). Back people who don't always back you.
   - "Ride for the brand," as the cowboys say. In other words, be loyal to your employer. (They can't be all bad; they hired you!)

16. Willing to admit mistakes:
   - Don't fear making mistakes, and above all don't fear confessing them.
   - Don't let setbacks negatively affect you in the slightest. In fact, seek out encumbrances and obstacles. That's where you challenge yourself.
   - Be thankful for problems.

17. Straightforward:
   - When you are talking with people they will only take away two or three things out of what you say. So say those two or three things clearly, purposefully, and exclusively. Don't

add fluff, bluff, needless, useless words or
sounds (e.g., uh, ah, okay).
- Keep people informed, particularly when you
  want to go in a new direction.
- Make shorter speeches.

18. Nice:
- Believe it or not, near-perfects are nice people.
  They are easy to talk to; that is why they got
  to the top.
- Understand your careless words or actions can
  hurt people and harm entire situations. You
  have a great deal of personal power to affect
  others. If you utilize thoughtfulness, you'll get
  things done so much quicker with far less car-
  nage in the wake.

19. Inquisitive:
- Don't assume people think like you. They
  don't always. Even if they look like you, act
  like you, come from the same neighbor-
  hoods—don't assume they think like you.
  They likely don't. More than ever, with diverse work-forces, you will be working with
  a group of less like-minded people. The
  biggest problem in relationships of any kind
  is that people take for granted that others are
  thinking a certain way and they aren't! Ask.
  Listen. Think about what you heard. Ask. Listen. Think about what you heard. Ask. Listen.
  Think about what you heard.
- Seek out, talk with, and listen to old men and
  old women more, for example. Nurture your
  network now. Twenty, thirty years from now

you'll be glad you did. Ask for advice. The more you are certain of something, the more you should seek counsel on it. Your certainty can impair your judgment: Wise advice lets you see dangers more objectively. (Being proud of having all the answers shows ignorance.)

20. Competitive:
    - Don't be foolish enough to think co-climbers are always looking out for your well-being. Accept the fact that whatever you attain someone is there desiring to take it from you (usually a friend).
    - Avoid being a victim, blaming parents, office politics, friends, wives, the weather, the economy, your height, age, sex, birth rank, the stars, or the competition for any of your problems. You won't like yourself and others will avoid you.

21. Flexible:
    - There is no one route through any problem or up any mountain. For example, you have to be as effective dealing with the computer as you are effective dealing with the customer.
    - Flexibility is strength.

22. A good storyteller:
    - Painting pictures with pertinent anecdotes makes for clearer communication among a larger group of people. Analogies, metaphors, similes, and examples cut through complicated issues while retaining the human side of business.

- Maintain a database of business stories. Add to it quarterly with new accomplishments, for example. Write up in a detailed manner what the situation was, what action you took, and what resulted. Use those stories on the telephone, in correspondence, on the Internet, with your boss, with co-climbers, in job interviews, in speeches, while selling, in performance appraisals, and any other time you are communicating.
- Be succinct. Be appropriate. Be amusing, if possible.

It's a tough climb to make it to the top of any mountain. With the right gear, you can be one of the few that do make it to the top. That's a guarantee.

Great climbs start here . . . and now.

A Special Thanks to . . .

Leonard Abramson, CEO and President, U.S. Healthcare

Nancy Albertini, CEO, Taylor-Winfield

Paula Ancona, Columnist, Scripps Howard News Service, Author of *SuccessAbilities*

Edmund N. Bacon, Director of Planning Commission, Philadelphia

Stan Bader, Wyoming Vice President, US West Communications

Jeff Barens, President, The Barens Group

Bob Berkowitz, Host, *Real Personal*

John Bianchi, Ph.D., Chairman of the Board, Bianchi International

Bill Blount, President, Power Motive Corporation

Denis Brown, CEO, Pinkertons

Curtis R. Carter, CEO, Mission Bay Investments

Linda Chambers, President and CEO, Corporate Direct Air

Franklin L. Child, Principal, Project Control, Incorporated

Patricia Child, Owner, Parklane

Douglas R. Conant, Group Executive Vice President, Nabisco, Inc.

Lodwrick M. Cook, Chairman and CEO, ARCO

Bob Cooper, President and CEO, Kennecott Corporation

Steve Cornforth, Partner, Price Waterhouse

Jeffrey Cunningham, Publisher, *Forbes*

Bill Daniels, Chairman, Daniels & Associates

Tim Day, CEO and President, Bar-S Foods

Julie Donahue, CEO and President, BBN Hark Systems Corporation

Henry Dubroff, Business Editor, *Denver Post*

Carolyn Duff, President, WomenWorks, Inc.

Perry Dye, President, Dye Designs International

Bill Eider-Orley, Vice President and General Manager, Hyatt Regency Scottsdale

Bob Elliott, President, Elliott Associates

Bill Fairfield, CEO, Inacom Corporation

Jack Falvey, CEO, Intermark

Bill Farley, COB, Fruit of the Loom

Michael Fields, CEO, OpenVision

Fred Florjancic, President, Brunswick Bowling and Billiards

Bill Frank, President, Careerlab

Robert Freiman, Artist

Neil Georgi, CEO, Neil Georgi & Associates, Inc.

Bill Graebel, COO, Graebel Companies

James M. Grier, Vice President and Dean of Seminary, Grand Rapids Baptist Seminary

Bob Hansford, President, US Sprint, Canada

Jerry Henry, Senior Vice President and CFO, DuPont

Don Hewitt, Producer, *60 Minutes*

Brian Hickey, President and CEO, Harlequin Enterprises

David M. Holland, Retired Senior Vice President, DSC Communications

Rick Holley, President and CEO, Plum Creek Timber Company

Paul Houston, President, Results, Inc.

Ernie Howell, Retired President, Packaging Systems International

Bob Hunter, President and CEO, Pepsico Food Systems

Larry Johnson, Chairman and CEO, Bank of Hawaii

Fred Kahn, Partner, Heidrick & Struggles

Mark Kimmel, President, Paradigm Partners

Larry Kirshbaum, President, Warner Books

Milan "Babe" Knezovich, President, K & Z Distributing

Hal Krause, CEO, Crestcom International

John Krebbs, President, The Parker Company

Karna Kruckenberg-Schofer, CEO, Poudre Valley Hospital

Joe Lamb, President and CEO, Golden Aluminum

Laurence Land, Attorney-at-Law, World Trade Center

Duane V. Larson, President, Children's World Learning Centers

Linn Leeburg, Executive Vice President and COO, WestGas

Wayne Lewis, CEO, The Lewis Group, Inc.

Marshall Loeb, *Fortune*

Jack Lundberg, President, Denver Sala/Svedala Industries, Inc.

Sirio Maccioni, Owner, Le Cirque

Harvey MacKay, author of *Swim with the Sharks*

Alex Mandl, CEO, Communications Services Group/ AT&T

Reuben Mark, COB, President and CEO, Colgate-Palmolive Company

Judy Marshall, President, Global Medical Review

Gay Mayer, President and CEO, MEM Company Incorporated

Richard McCormick, Chairman and CEO, US West, Inc.

Marie McDonald, President, Access Disability Advisors/McDonald Elevator

Marti McMahon, President, Pacific Marine Yachts

Jerry McMorris, COB, CEO and President, NW Transport, Owner, Colorado Rockies

Jim Mead, President, James Mead & Company

John C. Meng, President and CEO, Schreiber Foods, Incorporated

Vic Milla, CEO, New Method Textile Services

Gregg Miller, President, RACOM Corporation

Brooks Mitchell, President and CEO, Aspen Tree Software, Inc.

John Moore, President, Electro-Test, Inc.

Eli Morgan, CEO, M-Financial

Dr. William E. Morgan, Retired President, Colorado State University

John E. Odegaard, Captain, United States Navy

Vincent Okamoto, COB and CEO, Pacific Heritage Bank

Art Oldham, President, Oldham Planning and Design

Duane Pearsall, Cofounder, Columbine Venture Funds

William Perry Pendley, President and Chief Legal Officer, Mountain States Legal Foundation

Herb Pinder Jr., President, Goal Group Companies

Mimi Posser, Owner, Art Services International

Dave Powelson, Chairman, CEO, and President, TRI-R Systems

Marcia P. Pryde, Vice President and Managing Director, A.T. Kearney

Bill Reagan, CEO, Reagan Companies

Roudy Roudebush, Telluride Horseback Adventures

Monte Roulier, President, Service Adventures Inc.

Jim Rupp, Attorney-at-Law

Sam Sanderson, President and COO, Rogers Network Services

George Scalies, CAO, National Semiconductor

Joel A. Schleicher, COO, Nextel Communications, Inc.

Rick Schleufer, President, Enterprise Systems Group

Lola S. Scobey, President, Audio-Therapy Innovations

Michael P. Scott, International Communications Manager, Pioneer Hi-Bred International, Inc.

Yap Lim Sen, Managing Director, IGB Corporation Berhad

Ed Shonsey, CEO, Northrup King

Steve Silk, President and CEO, The Estee Corporation

Tim Stack, President and CEO, Borgess Health Alliance

Hugh Sullivan, President, Sullivan and Associates

Chuck Theisen, President, Phoenix Motor Company

Barbara Thomas, President, Pillsbury Canada Ltd.

Tammy Tierney, Editor, *Kansas City Business Journal*

Bill Tilley, CEO, Jacmore Companies

Inge Trump, President, Trump Property Management

Gary Van Dyke, President and CEO, Office Pavilion

David E. Vogel, President, David E. Vogel & Associates, Inc.

William B. Wallace, Retired Vice Chairman and COO, Phoenix Home Life

Mike Wilfley, President, A. R. Wilfley & Sons, Inc.

Phil Wilkinson, Principal, Network Programs, Inc.

Brad Williams, President, Dakota Beverage Company, Inc.

Cheryl R. Williams, Principal, ReArt Business Consultants

John P. Wilson, President, USC

W. Ted Wright IV, Managing Director, The Regent of Sydney

Dennis Wu, Partner, Deloitte Touche L.L.P.

Susan Yager, President, Domestications

Elmo R. Zumwalt Jr., Retired Admiral and Chief of Operations, U.S. Navy

and

Forbes, Fortune, and the *Wall Street Journal*